Carpentry For

M000275387

Nail Sizes

Penny (d)	Length (in inches)
2d	1
3d	$1\frac{1}{4}$
4d	$1\frac{1}{2}$
5d	$1\frac{3}{4}$
6d	2
8d	$2\frac{1}{2}$
10d	3
12d	$3\frac{1}{4}$
16d	$3\frac{1}{2}$
20d	4

Nail Types and Their Uses

Nail Name	Typical Uses	Comments
Common	General framing, heavy applications	
Box	General construction, light-duty applications	Thinner shaft makes this nail less likely to split wood, but it bends easier
Cement-coated (CC) sinkers	General construction	Adhesive coating for greater holding power
Finishing	Interior and exterior trim	Small head easily set below the surface
Casing	Interior and exterior trim	Similar to finishing nail, but its larger head gives more holding power
Brads	Plywood edging or any thin wood	Diameter measured as for wire gauges from No. 20 to No. 14, with 20 being the thinnest
Special-purpose nails, named according to use	Roofing, drywall, siding, masonry, flooring	Quality assured because they are engineered for a specific task

Carpentry For Dummies®

Cheat Sheet

Linear Measure

To make basic conversions, a carpenter typically needs to know the following equivalents:

- 12 inches = 1 foot
- 3 feet = 1 yard
- 10 millimeters = 1 centimeter
- 100 centimeters = 1 meter
- 1 mil (not to be confused with millimeter) = $1/1000$ of an inch
- Circumference of circle = diameter x 3.1416
- Radius of circle = $1/2$ diameter

Area Measure

Areas for the following shapes are expressed in square units, such as square inches:

- Square: Area = Side x Side
- Rectangle: Area = Side 1 (length) x Side 2 (width)
- Triangle: Area = Base x Height x $1/2$
- Circle: Area = 3.1416 x Radius x Radius (or R^2)
- 144 square inches = 1 square foot
- 9 square feet = 1 square yard

Volume Measure

Here's what you need to know to measure volume:

- Rectangular solid or cube: Volume = Length x Width x Height
- Cylinder: Volume = 3.1416 x Radius of the base^2 x Height
- 1728 cubic inches = 1 cubic foot
- 27 cubic feet = 1 cubic yard

IDG BOOKS WORLDWIDE

...For Dummies®: Bestselling Book Series for Beginners

Praise for Carpentry For Dummies

"When remodeling, it's easy to become overwhelmed by all the choices and possibilities. *Carpentry For Dummies* is a terrific guide to stay on the right track."

— Richard Karn, "Al Borland" *Home Improvement*

"Don't despair over household repairs. Gene and Katie Hamilton's easy-to-read how-to manual will make you feel like you can make repairs and maintain your home like a pro!"

— Chris & Beverly DeJulio, hosts of *HandyMa'am®* on PBS (author of the book, *HandyMa'am®*) and *HomeWise* on HGTV

"*Carpentry For Dummies* is probably the most useful tool to have in the home workshop — solid information about everything from buying lumber to finish carpentry is right at your fingertips.

— Don Geary, freelance how-to writer, book author, and President of the National Association of Home & Workshop Writers

Praise for Painting and Wallpapering For Dummies

"The Hamiltons do everything but roll on the paint or paste the paper for you. Here is specific, detailed, accurate information, problem-solving and trouble-shooting. Even a first-timer will feel confident about picking up a brush and transforming a room."

— Judy Stark, Home Editor, *St. Petersburg Times* and President, National Association of Real Estate Editors

"The thickness of a coat (only about 2/1000ths of an inch) is all that stands between your most costly investment and the environment. Before you expose your house to the next season, get seasoned advice. Brush-up with Gene and Katie Hamilton's *Painting and Wallpapering For Dummies*. It's a smart way to start your next project!"

— Thomas A. Kraeutler, Home Improvement Columnist and Radio/TV Host

Praise for Gene and Katie Hamilton

 ™

References for the Rest of Us!™

CARPENTRY
FOR
DUMMIES®

by Gene and Katie Hamilton
with Roy Barnhart

IDG
BOOKS
WORLDWIDE

IDG Books Worldwide, Inc.
An International Data Group Company

Foster City, CA ◆ Chicago, IL ◆ Indianapolis, IN ◆ New York, NY

Carpentry For Dummies®

Published by
IDG Books Worldwide, Inc.
An International Data Group Company
919 E. Hillsdale Blvd.
Suite 400
Foster City, CA 94404
www.idgbooks.com (IDG Books Worldwide Web site)
www.dummies.com (Dummies Press Web site)

Library of Congress Catalog Card No.: 99-63189

ISBN: 0-7645-5175-2

Printed in the United States of America

10 9 8 7 6 5 4 3 2 1

1B/SQ/QY/ZZ/IN

Distributed in the United States by IDG Books Worldwide, Inc.

Distributed by CDG Books Canada Inc. for Canada; by Transworld Publishers Limited in the United Kingdom; by IDG Norge Books for Norway; by IDG Sweden Books for Sweden; by IDG Books Australia Publishing Corporation Pty. Ltd. for Australia and New Zealand; by TransQuest Publishers Pte Ltd. for Singapore, Malaysia, Thailand, Indonesia, and Hong Kong; by Gotop Information Inc. for Taiwan; by ICG Muse, Inc. for Japan; by Norma Comunicaciones S.A. for Colombia; by Intersoft for South Africa; by Eyrolles for France; by International Thomson Publishing for Germany, Austria and Switzerland; by Distribuidora Cuspide for Argentina; by LR International for Brazil; by Ediciones ZETA S.C.R. Ltda. for Peru; by WS Computer Publishing Corporation, Inc., for the Philippines; by Contemporanea de Ediciones for Venezuela; by Express Computer Distributors for the Caribbean and West Indies; by Micronesia Media Distributor, Inc. for Micronesia; by Grupo Editorial Norma S.A. for Guatemala; by Chips Computadoras S.A. de C.V. for Mexico; by Editorial Norma de Panama S.A. for Panama; by American Bookshops for Finland. Authorized Sales Agent: Anthony Rudkin Associates for the Middle East and North Africa.

For general information on IDG Books Worldwide's books in the U.S., please call our Consumer Customer Service department at 800-762-2974. For reseller information, including discounts and premium sales, please call our Reseller Customer Service department at 800-434-3422.

For information on where to purchase IDG Books Worldwide's books outside the U.S., please contact our International Sales department at 317-596-5530 or fax 317-596-5692.

For consumer information on foreign language translations, please contact our Customer Service department at 1-800-434-3422, fax 317-596-5692, or e-mail rights@idgbooks.com.

For information on licensing foreign or domestic rights, please phone +1-650-655-3109.

For sales inquiries and special prices for bulk quantities, please contact our Sales department at 650-655-3200 or write to the address above.

For information on using IDG Books Worldwide's books in the classroom or for ordering examination copies, please contact our Educational Sales department at 800-434-2086 or fax 317-596-5499.

For press review copies, author interviews, or other publicity information, please contact our Public Relations department at 650-655-3000 or fax 650-655-3299.

For authorization to photocopy items for corporate, personal, or educational use, please contact Copyright Clearance Center, 222 Rosewood Drive, Danvers, MA 01923, or fax 978-750-4470.

About the Authors

Gene and Katie Hamilton are the husband-and-wife author team of the newspaper column "Do It Yourself . . . or Not?," *Home Improvement For Dummies*, and over a dozen best-selling books on home improvement. They're also the founders of www.housenet.com, the largest home and garden Web site for homeowners and do-it-yourselfers on the Internet. The Hamiltons have been featured in numerous publications and television shows, including HGTV CNN, *Today*, and *Dateline*. In their 20 years as home-repair experts, they've successfully remodeled 14 homes (and they're still married!).

Roy Barnhart is a lifelong do-it-yourselfer and former professional building and remodeling contractor. He enjoyed eight years as Senior Building and Remodeling Editor for two national home improvement magazines. For the last nine years, he has worked as a freelance writer, editor, and consultant. Roy has contributed articles to over a dozen home improvement magazines, including *American Homestyle, American How-To, Family Handyman, House Beautiful, Remodeling, Today's Homeowner,* and *Women's Day*. He has also contributed to three books, including *The New Reader's Digest Complete Fix-It-Yourself Manual, The Stanley Book of Home Improvement,* and *The Reader's Digest Book of Skills and Tools*. He is currently the author of a weekly column on HouseNet (Gene and Katie's favorite Web site).

ABOUT IDG BOOKS WORLDWIDE

Welcome to the world of IDG Books Worldwide.

IDG Books Worldwide, Inc., is a subsidiary of International Data Group, the world's largest publisher of computer-related information and the leading global provider of information services on information technology. IDG was founded more than 30 years ago by Patrick J. McGovern and now employs more than 9,000 people worldwide. IDG publishes more than 290 computer publications in over 75 countries. More than 90 million people read one or more IDG publications each month.

Launched in 1990, IDG Books Worldwide is today the #1 publisher of best-selling computer books in the United States. We are proud to have received eight awards from the Computer Press Association in recognition of editorial excellence and three from Computer Currents' First Annual Readers' Choice Awards. Our best-selling ...For Dummies® series has more than 50 million copies in print with translations in 31 languages. IDG Books Worldwide, through a joint venture with IDG's Hi-Tech Beijing, became the first U.S. publisher to publish a computer book in the People's Republic of China. In record time, IDG Books Worldwide has become the first choice for millions of readers around the world who want to learn how to better manage their businesses.

Our mission is simple: Every one of our books is designed to bring extra value and skill-building instructions to the reader. Our books are written by experts who understand and care about our readers. The knowledge base of our editorial staff comes from years of experience in publishing, education, and journalism — experience we use to produce books to carry us into the new millennium. In short, we care about books, so we attract the best people. We devote special attention to details such as audience, interior design, use of icons, and illustrations. And because we use an efficient process of authoring, editing, and desktop publishing our books electronically, we can spend more time ensuring superior content and less time on the technicalities of making books.

You can count on our commitment to deliver high-quality books at competitive prices on topics you want to read about. At IDG Books Worldwide, we continue in the IDG tradition of delivering quality for more than 30 years. You'll find no better book on a subject than one from IDG Books Worldwide.

John Kilcullen
Chairman and CEO
IDG Books Worldwide, Inc.

Steven Berkowitz
President and Publisher
IDG Books Worldwide, Inc.

WINNER

Eighth Annual
Computer Press
Awards ≥1992

WINNER

Ninth Annual
Computer Press
Awards ≥1993

WINNER

Tenth Annual
Computer Press
Awards ≥1994

WINNER

Eleventh Annual
Computer Press
Awards ≥1995

IDG is the world's leading IT media, research and exposition company. Founded in 1964, IDG had 1997 revenues of $2.05 billion and has more than 9,000 employees worldwide. IDG offers the widest range of media options that reach IT buyers in 75 countries representing 95% of worldwide IT spending. IDG's diverse product and services portfolio spans six key areas including print publishing, online publishing, expositions and conferences, market research, education and training, and global marketing services. More than 90 million people read one or more of IDG's 290 magazines and newspapers, including IDG's leading global brands — Computerworld, PC World, Network World, Macworld and the Channel World family of publications. IDG Books Worldwide is one of the fastest-growing computer book publishers in the world, with more than 700 titles in 36 languages. The "...For Dummies®" series alone has more than 50 million copies in print. IDG offers online users the largest network of technology-specific Web sites around the world through IDG.net (http://www.idg.net), which comprises more than 225 targeted Web sites in 55 countries worldwide. International Data Corporation (IDC) is the world's largest provider of information technology data, analysis and consulting, with research centers in over 41 countries and more than 400 research analysts worldwide. IDG World Expo is a leading producer of more than 168 globally branded conferences and expositions in 35 countries including E3 (Electronic Entertainment Expo), Macworld Expo, ComNet, Windows World Expo, ICE (Internet Commerce Expo), Agenda, DEMO, and Spotlight. IDG's training subsidiary, ExecuTrain, is the world's largest computer training company, with more than 230 locations worldwide and 785 training courses. IDG Marketing Services helps industry-leading IT companies build international brand recognition by developing global integrated marketing programs via IDG's print, online and exposition products worldwide. Further information about the company can be found at www.idg.com.   1/24/99

Dedication

We dedicate this book to volunteers everywhere who practice their building and carpentry skills to help their neighbors and community. We want to applaud the thousands of volunteers who help patch a roof or fix a broken fence gate for a neighbor, or the teams of volunteers in organizations like Christmas in April or Habitat for Humanity, who build or remodel a house for someone less fortunate. Their skills and talent range from budding do-it-your-selfers, with more enthusiasm than expertise, to seasoned professionals who practice their craft on weekends and after hours to help others. We continue to support and admire these volunteers with tools in hand and goodness in their hearts.

Authors' Acknowledgments

Our thanks to the experts who have encourage our interest in carpentry all these years. Contractors, tool-gurus, and friends along the way have taught us their special techniques, passed along their well-heeled advice, and shared their time and talents with us, and for that, we're grateful.

We appreciate the help and expertise of Tim Green, whose skilled eye gave a careful look to all the material in the book. As the technical reviewer, he made sure we got all the details right. And many thanks to our good friend Joe Truini, who contributes his own unique brand of wit and wisdom to make this book enjoyable, often laughable, as well as enlightening.

At IDG Books, we found new friends and kindred spirits in Project Editor Tim Gallan and Acquisitions Editor Holly McGuire, who maintained a steady head and steadfast hand to keep us on track.

As always, we are indebted to our agent Jane Jordan Browne, who continues to be our guiding light and good friend.

Publisher's Acknowledgments

We're proud of this book; please register your comments through our IDG Books Worldwide Online Registration Form located at http://my2cents.dummies.com.

Some of the people who helped bring this book to market include the following:

Acquisitions and Editorial

Senior Project Editor: Tim Gallan

Acquisitions Editor: Holly McGuire

Copy Editors: Patricia Pan, Donna Love, Tina Sims

Technical Editor: Tim Green

Editorial Coordinator: Maureen Kelly

Editorial Manager: Seta K. Franz

Editorial Assistant: Alison Walthall

Production

Project Coordinator: Tom Missler

Layout and Graphics: Amy Adrian, Angela F. Hunckler, Kate Jenkins, Dave McKelvey, Barry Offringa, Brent Savage, Jacque Schneider, Brian Torwelle, Mary Jo Weis, Dan Whetstine

Illustrator: Precision Graphics

Proofreaders: Christine Berman, Betty Kish, Marianne Santy

Indexer: Sharon Hilgenberg

General and Administrative

IDG Books Worldwide, Inc.: John Kilcullen, CEO; Steven Berkowitz, President and Publisher

IDG Books Technology Publishing Group: Richard Swadley, Senior Vice President and Publisher; Walter Bruce III, Vice President and Associate Publisher; Steven Sayre, Associate Publisher; Joseph Wikert, Associate Publisher; Mary Bednarek, Branded Product Development Director; Mary Corder, Editorial Director

IDG Books Consumer Publishing Group: Roland Elgey, Senior Vice President and Publisher; Kathleen A. Welton, Vice President and Publisher; Kevin Thornton, Acquisitions Manager; Kristin A. Cocks, Editorial Director

IDG Books Internet Publishing Group: Brenda McLaughlin, Senior Vice President and Publisher; Diane Graves Steele, Vice President and Associate Publisher; Sofia Marchant, Online Marketing Manager

IDG Books Production for Dummies Press: Michael R. Britton, Vice President of Production; Debbie Stailey, Associate Director of Production; Cindy L. Phipps, Manager of Project Coordination, Production Proofreading, and Indexing; Shelley Lea, Supervisor of Graphics and Design; Debbie J. Gates, Production Systems Specialist; Robert Springer, Supervisor of Proofreading; Laura Carpenter, Production Control Manager; Tony Augsburger, Supervisor of Reprints and Bluelines

◆

The publisher would like to give special thanks to Patrick J. McGovern, without whom this book would not have been possible.

◆

Contents at a Glance

Cartoons at a Glance

By Rich Tennant

"Oh Dave is very handy around the house. He manually entered the phone numbers for the electrician, the carpenter and the plumber on our speed dial."

page 5

page 47

"To preserve the beauty and durability of the dental molding, we put fluoride in the trim paint."

page 137

"I swear, Frank, it's not a pyramid scam. You help a few guys with their home improvements and then, after you bring in ten friends, you'll be enjoying each and every Saturday as much as I do."

page 221

Fax: 978-546-7747 • **E-mail:** the5wave@tiac.net

Table of Contents

. . . .

Introduction

· ·

*F*inding a carpenter who does quality work — at a reasonable price and in a timely fashion — can be a real challenge. For little jobs, you can spend more time on the phone (or waiting for someone to return your calls) than you would doing the job yourself, if you only had some basic tools and carpentry skills.

Over the years, the ability to handle small carpentry jobs can save you a great deal of money. Perhaps more important, you can make small repairs before they turn into big ones. In addition, you'll probably make a lot of little improvements that you might not have if you had to hire someone to do the work.

It is our intent to provide a carpentry reference source for the essential information on safety, tool use, and standard joinery techniques that will enable you to take on projects with the confidence that you will do a good job, save money, and hopefully enjoy the work and the satisfaction of knowing that you did it yourself.

We can't always guarantee that you'll find information on your specific project or even a similar one in *Carpentry For Dummies*. No one source will cover every project under the sun, and if one did, you could be sure it would be too superficial to be of any real value. For this reason, *Carpentry For Dummies* focuses on skill development. With this reference book, you will often be able to figure out what a particular repair or project requires, and then handle the task with confidence, even if it is not covered in this or other resources at your disposal.

Who Should Read This Book

Although we expect that everyone, even seasoned do-it-yourself carpenters, would benefit from reading many sections of *Carpentry For Dummies*, the book is primarily a reference for people with little or no experience with carpentry tools, repairs, and home improvements. In other words, the book is for those who want to go beyond the beginner's toolkit and simple shelf installations, and build on their DIY (do it yourself) experience to tackle more involved projects.

Perhaps it would also be helpful to point out that this is *not* the book for someone who wants a reference on building a home or an addition to one, on kitchen cabinet installation, on deck building, and similar projects. Typically, these projects require that you already have basic carpentry skills and are familiar with most of the material in this book. In fact, people contemplating

such projects should choose books and other resources that focus specifi-
cally on the type of project they intend to build, such as *Home Remodeling
For Dummies,* by the Carey Brothers, and *Decks & Patios For Dummies,* by
Robert Beckstrom, both published by IDG Books Worldwide, Inc.

How to Use This Book

We hope that *Carpentry For Dummies* becomes the first tool that you reach
for when you contemplate taking on a home improvement project that
includes carpentry or work with tools. Check out the materials section for
information relating to the intended work or the tool chapters for tips on
using the tools that will be needed for the project.

The book covers many of the most popular home improvement and repair
projects so certainly check to see if it specifically covers the work you are
about to undertake. If your project is not covered, however, don't put the
book back on the shelf. The projects in *Carpentry For Dummies* were chosen
in large part because they incorporate general skills and techniques that can
be applied to a wide range of projects. So browse topics that involve similar
materials, tools or techniques, even if the project is different.

Finally, we won't be offended if you choose to read the book from cover to
cover, flagging the pages or highlighting the text that have information that
you know you'll want to come back to in the near future.

How This Book Is Organized

Carpentry For Dummies is divided into four parts to help you easily find the
information you need. Parts I and II contain basic information and skills you
need for the interior home improvement projects described in Part III. In Part
IV, we get to make some personal recommendations for other valuable
resources and for projects we know from experience are among the most
rewarding you'll likely take on.

Part I: Carpentry 101

This part focuses on the background information you'll need before you ever
pick up a tool. Start with an overview of house carpentry from frame to
trim — just the big picture, mind you — as well as a description of the lumber
and other carpentry materials that go into a home. Then discover how to
draw basic project plans and brush up on basic math skills to help you with
those measurements and figuring. Get our advice on the best way to start and
grow your hand and power tool collection. Finally, take a close look at the
tips that will keep you safe and protect your home.

Part II: Tools and Techniques

If you were lucky enough to handle tools as a child, you probably pounded nails, lots and lots of nails, into just about anything, and planed wood just to watch the shavings curl. Well, the tool sections in this part remind us of that approach, which requires practicing techniques. Of course, producing something is the ultimate goal, so this part also covers the rough and finish carpentry techniques that turn lumber into walls or bookcases.

Part III: Interior Home Improvements

If you were to check out of the library ten years of back issues for a half dozen how-to magazines for homeowners, you'd notice that the same projects are covered by each publication again and again. In this part, you'll get step-by-step instructions for some of the most popular home improvement projects.

Part IV: The Part of Tens

With a growing tool collection and the skills to use them, it's time to go to work. We know you probably have more projects than time to do them. In this part you'll find some of our favorites resources for the additional information you may require and a sampling of some of the most rewarding carpentry projects that we've done over the years.

Icons to Draw Your Attention

Those funny little pictures in the margins of this book are our way of telling you that there's some information that we wouldn't want you to miss. Here's what each icon means:

Experience is the best teacher, especially when it comes to learning all the little things that you can do to make your work much easier or produce superior results. We have many years of remodeling experience, and thanks to our position as founders of HouseNet (a top-rated Internet site for do-it-yourselfers), we also have the benefit of many hundreds of tips from professionals and everyday folk who share their experience on the Web site. Here's our chance to share them with you.

When we want to get a specific point across, we use this icon. Granted, we'd like you to remember the whole book, but we've decided to be selective and have picked out a handful of facts and figures that you shouldn't forget.

The tools and techniques described in this book won't hurt you if you use them properly and take appropriate precautions. This icon reminds you about particularly important safety procedures. Be sure to read tool manuals, manufacturer's instructions, product labels, and other related sources of safety information.

We know an awful lot about carpentry, and we've heard and been a part of lots of stories over the years. When we decide to bore you with a story, we use this icon.

This icon lets you know that what you are about to read is a bit technical, and you can skip that paragraph if you want to.

When you see this icon, always take very special care. We use this icon when we know that a particular injury is commonly associated with a certain tool or technique and is, therefore, predictable to a degree. The icon also flags your attention when the degree of an injury is particularly serious or life threatening. We don't mean that you shouldn't use the tool or technique; just go into it with your eyes wide open. On the other hand, you should not use any tool or technique that you don't feel comfortable using.

This icon is meant to dispel any doubt that you may have about whether a tool or technique described in the adjacent paragraph is appropriate for a beginner. Not only are they appropriate, we highly recommend them.

One Last Thing . . .

Carpentry isn't the safest hobby in the world. That said, here's a little disclaimer:

In describing tool use for specific projects throughout this book, the authors and IDG Books staff have done their best to emphasize the importance of working safely. They point out key safety issues associated with particular tools or projects and encourage readers to read labels, tool manuals, and the like for additional safety information. However, what is safe for one person under certain circumstances may not be safe for another person under the same or different circumstances. Readers must make a considered judgment about the appropriateness of particular projects, tools, or procedures, and then undertake the work at their own risk.

Part I
Carpentry 101

The 5th Wave   By Rich Tennant

"Oh Dave is very handy around the house. He manually entered the phone numbers for the electrician, the carpenter and the plumber on our speed dial."

In this part . . .

A h, the pleasure of walking through a lumberyard with sawdust dusting the sole of your shoe and the aroma of fresh-sawn pine in the air. Capture the moment because it's that sense of new beginning and discovery we hope you'll find in these chapters, along with some facts and information to help you make lumber and tool buying decisions.

In this first section of the book, we'll take you through the basics of choosing lumber and material, and we'll look at a variety of toolkits for different uses. We hope to demystify some of the choices so you'll feel more self-assured as you shop and make decisions.

Chapter 1

Starting Off on the Right Foot

Experience is the best teacher. Indeed, most homeowners who are interested in knowing more about carpentry so that they can have a greater degree of independence when it comes to the repair, maintenance, or improvement of their home, learn practically everything on the job. There are some things, however, that you need to know or do before you start a project.

You got off to the right start when you purchased this book. (I know we're prejudiced, but we'd say the same if you had purchased another good reference book on carpentry.) This chapter is the first trimester of Carpentry 101, which is a prerequisite for the work that follows (Chapters 2 and 3). With an understanding of the basic information in these first three chapters, you'll probably make fewer mistakes, waste less time, save more money, and be less likely to incur an injury.

Defining Carpentry

The earliest "carpenters" were wagon makers by trade, but over the centuries the term carpenter has come to mean a tradesperson who builds (or repairs) wooden things, especially structures.

The work of the house carpenter (or the homeowner/would-be carpenter) divides into *rough* carpentry and *finish* carpentry. Rough carpentry covers all the work beginning with the construction of a wood frame on a foundation and ending with the completion of the skin on the exterior walls and roof, and the installation of the subflooring. Finish carpentry includes wood-related cutting, fitting, assembly, and installation that follow. A carpenter so often dabbles in other trades such as roofing and drywall installation and finishing, that these, too, might be considered tasks that a carpenter would be competent doing. Finally, finish carpenters also install accessories such as towel bars, closet shelving systems, shower doors, and other nonwood materials and products.

Roughly Speaking

Although most carpentry repairs and improvements in and around the home are limited to what are called finish materials, there are plenty of home repairs that do involve minor new construction or work on the elements that make up the structural shell of the home. So even if you never build or remodel a home you should know the basic elements that make up its shell, what role they play structurally, and how they are fastened together.

From the ground up, the shell of a house includes the following elements:

- ✔ **The foundation walls.** Foundations are usually made of concrete, concrete block or, in some old homes, stone. The walls, whether full height *basement walls* or shorter *crawl space walls*, rest on a wide base, called a *footing*, which in turn rests on solid, undisturbed earth.

- ✔ **The framing.** These numerous sticks of *dimensional* lumber make up the framework of the skeleton of the house. The principal players are joists (horizontal floor and ceiling members); studs and posts (vertical wall members); and rafters (sloped roof members) or truss roof assemblies, which are prefabricated units that are both roof and ceiling members. *Member* is just a fancy way of referring to any structural piece.

- ✔ **The subflooring and sheathing.** These elements, usually made of plywood or other 4x8' panel goods, add strength and rigidity to the system and for the floor, exterior wall, and roof surfaces.

As you read the sections that follow, refer to the simple structure described in Figure 1-1.

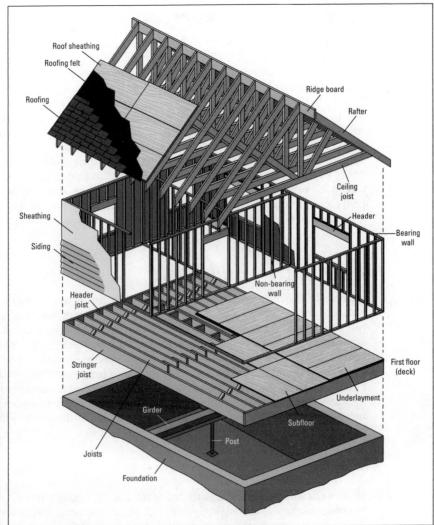

Roof sheathing

Roofing felt

Roofing

Ridge board

Rafter

Ceiling joist

Header

Bearing wall

Sheathing

Siding

Header joist

Non-bearing wall

First floor (deck)

Stringer joist

Underlayment

Girder

Subfloor

Joists

Post

Foundation

Figure 1-1:
Of the three
types of
house-frame
systems,
platform
framing is
the most
common.

Learning the Shell Game

Constructing the shell of a house is known as *framing*. Proper framing is critical to the integrity of the structure and to the life and safety of its occupants. Never make modifications to a structure unless you know what you are dealing with and how to go about making the modifications properly. Depending on the task at hand, that often means consulting a licensed building contractor, an architect or structural engineer, or a building inspector.

Three common approaches

There are three widely used types of house frames in one- and two-family residential construction. Of the traditional approaches — *platform-frame* and *balloon-frame* — platform-frame is by far the most common. In platform framing, each floor (platform) is completed and the walls are then built for that floor. In balloon framing, however, studs extend from a wood sill on the foundation to the roof. This type is typically limited to homes constructed prior to the 1940s. Walls, floors, ceilings, and roof members in both types of frame are typically spaced 16 inches apart, from center-to-center (called *16 inch on center*, or just *16" OC*). In *post-and-beam* construction, the sturdy frame and thick plank floors and roofs provide the structural integrity, and often much of the structure is left exposed to interior view. By the same token, exposed beams or 4x4 posts and top plates in walls don't necessarily indicate post-and-beam construction, so don't jump to conclusions that can get you in trouble.

Foundation and floors

Ultimately, the weight of the entire building is transferred to the *foundation,* either to the concrete or concrete block walls at the perimeter or to concrete pier *footings*. The wood *mudsill,* which rests directly on the concrete, is pressure-treated to resist damage from rot and insects due to moisture from the concrete. The *floor joists* are covered with a *subfloor* — plywood or another engineered panel product in newer homes, and tongue and groove boards in older homes. *Underlayment* provides additional strength and a smooth surface for carpeting, vinyl, wood, and similar finish flooring. Thicker wood floors may be installed directly over a subfloor perpendicular or diagonal to the joists.

Walls

Most walls are constructed with 2x4 *studs,* but new construction (especially in colder climates) increasingly uses 2x6 lumber in order to achieve greater insulating values. Spacing may be increased to 24 inches with 2x6 framing. *Bearing walls* are those that support any vertical weight (*load*) in addition to their own weight. *Nonbearing partitions* and walls do not support any more than their own weight. Framing requirements for the two types differ. To create a large opening in a *bearing* wall, for example, a substantial beam (*header*) must span the top of the opening and the weight on it must be transferred to the floor below through posts at each end. The best advice is to consult with a building professional or inspector before modifying any wall.

Foundation walls are typically concrete block or poured concrete. Interior finishing, when desired, is usually done in two ways:

✔ Building 2x4 walls in front of them, which has the advantage of providing space for fiberglass insulation, electrical wires and boxes, plumbing pipes, and heating ducts.

✔ Fastening furring strips to the wall as nailers for a finish wall material such as drywall or wood paneling.

Roofs

There are two basic approaches to roof framing. In the conventional roof, the *rafters* (the inclined members) and the *ceiling joists* (the beams that support the ceiling load) are assembled in place, piece-by-piece. In a *structural ridge,* a substantial *ridge beam* spans from end to end, transferring the weight of the roof to posts and ultimately the foundation. A *nonstructural ridge* has a *ridge board,* which serves little more than as a convenient place to fasten the rafters. It does not support the weight of the rafters, so *collar ties* are required to counter the forces pressing down on the rafters and out on the side walls they rest on.

In *trussed roof construction,* prefabricated engineered assemblies (roof trusses) rest on outer walls, providing both a roof and ceiling frame. Every member of a truss (and the special gussets or plates used to join them) is essential to the assembly's overall strength and performance. Unlike rafters and ceiling joists, which can be cut if the load on them is transferred to adjacent rafters or joists, trusses should never be cut or modified without consulting a structural engineer.

Finishing School

Once the shell is up, the finishing materials are applied: first the exterior basics, including roofing, siding, windows and exterior doors, and trim; and then insulation and interior finishing materials such drywall, tile, finish flooring, interior doors, trim, cabinets, and closets. (Plumbing and electrical work is similarly done in rough and finish stages.) The rough work is quickly concealed by drywall and flooring, but now that you know what's supposed to be there, it's easier to locate the framing when it is required as a nailing base for many finishing materials such as trim or cabinets.

Workmanship and Building Codes

Despite the name "rough," the workmanship required for rough carpentry is just as demanding as that for trim carpentry, although in a different way. Appearance may not be as important, but strength is critical. A structure must be plumb, level, and square; and framing members must be properly sized and fastened together. Nail sizes and spacing matter. A whole series of regulations (building, mechanical, and electrical codes) and accepted standards for the quality of materials and products, such as those set by the American Society of Testing Materials (ASTM), Underwriters Laboratories (UL), and other bodies apply to virtually every aspect of home construction. You need to know about ones that apply to the work you are undertaking.

Codes

Strict building codes establish *minimum* standards that assure that a structure will withstand loads and forces placed on it by its own weight (*dead load*) and nonpermanent weight factors, called *live load,* such as the persons occupying it and snow on a roof. In some regions, the stresses caused by earthquakes and high winds must also be provided for. Other codes, such as the ones that require clearance between framing and a chimney or firestops between floors, protect against the rapid spread of fire. Your local building inspector is the best resource for code information.

Permits

Building permits may be required for all but the simplest repairs and non-structural improvements. Don't underestimate their importance. Ignoring what seem to be unimportant details can put you at risk of personal injury. All across the country, for example, people turn basements into living spaces without providing the code-required secondary means of safe egress, such as a door or large window. If stairs are blocked by fire, people can be trapped.

Any work done on a house that does not meet code can also jeopardize your insurance coverage in the event of a problem, leaving you personally liable should someone be injured, even years later, due to unpermitted work. Such work can also jeopardize the timely sale of a house.

Inspections

Any job that requires a permit may also require a timely inspection and in the case of new construction or an addition, a final stamp of approval, called a *certificate of occupancy*. Make sure you adhere to the schedule. If you cover up work that required inspection, you will likely need to undo your work — a costly and depressing process.

Do it yourself or hire a pro?

By supplying your own labor you can expect to save anywhere from 20 percent to 100 percent of the cost of a job. Over the years, the collective experience of the authors suggest that new work seemed to run about 50-50, labor and materials, while savings on repairs were quite a bit higher. It depends on the cost of the material.

You won't save much, however, if you botch the job. Avoiding that is largely a matter of allowing sufficient time to carefully research the proper ways of doing something and an honest evaluation of your own skills and tool limitations. Make your own personal safety a priority and think twice about jobs that put you at serious risk, such as roof repairs.

Before you undertake any project, gather whatever information you can and consult with suppliers or professionals until you are confident that you know what to do. In many cases, especially when replacing or repairing something, it may be obvious what needs to be done. Manufacturers, suppliers, or building trade associations provide (or have available) plans and detailed instructions for many projects ranging from workbenches to decks. For more involved projects, such as basement remodeling or modifying or removing interior walls, you'll want to explore other books, magazines, and Internet resources for design ideas, information on the latest materials, and detailed how-to guidelines.

If you're a rookie, the best way to get experience is to *start small*. Build some basement storage shelving before you tackle a living room bookcase. Consider also the required investment in tools and materials or your time. Build your skills, tool supply, and confidence on your successes or on modest failures — not on white elephants or disastrous results.

Don't start any jobs by yourself with a deadline dictated by an important event like a wedding or the birth of a baby rather than a reasonable assessment of the job and a healthy allowance for the unexpected. Assume Murphy's Law will prevail.

Spend a lot of time researching a project and planning the work. You'll find that it pays off many times over. You'll avoid mistakes and delays and discover better tools or materials or better and faster ways to do things. You may learn what work might better be handled by a pro. In short, the preliminary work can be largely responsible for making a job go smoothly.

Drawing Plans

A carefully drawn plan is worth every minute you spend on it. It's a time of discovery. As you draw, you are actually "building" your project on paper and so have a visual clarification of the construction. You then can foresee and resolve many problems and find out what you don't know so you can get the answers before you start. Because you have already "built" the project, doing it the second time goes much smoother because you don't have to stop every other minute to figure out what you need or how to do something.

In addition, making a plan is the first and often necessary step in generating a materials list, making cost/time estimates, and creating a cutting list for woodworking.

So gather some drawing supplies including paper, a drawing pencil, a triangular "architect's" scale and a 45- and 30-degree clear plastic triangle. Don't forget a good eraser, too. It's also very handy to have either a simple drawing board and a T-square, or a drawing board with a sliding horizontal straight-edge. If angles or circles are involved, pick up a protractor to lay out and measure angles, and a compass to draw circles. All these items may be available more economically in kit form.

Understanding how to use most of the tools is self-evident. The one you may not be familiar with is the *scale*. A scale enables you to easily make drawings smaller than the actual project. An *architect's scale* includes five scales ranging from ³⁄₃₂" = 1' to 3" = 1', and a standard 12-inch ruler. On each scale, a measurement in inches or fractions of an inch represents a larger actual dimension. The first "foot" on a scale is divided into inches and, with larger scales, fractions of an inch.

Even if you are generally familiar with these tools, we recommend that you visit a library or bookstore and pick up a book on basic drafting for handy tips, more information about the various styles of drawings, techniques, and the standard way that dimensions and objects are represented on paper.

You should understand how to draw the following four basic types of drawings, each of which represents various *views* of an object, whether it is a house frame or a bookcase:

- A *plan* or *overhead view* is a two-dimensional representation of what the object would look like when viewed from overhead.

- An *elevation* is a two-dimensional view of what the object would look like from the front, back, or either side.

- A *section* view is an elevation of what the object would look like if you were to slice through it at any particular point.

- A *projection* is a three-dimensional view of the object viewed at an angle. Typically, you will see three sides of the object at once, but may also draw dashed lines to indicate the location of the other three sides or any internal components.

To "see" the design of a project and know how it is constructed, or to communicate those concepts to other people, you may need one or all of the drawings described above and shown in Figure 1-2. The amount of detail you put into each drawing will vary, and you can also add what are called *detail drawings* that show a close-up view or more information of a particular small area in a larger drawing. Typically, you would indicate such details on the main drawing with a letter that corresponds to a label on the detail drawing. Details, which can be drawn in any of the four views just described, might, for example, show exactly how two members that are represented by simple lines on a larger drawing are actually joined. It may even show the fasteners used.

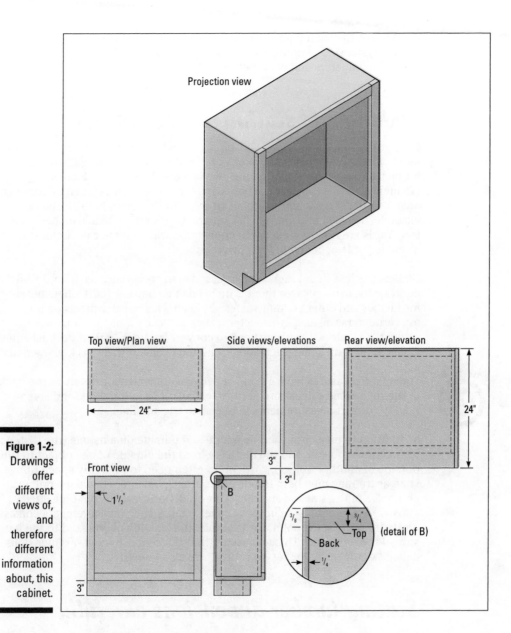

Figure 1-2: Drawings offer different views of, and therefore different information about, this cabinet.

Basic Carpentry Math

Carpentry involves a lot of work with measurements and some basic calculations. You need some basic math skills, formulas, and maybe a decent calculator to plan a carpentry project and then to create a materials list and build it. For the most part, measurements are made in inches and feet (the *English* system). One notable exception is European-style cabinets, which are sized in millimeters and centimeters (the metric system).

Making and stating measurements

Carpentry dimensions, especially ones over 8 feet, are usually expressed in units of feet and inches, for example, 6 feet 3 inches, or (using the symbols for inch and foot) 6'3"; but dimensions may also be stated in inches only (75 inches, in this example). When using formulas, such as when calculating area, use all the same units (inches or feet) for the terms in the formula, for example, 6 inches x 16 inches = 96 square inches rather than 6 inches x 1.3 feet. Yards are not used except in connection with volume calculations, such as cubic yards of concrete for a driveway.

Dimensions less than 1 inch are expressed in fractions such as 3⁄16" or decimal equivalents. In most cases there is no need to go beyond 16ths when measuring lumber and other building materials. Even when greater precision is called for, carpenters will usually use a term such as "a fat 3⁄16" or "a hair over 3⁄16" rather than state 7⁄32". You may need to convert fractions to their decimal equivalents to perform some calculations, and then convert them back to fractions.

Some tape measures have a table of decimal equivalents printed on the back of the rule. Some calculators perform calculations in fractions, and some readily convert measurements between metric and English.

In addition to measuring simple inside and outside dimensions (the distance between two objects and the distance from the outside of one object to the outside of another object), carpenters often need to regularly space things such as framing members (studs and rafters), balusters in a deck railing, and holes in the sides of an adjustable-shelf bookcase for pin-type shelf clips. To avoid confusion in these cases, makes such measurements consistently from the same point, for example, the left side of one stud to the left side of the next stud. This will assure that the center-to-center dimensions, called "x-number of inches on center" are also consistent.

Stating lumber dimensions carefully

Both *nominal* (name-only) and *actual* dimensions are used to describe lumber, such as *board* and *dimensional* lumber. (See Chapter 2 for information on lumber.) For example, when you hear or see the term 1-by-6 (written, 1x6), it refers to the nominal dimension. In fact, a 1x6 measures 3⁄4 x 5½ inch. Similarly, you may hear or see the term 1-by or 2-by (written 1x and 2x). This refers to a 3⁄4- or 1½-inch-thick board of any width.

To make matters more confusing, actual dimensions are less than the nominal dimensions for board lumber, but are identical for panel goods, such as a 4x8 sheet of ¾-inch plywood, which actually measures 4 feet by 8 feet.

Notice that when dimensions are nominal, the "inch" or "foot" is not stated. For example, a 4x8 is either a heavy timber that measures 3½ x 7¼-inches, or a panel that measures 4x8-feet. (You're expected to know which by the context.) When you need to describe a particular length or a standard board, it is standard practice to mix nominal and actual dimensions — for example, "Cut me a 47" 2x4."

If there is any chance of confusion between two people working together, you'd better spell out what you mean. For example, if you want a block of wood with an actual dimension of 2x4x32", say "I want a block that measures 2 inches by 4 inches by 32 inches," not "I want a 2 by 4 by 32 inch block." When you are *dimensioning* a drawing of a project such as a bookcase, or writing out its *cutting list,* always use actual dimensions to avoid confusion. State the thickness, width, and length in that order — for example, ¾ x 5½ x 32".

Nailing down those formulas

The nature and scale of most carpentry work limits the number of calculations that you're likely to encounter. Here are some of the most commonly used ones:

Linear measure

The most basic and commonly used measure is *linear measure* — that is how long, wide, high, or thick something is. To make basic conversions, a carpenter typically needs to know the following equivalents:

- 12 inches = 1 foot
- 3 feet = 1 yard
- 10 millimeters = 1 centimeter
- 100 centimeters = 1 meter
- 1 mil (not to be confused with millimeter) = $\frac{1}{1000}$ of an inch
- Circumference of circle = diameter x 3.1416
- Radius of circle = ½ diameter

Area (A) measure

Square measure is used to describe areas, such as the number of square feet of wall area or square yards of vinyl flooring. Areas for the following shapes are expressed in square units, such as square inches:

✔ Square: Area = Side x Side

✔ Rectangle: Area = $Side_1$ (length) x $Side_2$ (width)

✔ Triangle: Area = Base x Height x ½

✔ Circle: Area = 3.1416 x Radius x Radius (or R^2)

✔ 144 square inches = 1 square foot

✔ 9 square feet = 1 square yard

Volume measure

Cubic measure is used to measure volume (V). Here's what you need to know to measure volume:

✔ Rectangular solid or cube: Volume = Length x Width x Height

✔ Cylinder: Volume = 3.1416 x Radius of the $base^2$ x Height

✔ 1,728 cubic inches = 1 cubic foot

✔ 27 cubic feet = 1 cubic yard

Circular measure

Circular measure is used to describe and calculate angles of all kinds, which are described in degrees. The most common circular measures you are likely to encounter are 45 and 90 degrees. Most things are built "square," meaning that members are perpendicular to each other (or at 90 degrees to each other). When two members meet at a right angle, such as the casing around a door frame, they each are often cut at 45 degrees so that they form a 90-degree angle when joined together. A degree is $\frac{1}{360}$ of the circumference of a circle, or 360 degrees = 1 circle.

3-4-5 right triangle rule

If you're working on a small project and need to assure that two boards, for example, meet at a right angle (90 degrees), you can use a square (see Chapter 4) to locate or verify the angle. However, when the scale of a project exceeds a few feet in size, such as building a fence or adding a partition wall, even a large framing square may be too small. For these occasions, carpenters use what is called the *3-4-5 right-triangle rule,* which states that a triangle with sides in the proportion of 3, 4, and 5 (inches, feet, or any other measure) will always be a right triangle, forming a 90-degree corner where the "3" and "4" sides meet.

To make sure that a new wall is perpendicular to an existing wall or new wall, for example, mark the existing wall at the point where the new wall will intersect and add a second mark 3 feet away. Adjust two tape measures, as shown in Figure 1-3, until the 5-feet mark on one tape crosses the 4-feet mark on the second tape. Snap a chalk line from that point to the first mark you made, and the line formed will be perpendicular to the wall. For larger projects, such as a deck or fence that you want to square to a house, you can substitute 6, 8, and 10 feet.

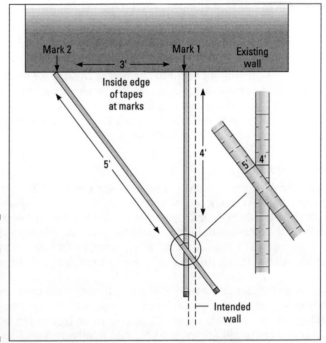

Figure 1-3:
Use a 3-4-5 triangle to square a new wall to an existing one.

Squaring things up

If you need to verify that any structure or construction (such as the forms for a concrete patio, the four sides of a bookcase, or the walls on a platform) is square, you need only measure the two diagonals. If they are both equal, the object is square. If diagonal measurements differ, then (depending on the project), you may be able to square the construction by making adjustments until the diagonal dimensions are equal.

Protecting Yourself and Your Property

Doing carpentry work yourself can save a great deal of money, but it won't if you injure yourself or damage your property in the process. In both cases, there are steps that you can and should take to protect your safety (and that of others who may be affected by your work) and your home.

General safety

We can't begin to list all the things that you might do for every project that will keep you and those around you safe — that's what common sense is for — but we can point out some general guidelines here. Look for additional safety information in our tool chapters (Chapters 4 through 7) and in adjacent Safety icons throughout the book.

Work habits

Just like skiing, more accidents occur at the end of the day when people are overtired. Take plenty of rest breaks. You're a little weaker and your concentration begins to fail you at the end of a hard day. At least put down the power tools and limit your end-of-the-day work to cleanup, sweeping, and making checklists for the following day's work.

Handling materials

Hey, you don't need to prove anything to anybody. Get help lifting or moving heavy or awkward items. Back injuries are the most common injury in carpentry. More people injure their backs than wound themselves with tools. Take advantage of appliance dollies as much as you can. When you do lift, remember the most basic rule of lifting: Keep your back as straight and vertical as possible; and to reach things low to the ground, bend at the knees.

Travel safely with lumber and materials loaded into or onto cars and trucks. Take full advantage of a home center's offer to help you secure your load. If you're hauling debris to the dump in a pickup or open trailer, cover your load. If anything were to fall off, even something relatively harmless, it could surprise a following driver and cause an accident. Whenever a board or similar material extends more than a couple of feet beyond the front or back of your vehicle, tie on a red flag or similar warning.

On the work site

Keep your work area clean and maintain solid footing. Much carpentry is site work involving work on uneven ground, ladders, or other less than ideal conditions. Take the time to set up properly and clear an area, or bring your work elsewhere. Pull or bend over nails in materials that you are removing as you work or place them out of the way in a pile or a trash container.

Electrical safety

Don't mess with live wires or leave outlet boxes and wires exposed. Always shut off the power at the main circuit breaker or fuse panel. (See "Tool safety" and "Demolition safety" later in this chapter for additional electrical warnings and precautions.)

Tool safety

Use tools for their intended use and read your manual. If people followed these two rules, tool-related accidents would be a tiny proportion of what they are today.

If you are using a power tool, keep in mind the following general tool safety tips:

✔ All tools with 3-prong grounding plugs must be used in grounded outlets only or with a properly installed adapter plug. (The connector on the end of the grounding wire must be secured under the cover-plate mounting screw.)

✔ If you do work in a basement or garage shop, make sure that all outlets are properly grounded. Considering the dampness of many concrete floors, it is also highly advisable (and my be required by code) to install ground fault circuit interrupter (GFCI) receptacles in all garage and basement outlets. A GFCI instantaneously shuts down a circuit if it detects a leak to ground, which would be the case if electricity began to flow through your body on its way to ground. Replacing a standard receptacle with a GFCI is easy. (Installation instructions are included with the GFCI.) For other damp conditions you can also buy extension cords with an integral GFCI.

✔ Remove the cord before adjusting tools or before removing or mounting an accessory such as a saw blade.

✔ Wear eye protection (safety goggles or safety glasses with side protectors).

✔ Switch off a tool before you unplug it, and always unplug a tool when the work is done.

✔ Check the switch on a tool equipped with a lock-on switch before plugging it in.

✔ Maintain tools, cords, and accessories in good condition.

✔ Use only sharp cutters, such as drill bits or saw blades.

✔ Don't remove or disable guards, such as the blade guard on a circular saw. Doing so puts you at great risk and voids the warranty on most tools.

✔ Whenever possible, use a dust collection system with a cutting or sanding tool. Some tools are equipped with dust bags or ports that connect to shop vacuums.

Demolition safety

Homeowners often tackle the demolition phase of a project to save some money. Generally speaking, the skills and tools required are within the reach of a rookie and, because the pro doesn't come on the scene until after the demolition work is complete, the homeowner is less likely to interfere with his scheduling.

Make sure that you know what you are dealing with before you start swinging a hammer or ripping things apart.

We had a good friend once — a college graduate at that — who demolished a wall between his dining room and kitchen. He wanted a more open, airy feeling. So he started on the dining room side and after exposing the wall studs, he smashed through the back side of the wall only to discover that he had just made an opening to his back porch, not the kitchen. He got his wish, sort of.

Look for electrical outlets and go to the floor above or below and look for heating registers, radiators, plumbing fixtures, or other indicators of things buried in the wall. You need to avoid all of these.

Don't remove any framing unless you are sure that it is not required structurally. Only an experienced building professional, such as a building contractor or inspector, should make that call.

Chapter 2

Buying Lumber and Other Materials

● ●

In This Chapter

▶ Buying the right lumber for your project

▶ Checking out gypsum drywall and accessories

▶ Keeping it all together with fasteners, anchors, adhesives, and caulks

● ●

*H*ome centers, lumberyards, and other outlets abound with materials for the carpenter, ranging from the most basic raw materials, such as rough-sawn boards from local mills to $2,000 prefinished entry door systems. We love this stuff and could go on and on and on . . . but our editors won't let us. Reluctantly, we draw the line. In this chapter we contain ourselves to describing basic lumber and drywall products and the products you use to hold things together — fasteners, anchors, adhesives, and caulk. These are the materials that you will use most often in your carpentry projects.

Sorting through Lumber

The first thing that you need to know when buying lumber is its intended use. Knowing that, you (or the lumber salesperson helping you) can then better determine the degree of importance that strength, appearance, and durability may have. Then you can decide whether to buy solid lumber or manufactured lumber products such as plywood, the wood species, the size, grade, and other qualities.

Lumber is described as either softwood or hardwood depending on the source. Softwoods (conifer trees such as fir, spruce, and pine) are used for virtually all house construction lumber, from framing to moldings (trim). The hardwoods (deciduous trees such as maple, birch, and oak) are known for their beauty. And because of the relatively high cost, hardwoods are rarely used for anything but finish carpentry projects, such as cabinets and moldings. Hardwoods also are more difficult to mill, cut, and nail than softwoods, so we focus primarily on softwoods in this book.

Sizing things up

Lumber is a general term for both solid wood and manufactured wood products. Dimensions for lumber are stated in thickness, width, and length, in that order. *Nominal* dimensions (which are different from the actual measurements) describe strip, board, and dimensional lumber. For example, after a 2x4 is milled it actually measures 1½ thick by 3½ inches wide — but it's still called a 2x4. *Actual* dimensions are used for panel goods. Fortunately, 8 feet still means 8 feet. In most cases, lumber is sold in even-numbered lengths. (One notable exception is a precut wall stud, which measures 91½ inches.) *Dimensional lumber* is available from 2 to 4 inches thick, and from 2 to 12 inches wide (for more information, see "Making the Grade, below).

Solid wood lumber falls into several categories according to its dimensions, as shown in Table 2-1. Lumber that measures more than 4 inches thick is called *timber*.

Table 2-1		Softwood Lumber Categories by Size in Inches	
Nominal Thickness	*Actual Thickness*	*Nominal Face Width*	*Actual Face Width*
Strips			
1	¾	2	1 ½
1 ¼ (⁵⁄₄)	1 ⅛	3	2 ½
Boards			
1	¾	2	1 ½
1 ¼ (⁵⁄₄)	1 ⅛	3	2 ½
1 ½ (⁶⁄₄)	1 ⅜	4	3 ½
2	1 ¾	5	4 ½
		6	5 ½
		8, 10, 12, and wider	¾ less than nominal
Dimensional			
2	1 ½	2	1 ½
4	3 ½	3	2 ½
		4	3 ½
		6	5 ½

Nominal Thickness	Actual Thickness	Nominal Face Width	Actual Face Width
		8	7 ¼
		10	9 ¼
		12	11 ¼

Stretching natural resources

Lumber manufactured from reconstituted wood makes more efficient use of our tree resources and often has superior qualities such as strength and consistency. No longer constricted by tree sizes, these products are available in large sizes such as 4x8 panels and 60-foot long beams. Table 2-2 describes some of the most common reconstituted wood products and typical uses.

Table 2-2	Manufactured lumber products	
Product	*Description*	*Typical Uses*
Plywood	Thin layers of wood, called *plies*, are glued up under pressure to form 4x8 panels	Subfloor, wall and roof sheathing, flooring under-layment, siding, cabinet carcasses, furniture, paneling
Particleboard (chipboard)	Very small wood particles and sawdust bonded to form a very stable, heavy panel	Underlayment, substrate for plastic laminates (for countertops) and plastic and wood veneers (for furniture)
Medium-density fiberboard (MDF)	A very dense, smooth panel made with fine wood fibers	Cabinet door panels, moldings
Hardboard (high-density fiberboard)	Dark brown, very dense material pressed in the shape of panels, doors, and siding panel. Available tempered (water-resistant) and untempered	Cabinet backs and drawer bottoms; hollow-core doors; paneling; perforated for use with clips (for example, Peg-Board); siding

(continued)

Table 2-2 *(continued)*

Product	Description	Typical Uses
Oriented-strand board (OSB)	Panels made with large chips with fibers in each layer oriented perpendicular to the adjacent layer	Wall and roof sheathing; subflooring
Flakeboard (waferboard)	Similar to OSB, but flakes are random and not as strong	Wall and roof sheathing; utility sheds and similar, less demanding, building applications

Making the grade

Lumber is graded at the mill according to wood characteristics that affect its strength or appearance. You pay more for better grades, so buy the lowest grade that meets your needs. If appearance is not important, you might choose No. 2 pine, which has knots, rather than a "D-select" grade, which has no knots. Similarly, if your need is plywood for wall sheathing, the appearance of the face veneer is not important.

Dimensional lumber is milled lumber intended primarily for structural use — house framing, outdoor constructions, and decks. It is, therefore, graded according to "characteristics" (or defects, if you will), such as knots, splits, and warps, that affect a board's strength or other performance qualities. Avoid *utility* grade for house construction projects, choosing instead *Standard, Construction,* or *Stud* grades.

Board lumber is used for general purposes and is graded for appearance. In effect, you don't need to know the grade if you are buying the lumber in person, but here's a quick look at grading, in case you want to know:

 ✔ **Select grades** are the best quality boards. They range from *B and better-select* (best quality) to the most commonly available *D-select.* Use this grade for trim, cabinets, and similar projects where appearance is a top priority.

 ✔ **Common grades** have knots and other normally less desirable characteristics. They range from *No. 1 common* (best) to *No. 5 common.* Most lumberyards stock only one or two common grades, with No. 2 being the most common. Use common grades for shelving and similar, less demanding, projects that will be painted.

Plywood panels are given *appearance* or *surface* grades for the veneer faces ranging from A (best looking) to D. Each side of a panel gets a grade, so you will see *AC, BC,* and so on. The panels are also given an exposure rating that tells you whether it can be left exposed outdoors (permanently or for a period of time) or should be used indoors only.

The three most commonly available exposure grades for plywood panels are:

- ✔ **Exterior.** All plies, including interior ones, are grade C or better and have a waterproof bond. It can be permanently exposed to the weather.

- ✔ **Exposure 1.** These panels have the same waterproof bond as exterior plywood but with lower quality interior plies. They can be exposed to weather during construction or when exposure is limited to the underside (a roof soffit, for example) but must eventually be covered.

- ✔ **Interior.** Interior plywood does not use waterproof glue and must only be used indoors.

Plywood and other panel goods, such as oriented-strand board and particleboard, are also given engineered grades such as Underlayment or Rated Sheathing, rated Sturdi-Floor or Rated Siding. Guess what they are used for?

Weathering well

Some woods are naturally more weather-resistant than others. Redwood and cedar are two notable, widely available examples. You may also find exotic rainforest hardwoods that are marketed for decks. If you buy exotic wood, look for the stamp of a certification program, such as the Rainforest Alliance's SmartWood program, that states that the lumber was responsibly harvested. (Check out the alliance's Web site at www.smartwood.org.) *Pressure-treated* lumber is impregnated with waterborne preservatives such as chromated copper arsenate (CCA) and borate to make the wood more decay- and insect-resistant.

Treated wood may not rot or be eaten by insects, but it is just as susceptible to cracking, splitting, and warping as other woods, and more so than some untreated species. Protect pressure-treated by regularly treating with a water repellent or water-repellent stain.

While many woods are pressure-treated, southern pine takes the treatment best. The amount of preservative retained by the wood, measured in *pounds per cubic foot* (pcf), determines the effectiveness of the treatment. For a*bove ground use,* that is, for wood not in soil contact, look for 0.25 pcf retention on the label. For *ground contact use,* that is for wood in contact with soil or fresh water, including sawn posts and columns supporting decks, look for 0.40 pcf.

Although CCA preservatives don't affect the ability of a wood to take a finish, the most widely treated wood, southern pine, does not hold paint well. Plan to use a stain rather than paint.

Working with Gypsum Drywall

Gypsum drywall (also called wallboard or, by one maker's trade name, Sheetrock), is the most widely used interior wall and ceiling surfacing material. The panels are available in various sizes and grades (see Table 2-3). Water-resistant panels (W/R) are good for bathrooms except under tub/shower enclosure tile, where special tile backer boards are recommended. Use fire-rated products as specified by local codes for increased fire resistance.

Table 2-3	Gypsum Drywall	
Dimensions	*Grades*	*Uses*
¼" x 4' x 8' or 10'	Standard	Covering existing surfaces and curved walls
⅜" x 4' x 8', 9', 10', 12', or 14'	Standard	Repair and covering existing surfaces
½" x 4' x		Good for single-layer wall; acceptable for single-layer ceiling
8', 9', 10', 12', or 14'	Standard	
8', 10', or 12'	Fire-rated	
8', 10', or 12'	Fire-rated W/R	
⅝" x 4' x		Best for single-layer wall and ceiling applications
8', 9', 10', 12', or 14'	Standard	
8', 10', or 12'	W/R	
8', 10', or 12'	Fire-rated	
8,10,12	Fire-rated W/R	

The joints between panels are concealed with joint compound, reinforced with paper or fiberglass tape. Fasteners also are covered with joint compound. And corners are first covered and protected with metal trim, then covered with compound.

Here's what you need to know about these drywall installation products:

- **Joint compound** is available in two premixed versions (regular and lightweight). The lightweight is faster drying but does not dry as hard; so we suggest the regular type. Joint compound is also available in powder form. While much less convenient, you'll get longer lasting results when patching cracks in plaster if you use the dry mix compound with perforated paper reinforcing tape.

- **Reinforcing tape** is available in two types: *Paper tape* is inexpensive and superior for plaster crack repair. *Self-adhering fiberglass mesh* costs more but is convenient and perhaps a little easier to use for DIYers with little taping experience. While some claim it is stronger, pros rarely use it.

- **Corner bead** (metal trim for corners) is available in several varieties. The all-metal type is the most common and is available in 10-foot lengths. Paper-and-metal and plastic types are available for rounded inside and outside corners, curved corners (such as arches) and non-right-angle corners.

Keeping It All Together

Fasteners, anchors, and adhesives are all used to hold things together. You need to match your needs and your materials to the properties of the fastener. Some of the principal factors that you need to consider are whether you want the material to ever come apart, how strong the bond must be, the materials involved, and whether the application is indoors or outdoors.

Choosing the right fasteners

The fasteners that carpenters use most often are nails, but screws are playing an increasingly large role in residential construction. Carpenters also need other fasteners and anchors for hollow walls, concrete, and masonry. The size and type you choose depends on the application. In some cases, the name of the fastener tells you its principal intended use — roofing nails and drywall screws, for example. Some names don't tell you much (common nail) or give a hint (finishing nail, exterior screw).

Nails

Nails are nails, right? Wrong. Each type of nail is engineered to perform differently. For example, some are galvanized for exterior use, and some have large heads or shanks that are deformed for better holding power. (See Table 2-4.)

For exterior uses, always use fasteners that are designated for such applications. Uncoated steel nails will rust and cause stains when exposed to the elements. A galvanized coating is the most common protection for exterior-use nails, and *hot-dipped galvanized (HDG)* coatings offer the best protection. Use stainless steel nails or HDG nails whenever the fastener will remain exposed, such as for certain types of siding installations.

Table 2-4	Nail Types and Their Uses	
Nail Name	*Typical Uses*	*Comments*
Common	General framing, heavy applications	
Box	General construction, light-duty applications	Thinner shaft makes this nail less likely to split wood, but it bends easier
Cement-coated (CC) sinkers	General construction	Adhesive coating for greater holding power
Finishing	Interior and exterior trim	Small head easily set below the surface
Casing	Interior and exterior trim	Similar to finishing nail, but its larger head gives more holding power
Brads	Plywood edging or any thin wood	Diameter measured as for wire gauges from No. 20 to No. 14, with 20 being the thinnest
Special-purpose nails, named according to use	Roofing, drywall, siding, masonry, flooring	Quality assured because they are engineered for a specific task

Generally, you want a nail to penetrate two-thirds its length into the base material. Nail sizes, shown in Table 2-5, are described by using *penny* — an antiquated weight that is abbreviated as *d.*

Table 2-5	Nail Sizes
Penny (d)	*Length (in inches)*
2d	1
3d	1 ¼
4d	1 ½

Penny (d)	Length (in inches)
5d	1 ¾
6d	2
8d	2 ½
10d	3
12d	3 ¼
16d	3 ½
20d	4

Once you have the right type and size nail, you need to know how many of them to use and where to use them. Each task in building construction calls for specific nailing practices, called a *nailing schedule.* This schedule specifies the type of nail, spacing or number, and other details, as shown in Table 2-6 for walls. For nonstructural items, just use your judgment as to the nailing requirements. But if you get involved with installing underlayment or structural work, consult your building inspector or other sources for the nailing requirements.

Table 2-6   Recommended Nailing Practices for Wall Framing

Location	Nailing Method	Nail size/frequency
Stud to soleplate	Toenail (framed in place)	8d/5 per stud
	End nail (framed and tilt up)	16d/2 per stud
Lower top plate to stud	End nail	16d/2 per stud
Upper top plate to lower one	Face nail	16d/16" OC
Soleplate to platform	Face nail	16d/10" OC
Corner studs to blocking	Face nail	10d/2 each side
Intersecting corner stud to blocking	Face nail	16d/12" OC
Doubled studs, jack/king studs	Face nail	10d/16" OC, staggered and angled
Doubled 2x header	Face nail	10d/2 at edges 12" OC on both sides

(continued)

Table 2-6 *(continued)*

Location	Nailing Method	Nail size/frequency
Built up beam/girder (3 members)	Face nail	20d/32" OC each side
End stud to intersecting wall	Face nail	16d/12" OC to each stud
½" plywood wall sheathing (applied vertically)	Face nail	8d/6" OC at edges, 12" OC at intermediate studs

Screws and other un-nails

Two revolutions in tool technology have vastly increased the use of screws in carpentry. The first is the development of power screwdrivers — particularly the cordless drill/driver, which eliminates the hassle of cords and takes all the effort out of driving a screw. The second is the straight-shafted, bugle-headed drywall screw. This type of screw generally does not require a pilot hole or a counter sink to recess the head, making it at least two steps up on the standard tapered wood screw, which requires three different holes: a pilot hole, a clearance hole, and a countersink. Although it is still called a drywall screw, this all-purpose screw is used indoors and outdoors in countless carpentry projects.

Table 2-7 gives details on a variety of screws and other valuable fasteners.

Table 2-7   Screws and Other Common Fasteners for Carpenters

Fastener	Description	Typical Uses
Drywall screw (also called multi-purpose, all purpose, carpentry)	Straight-shaft, bugle-head, in coarse thread for wood and fine thread for thin metal	Drywall installation, general interior and exterior construction. Has largely replaced the tapered wood screw
Exterior screw	*Rust-resistant* coarse-threaded drywall screw with galvanized or polymer coating. Stainless steel version is rustproof	General exterior construction, decking, fences and gates, outdoor furniture
Wood screw	Tapered shaft, partially threaded shank	General rough and finish, interior and exterior applications depending on finish or alloy. Largely being replaced by the drywall screw

Fastener	Description	Typical Uses
Masonry screw	Thin, sharp, widely spaced high/low threads, straight shaft	Attaching things to masonry
Sheet metal screw	Shank threaded from tip to head in steel or aluminum, usually self-tapping	Wood-to-metal, metal to wood, and metal to metal (storm doors)
Lag screw	Large shank (¼" minimum), wood screw with hex-head	General construction, heavy duty applications, deck construction, used with anchor in concrete and masonry
Machine bolt	Large shank (¼" minimum) machine-thread bolt with square or hex heads and square or hex nuts	General construction, decks, heavy duty framing anchors

Anchoring in hollow walls and concrete

Carpenters often face the task of fastening items to hollow walls, concrete, masonry, and other nonwood substrates. Usually a special fastener, or anchor to be used in conjunction with a fastener, is required.

A huge variety of these anchoring systems are stronger, faster, and easier to install than old plastic and lead sleeves. With many outdated systems you have to carefully lay out the anchor locations, called *holespotting,* install the anchor, and then install the fixture. (A *fixture* is the term used by the anchor industry to describe whatever is being anchored to a wall.) With most new systems, you install the anchor and the fixture at the same time.

Table 2-8 shows many of the available anchoring systems. Choose one that is easy to install and adequate for the load or force you intend to place on it.

Table 2-8	Anchors and Fasteners	
Anchor	*Duty Range*	*Applications (see key)*
Friction		
Masonry nail	Light	1, 2, 5
Masonry screw	Light-Medium	1, 2, 5

(continued)

Table 2-8 *(continued)*

Anchor	Duty Range	Applications (see key)
Friction		
Plastic plug	Light	1, 2, 5
Alligator brand	Light-Medium	1, 2, 5
Drive-screw wallboard anchor	Light	3
Compression		
S-shank hammer	Medium-Heavy	1, 2
Split-shank hammer	Medium	1
Nail-in or screw-in pin	Light	1, 2, 5
Lag screw shield	Medium	1, 2
Machine screw	Medium	1, 2
Double-wedge expansion bolt	Medium	1
Clamping		
Spring-wing toggle	Light-Medium	3, 4, 5
Toggler brand toggle	Light-Heavy	3, 4, 5
Plastic toggle/screw	Light-Medium	1, 2, 3, 4, 5
Molly (standard)	Light-Medium	3, 4
Molly (drive)	Light-Medium	3
Undercut		
Wedge stud	Heavy	1, 2
Wedge bolt	Heavy	1, 2
Chemical/Adhesive		
Epoxy	Heavy	1, 2

Key to Table 2-8:

1 = concrete

2 = brick, block

3 = drywall

4 = plaster wall

5 = hollow block wall

Framing hardware

Framing anchors are used widely in house, deck, and fence construction for every conceivable wood-to-wood and wood-to-concrete framing connection. These anchors offer more consistent strength than nails, less wood splitting, and easy installation. Several varieties are shown in Figure 2-1.

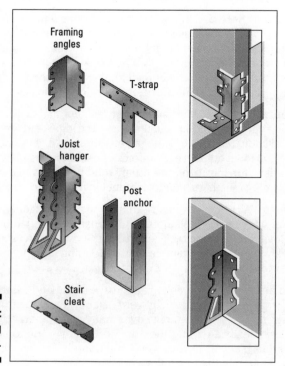

Figure 2-1:
Framing
anchors.

Undernailing is the most common mistake. As a general rule, put a nail in every round hole that the anchor has. With most makes, other shape holes (diamond, square, oval, and so on) are optional and should be used as required by the engineering of the project. Use only the size nails recommended by the manufacturer, and use hot-dipped galvanized nails for outdoor projects.

Glues and adhesives

Adhesives is a general term that includes adhesive, glue, mastic, epoxy, and dozens of other types of materials that bond one surface to another. The adhesive bond is often stronger than the materials being bonded. There are dozens of types and perhaps thousands of glues and adhesives but, in the carpentry world, most fall into two categories: construction adhesives and woodworking glues. You'll likely encounter and use most often the following:

- ✔ **Adhesive caulk.** The emphasis here is on the caulk, but unlike other caulks this type bonds a wide variety of materials together. It would only be used where using adhesives would produce an unattractive dark glue line. Example of use: Adhere counter backsplash to drywall.

- ✔ **Aliphatic resin adhesive.** Usually called carpenter's glue or just yellow glue, this is the most widely used glue used in finish woodwork. The bonded materials must be held together under pressure with clamps or fasteners. A water-resistant variety can be used in damp (not wet) locations. Examples of use: Used to bond all joints in moldings, cabinetmaking, and general interior woodworking projects.

- ✔ **Construction adhesive.** A thick, somewhat resilient mastic that remains flexible. Most types are sold in caulking-gun cartridges and are waterproof. Special subcategories include panel adhesive, drywall adhesive, and polystyrene foam adhesive. Examples of use: Bonding plywood subfloor to joists, furring strips and other wood members to concrete, drywall to framing members, and foam panel insulation to concrete walls.

- ✔ **Contact cement.** A rubbery adhesive that bonds on contact and so does not require any fasteners or clamping. It is brushed or rolled on both surfaces, allowed to become tacky and then the two surfaces are brought carefully together. Example of use: Bonding high-pressure plastic laminates to a base material for countertops.

- ✔ **Epoxy resin adhesive.** This two-part adhesive (resin and catalyst) is very strong, non-flexible and usually very fast curing. Aside from its renowned strength, a key advantage over many other alternatives is that it bonds to practically anything and, therefore, allows you to bond dissimilar materials, such as porous wood and nonporous steel. Example of use: Adhering ceramic tile to subfloor.

- ✔ **Hot-melt adhesive.** This fast setting adhesive that is dispensed by an electric heat gun is available in various forms for a wide variety of materials. The glue cures very quickly so you only need to hold parts together momentarily. Example of use: Bonding pieces of trim work that either cannot be accessed for nailing or that are so small or thin that a fastener would likely crack the wood.

- ✔ **Mastics.** Although these technically include construction adhesives, they are usually thought of as flooring adhesives that come in cans or buckets and are spread with notched trowels or similar spreaders. Different types are available for a wide variety of materials, including wood and vinyl. Some products specify a particular brand/type for warranty protection. Examples of use: Parquet and other glue-down wood flooring, vinyl tiles, and sheet flooring.

✔ **Polyurethane adhesive.** A very strong waterproof adhesive. Messy to use but a good choice for bonding wood exposed to the weather or other sources of moisture. Example of use: Exterior trim work.

Caulks

Sealing for energy efficiency, appearance, or for watertight connections are some of the most common uses of caulks. Caulk comes in small, squeezable tubes and in tubes that fit into a dispenser called a *caulking gun*. Always read the label; for long-lasting results, buy the best quality that you can afford.

The following list shows the types of caulk most often used by carpenters:

✔ **Acrylic latex**

   Best use: The painter's caulk, it seals narrow gaps and joints in interior painted trim

   Comments: Fairly flexible, adheres to damp surfaces, inexpensive and very easy to use

✔ **Silicone**

   Best use: Bathtub/tile joint, wood-to-masonry joints, and any demanding application that will not be painted

   Comments: Very flexible and long lasting; messy to use, does not bond well to cedar, cannot be painted over, available in clear and colors

✔ **Siliconized acrylic latex**

   Best use: Most interior and exterior applications

   Comments: More flexible, bonds better to more surfaces, and longer lasting than acrylic latex; available in clear and colors; paintable; less messy and easier to use than silicone

✔ **Butyl rubber**

   Best use: Sealing to metal

   Comments: Inexpensive, flexible, and messy to use

Chapter 3

The Tools You Need

Y ou can't expect to do carpentry projects around the house without reliable tools. If you think of every tool that you buy as a long-term investment, you'll gradually acquire a reliable stash that can get you through most home repairs and improvements.

People take different approaches to owning tools. Tool-obsessed individuals look for any excuse to add to their collection — these folks simply can't own too many tools. "Oh boy, a metric hammer. I gotta have that," they say when they spy this tool in the hardware store. The more practical do-it-yourselfers want to own only what they need to do the job. Both approaches have their place. But whichever your persuasion, you need a stockpile of core tools that are suited to the amount of "homework" you plan to do — whether it's just taking care of emergencies and small repair tasks or tackling serious home improvement and woodworking projects. Then there's the do-it-yourself survivalist. You know the type: He drives screws with a butter knife and pounds in nails with a saucepan. Do not loan tools to this fellow.

In this chapter, we walk you through the basics. We discuss the tools that you need based on your level of do-it-yourself involvement, offer tips on when and where to buy your tools, and give you some ideas for convenient, safe tool storage. You can also find tips about workbenches and advice about when renting tools is preferable to buying them. Subsequent chapters get into more details, including how to use the tools.

A Place of One's Own

Carpentry repairs and home improvement jobs are largely site-based work. Oh, you may set up sawhorses outdoors or in the garage for cutting, sanding, painting, and doing other dirty work, but to make the job easier and faster, we recommend that you set up shop as close to your work as possible. Depending on the project, your "shop" may be nothing more that a bucket of tools and an old blanket or drop cloth to protect the floor. If you show up with only a bucket of chicken, however, you're not going to have a very productive day.

Regardless, you need a permanent place to stow your tools and organize fasteners and other supplies. You may dream of a workshop like Norm's on "This Old House," but in the real world, most of us are hard-pressed for space and don't have advertisers sending us free tools. At the bare minimum, find room for a designated workspace somewhere in your house, garage, basement, or shed. (Your spouse's walk-in closet is not an option.) Your workspace doesn't have to be fancy — anywhere with good lighting and electrical power will do. Find someplace bigger than the kitchen junk drawer to stow your tools, and make sure there is a nearby outlet to plug in a charger for power-tool batteries. If you have the room, it's also nice to have a workbench where you can glue up a broken drawer, lay out a window frame that needs new screening — or play poker (after completing your work, of course).

Tool Storage

Concentrate first on providing storage space for your tools. We suggest that you keep a fairly large toolbox, a tool bucket, and provisions to store these items and other tools, including any power tools, in the workshop. Here's what works well for us:

- ✔ **Keep a stash of the tools you use most often in some kind of portable toolbox.** Some toolboxes even provide a sturdy surface to stand on, which comes in handy. Ideally, it has two or three divided drawers. Use one drawer for screwdrivers, pliers, pencils, utility knives, and other small tools that you use most often. In the other drawers, organize a handful of various sizes and types of screws, nails, hollow wall and masonry anchors, picture hooks, a few adhesive bandages, and other such things in divided compartments. The purpose of this toolbox is to provide a small supply of just about anything you might need when you bring your toolbox to the area where you're working. Warning: Resist the temptation to buy or build a big toolbox for all your tools and supplies. Why? In a word: hernia.

- ✔ **Buy or salvage a 5-gallon bucket.** At times, you know that you'll need only a few specific tools and supplies. For those occasions, we suggest salvaging an empty 5-gallon drywall compound bucket. (Check out any building or remodeling site in the late stages of the project, and you're sure to find one.) Fill it with water to soften any dried compound, wash it out, and you've got a nice sturdy bucket. Or ask for a bucket at a local doughnut shop. (Do you think they actually make that jelly filling themselves?) Gather only the tools and supplies that you know you will need and toss them in the bucket.

Tool stores, home centers, and mail-order outlets sell fabric tool pouches that are specifically designed to fit on 5-gallon buckets. You can insert numerous tools in pouches around the outside of the bucket and keep the inside for power tools, sandpaper, glue, extension cords, or other items that you need for the project at hand.

✔ **Use tool and nail pouches for items you need to carry.** Many tasks require that you carry a few tools and perhaps one or two types of fasteners with you. Buy a decent cloth-style apron that's a step up from the simple give-away two-compartment nail pouches. A belt that holds a holster for a hammer or portable drill is worth considering. If you get involved in full-scale remodeling work, you may want heavy-duty cloth or leather tool belts with numerous pouches and provisions for tools such as hammers, tape measures, nail sets, and so on. The best thing about tool belts is that you no longer need to carry around ten tools and a pound of nails in your pants pocket.

✔ **Provide storage in the shop.** Finally, you need to provide a place to store your toolbox, tool bucket, tools that you don't use often, tools that you use only at the workbench, and tools that don't fit into your toolbox. Some combination of *open storage*, such as hooks on walls or Peg-Board and open shelving, and *closed storage* such as drawers of various depths and cabinets, works best.

If you have young children in your home (or, for that matter, older ones who never remember to put tools back where they belong), consider having at least one lockable cabinet for tools and supplies that may be dangerous.

Zillions of perfectly serviceable kitchen cabinets are tossed out with the trash. Perhaps you can snag a couple for your shop. Hang an upper cabinet on the wall (see Chapter 14) and set up a drawer base below it. Secure a wall cabinet with screws through the nailers (the thicker strips of wood at the top and bottom of the cabinet) and into studs or anchors in concrete walls. Take time to level and plumb a base cabinet by using shims (or other thin pieces of wood) under or behind the cabinet, as needed. If your shop is in your garage, install shallow shelves by nailing 1x4 boards in the spaces between the wall studs. If your workbench is anywhere else, you can create extra storage space by making a simple bookcase-style shelf unit.

Inexpensive drawer hardware and a piece of plywood are all you need to install a rollout shelf in your secondhand cabinet. Just cut the plywood shelf *exactly* 1 inch narrower than the width of the cabinet (or as directed by the slide installation instructions). Attach half the slide to the cabinet wall and the other half to the edges of your shelf.

Workbenches

If you've been working off the hood of your car, then you know how important it is to have one small work surface, such as a workbench or a base cabinet with a counter. If you're really tight for space, try a collapsible work table, such as The Workmate made by Black & Decker. Or hinge a piece of plywood on the wall so that you can pop it up when you need it and drop it down out of the way when you don't. Although a permanent workbench is convenient, more often than not, such a surface is either too small or so cluttered that you use it only occasionally.

You can buy a ready-to-assemble workbench or make one from scratch. The advantage of making your own is that you control the size and can build in features such as drawers or shelves underneath. Using the right hardware makes the assembly easier and guarantees a sturdy result.

If you're going to build a workbench for a basement shop, be sure that it's not too big to fit through the doorway.

Although a permanent bench is handy, you may find that a large, temporary table is even more useful. Have on hand a pair of 36-inch-tall, sturdy sawhorses and some sort of flat surface for a top. Typically, sawhorses are closer to 24 inches tall, which is a fine height for the work that they derive their name from but too low for a worktable or counter. A salvaged flush door (one without any raised panels) is big enough for most projects, yet small enough to handle easily and store on-end. Or a 6- or 7-foot length of 30-inch-wide, ¾-inch-thick B/C-grade plywood works well.

If you're going to use a piece of ¾-inch-thick plywood for your workbench top, take a few minutes to nail and glue strips of 1x2 pine all around its edge. These pine strips stiffen the plywood and protect the edges from damage and splintering. Cut strips for the short sides first and nail them to the glued edge of the plywood with 4d finishing nails every 8 to 12 inches. The pine strips should be flush with the smooth, "good" side of the plywood. Then measure and cut the strips for the long front and back edges and fasten them the same way as the short sides. Sand the surface and seal both sides with a clear sealer or varnish to prevent it from warping and to make it easier to clean up spills. If you plan to hang the plywood panel on the wall, consider installing a pair of eyebolts in the edge of the top and a mating pair of hooks on a cleat attached to your wall.

The Top Tools for Any Home Carpenter

Shop for home carpentry tools in home centers, hardware stores, or large discount department stores. Don't try to buy all the tools that you'll ever need at one time; instead, buy tools as you need them. Focus on quality rather than quantity, and buy the best-quality tools you can afford. After all, you need good performance at least as much as a pro does and maybe more: The pro goes home when the project's done, but you have to live with it.

As competitive as the tool industry is, you can pretty much tell the quality of a tool by the price. Although a less expensive tool may sometimes do a perfectly adequate job and be durable enough for a home carpenter's needs, you probably can't judge a tool's performance unless you have a chance to try the tool (and that's not usually an option). Tool performance and durability often go hand in hand, but you should focus on performance. You can't get around the fact that a $200 portable jigsaw is going to do better work than a $30 one. As a do-it-yourselfer, you may not need the durability that a professional carpenter does, but a novice needs a tool that produces quality results as much as a professional does. Bottom line: You get what you pay for.

The tool-buying experience can be daunting for a first-time home carpenter. As you roam the aisles of mega-stores, don't let the overwhelming selection intimidate you. Ask a salesperson for help and explain that you're new to the do-it-yourself scene. A knowledgeable salesperson can help you make your decision by explaining how the wide range of prices reflect the quality, features, and materials of various tools.

The following sections present the three basic tool kits you need as you travel the road of home carpentry adventures. The tool suggestions are based on more years of experience than we — as homeowners, do-it-your-selfers, and professionals — care to admit. We describe these tools in some detail in the next few chapters.

A beginner's DIY tool kit

This beginner's tool kit includes tools that you definitely don't want to be without. This list contains the basic supplies for handling emergencies and for performing simple, everyday, carpentry-related repair, maintenance, and installation tasks. You should get these tools before you really need them so that you always have them on hand.

Adjustable wrench	Dust mask	Magnetic bit holder with #1 and #2 Phillips bits
Caulking gun	Hacksaw	
Claw hammer (16-ounce)	Hex wrench set	Nail pullers (2 sizes)
	Locking pliers (Vise-Grips)	Needle-nose pliers (6-inch)
Cordless drill/driver (⅜-inch)		Neon circuit tester

Nail sets (set of 3)

Putty knife

Retractable tape measure (16-foot)

Rubber sanding block

Safety goggles/glasses

Screw/nut driver (6-in-1)

Slip-joint pliers

Toolbox saw (aggressive or fast-cutting)

Torpedo level

Twist bit drill index (15-piece)

Utility knife

Home maintenance and repair tool kit

You can expand the beginner's tool kit by adding the following tools, which will equip you to handle most carpentry-related maintenance and repair tasks. Here's where you really start to buy tools more on an as-needed basis as opposed to a "gee-whiz-look-at-that" basis. When you are about to undertake a project and are putting together your shopping list, think through the process or read directions to determine what tools you'll need.

Carpenter's level

Chalk line

Combination square

Compass/scribe

Coping saw

Drywall taping knife (6-inch)

Ear protection (plugs or muffs)

End-cutting pliers ("nippers")

Extension cord (25-foot)

Knee pads

More drill accessories: set of spade bits and set of masonry bits

Random-orbit sander

Rough pry bar

Set of contractor-grade wood chisels ($\frac{1}{4}$-, $\frac{1}{2}$-, $\frac{3}{4}$-, and 1-inch)

Socket wrench set

Spring clamps and speed clamps

Staple gun

Surform rasp

Trim pry bar

Independent homeowner's tool kit

Here's a tool kit for the aspiring carpenter/woodworker who wants to take care of all carpentry-related maintenance and repair tasks but who also wants to tackle more involved home improvements, such as building and installing storage solutions, upgrading doors or windows, trimming rooms, installing cabinets, and removing shutters from the neighbor's house. Make the following additions to the above tool kits, and you'll be well equipped.

Belt sander

Block plane

Drywall square

Electric drill ($\frac{1}{2}$-inch)

Framing square with stair gauge

Hammer drill

Hole saw (2 $\frac{1}{8}$-inch, for starters)

Hot-melt glue gun

Lineman's pliers

More clamps: Pipe clamps, hand screw, quick bar clamps

More drill accessories: combination drill/countersink, self-centering bit

Pole sander

Portable circular saw (7 ¼-inch)

Protractor guide/speed square

Respirator

Retractable tape measure (25-foot x 1-inch)

Ripping hammer (20-ounce)

Sabre saw (portable jigsaw)

Screen spline installing tool

Set of butt hinge marking gauges

Sliding T-bevel

Staple gun

Water level

Wet/dry shop vacuum

Window zipper

Zip tool (for vinyl siding repair)

Renting May Be the Way to Go

Unless you're tackling a major remodeling project that involves the full gamut of work, you're likely to use some power tools only once a year or so. Visit your local tool rental outlets and bring home a list of available tools. Naturally, the primary motivation for renting is that it's usually a lot cheaper than buying if you rarely use the item. But perhaps an additional benefit of renting is that the tool you rent is usually a much higher-quality tool than one you'd likely buy. Better tools usually have more features and perform better, which means better-quality work accomplished in less time. Here are just a few of the many great tools that you may want to rent:

- **Miter saws and sliding compound miter saws.** The only way to go when trimming a room. They produce incredibly accurate angle cuts in a fraction of the time that it takes to cut them by hand using a miter box.

- **Reciprocating saw.** A virtual necessity in a significant demolition/remodeling project. With blades of all sizes designed to cut all sorts of materials, it works in places that handsaws can't go.

- **Router.** Often used in woodworking projects. If you find that you do this work more than once a year, move it into the independent homeowner's tool kit. But for one-time efforts, such as building bookcases for your new home office, consider renting.

- **Builder's level.** Looks like a transit that you see land surveyors use. This level has one primary function: to determine the relative level of one point to another, generally over long distances that cannot easily be done with a spirit level. It is very accurate and handy but not the type of tool you need more than once or twice.

Part II
Tools and
Techniques

The 5th Wave   By Rich Tennant

In this part . . .

You're gonna love this part of the book, especially if you're tool-deprived, because you'll find out about all kinds of tools you're sure to covet. And along with a description and explanation of the tools, we show you how to use them. We've grouped the tools according to general function. For example, there's an array of measuring, marking, and layout tools, many of which should be a mainstay in your toolbox. Cutting, shaping, and smoothing wood and materials are the categories of tools you'll find a lot of use for. The same goes for fastening and unfastening tools. And no tool section would be complete without "miscellaneous" (Chapter 7), where some of our favorites are featured. We round out this part of the book by putting those tools to work with descriptions of rough and finish carpentry skills that we hope you'll master.

Chapter 4

Measuring, Marking, and Layout

· ·

In This Chapter

▶ Getting accurate measurements

▶ Making things square, level, and plumb

▶ Finding out about marking tools

· ·

*I*n virtually all carpentry projects, accurate measuring is crucial to the success of your project. Accurate measuring gives you the existing dimensions of your situation so that you can successfully plan and execute future tasks. For example, measuring helps explain why that 4-foot-wide window doesn't fit into that 46-inch-wide wall opening. And you can use the tools that help you measure dimensions and check whether things are square, plumb, or level in other ways. For example, you can use them to accurately measure how far *off* plumb things are, or to build roofs, stairs, and diagonal counters at a specified angle or slope. So in many (if not all) cases, the tools in this category serve more than one purpose. Want another example? In addition to measuring simple dimensions, a tape measure or framing square may tell you whether something is square or help you quickly locate wall studs. We'll tell you how.

Today, you can buy fancy laser levels, electronic distance-measuring devices, and a slew of other specialized tools. Some are essential for certain tasks, some let you do a job faster or easier, and some just take up space (like that rowing machine rusting in the garage). Fortunately, you really need to know how to use only a few of these tools. This chapter focuses on these few tools.

How to Measure Up

For convenience and ease of use, the primary tool for measuring is a retractable tape measure. This flexible metal ruler rolls up inside a palm-size case. The blade extends when you need it and retracts when you don't. It sure beats walking around with a 16-foot ruler into your pants pocket! The tool is marked in ⅟₁₆-inch increments and also has special layout markings (usually colored arrows) every 16 inches that coincide with the most widely used framing spacing, 16 inches on center. Some tape measures have handy information printed on the backside, too, such as decimal equivalents of commonly used fractions.

A hook on the tape end is made to slide back and forth a bit so that you can take an accurate measurement whether you are hooking the end over the edge of an object or butting the end of the tape to an object.

Tape measures that are 16 feet and longer all have a mechanism that lets you lock the extended tape at any desired position. When the lock is released (or the unlocked tape is unhooked from an object), a strong spring rapidly rewinds the tape back into the case.

Although a tape measure is relatively harmless, the closing force can snap the hook right off the end of the rule or pinch fingers if you let it retract at full speed back into the case. It can even snap the blade back into your face. So when using a tape measure, always wear goggles and use the locking mechanism as a brake to slow down the blade as the end nears the case. If you let your children use it, show them how and when to apply the brake, too.

A 16-foot tape measure with a ¾-inch-wide blade is sufficient for most small carpentry projects around the home and in the shop. You need a 25-foot tape with a stiffer, 1-inch-wide blade for larger construction projects such as building a deck or a fence or installing exterior house trim.

The tool is flexible in more than one sense. Figure 4-1 and the following list explain several ways to use a tape measure:

- ✔ Butt the end of the tape against one surface and extend the tape past the other point; read the measurement where the tape passes over that point. This outside-to-outside approach is the most exacting way to measure a piece of lumber or plywood.

- ✔ Extend the tape between two surfaces, with the butt end against one surface and the tape case against the other; read the dimension at the mouth of the case and add the length of the case (it's printed on the side). This is a good way to make accurate measurements of things like window frames, door openings, and cabinets.

- ✔ Butt the end of the tape against one surface, extend the tape, and bend it when you reach the opposite surface. Estimate which marking would fall at the corner. If you look straight into the corner across your tape and line up a marking with the corner, your "guesstimate" will usually be accurate within ¹⁄₁₆ inch. This method is best used for measurements that don't have to be perfectly accurate, like when you need to know the dimensions of a room.

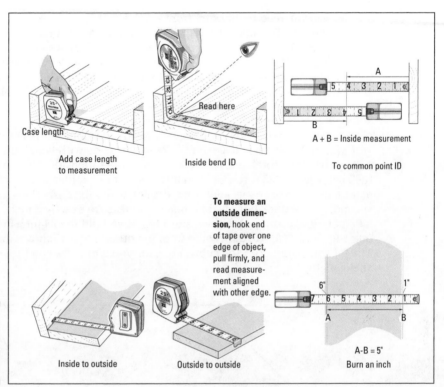

Case length

Add case length to measurement

Read here

Inside bend ID

A

B

A + B = Inside measurement

To common point ID

To measure an outside dimension, hook end of tape over one edge of object, pull firmly, and read measurement aligned with other edge.

6"

1"

A

B

A-B = 5"

Burn an inch

Inside to outside

Outside to outside

Figure 4-1: Measuring with a tape measure.

✔ For greater accuracy when taking an inside measurement between, say, two interior walls or two sides of a closet, take two measurements — one from each end to a common point between them, and add the results. To make adding in your head easier, make the first measurement a nice round number like 4 feet or 10 feet, not 9 feet 7³⁄₁₆ inches.

✔ When you are measuring from a mark, rather than a corner or edge that you can either hook over or butt into (like in the middle of a piece of plywood), you may want to "burn an inch." No, we're not talking Jenny Craig here. Position the tape so that the 1-inch marking is on your pencil mark. Read your dimension at the other end of the tape and then subtract the inch that you added because you started your measurement at 1 inch instead of at the end of the tape.

Although this works beautifully, it's also the cause of all too many boards being cut exactly 1 inch shorter than intended. Remind yourself out loud to "Burn an inch, burn an inch. . . ." as you take the measurement and again as you transfer it to the workpiece. You don't want to hear yourself saying, "I cut it twice and it's still too short."

✔ When you need to measure from a point that is out of reach (like to the far end of a box-filled crawlspace), you can extend a tape measure through the air. Most tape measures extend a long way before they droop. By the way, a 1-inch-wide blade is stiffer and, concave-face-up, can be extended much farther without support than a ¾-inch-wide blade. Blade stiffness varies by tool brand and the age/wear of the blade, too.

Sometimes you need to determine how long to make a board that, when placed between two others, will equal a particular dimension. For example, if you want to build a bookcase that is 24 inches wide with ¾-inch-thick sides, you subtract the total side (2 x ¾ = 1½) from the total width (24) to determine the shelf width (22½). You can run into two complications here: First, you can make a math error (especially when dealing with mixed fractions), and second, ¾-inch-thick boards do not always measure exactly ¾ inch. To eliminate potential error, put the two sides together, hold the 24-inch mark against one edge and read the dimension from the other edge, as shown in Figure 4-2. The tape measure does the subtracting for you and gives you the required shelf length.

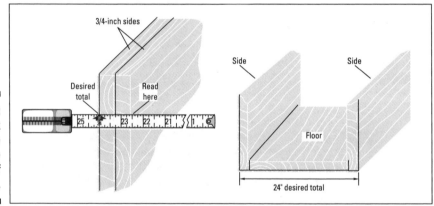

Figure 4-2:
A no-risk approach to determine proper shelf width.

How to Be Level-Headed

With a few exceptions — most notably, the roof — a house and all its various elements are built *square* (90-degree corners), and either *plumb* (truly vertical) or *level* (truly horizontal). Nothing sticks out more than a built-in bookshelf that is a little racked, a wall that leans out, or a countertop that runs downhill. To make sure everything you do is square, plumb, or level, you have to know how to use several different kinds of levels.

When you need to check horizontal surfaces for level and vertical surfaces for plumb, a *spirit level* is the tool to use. Spirit levels have a metal or wood frame with one or more slightly curved glass vials that contain a clear fluid and an air bubble. The vials are set precisely parallel, perpendicular, or at a 45-degree angle to the frame. Because air tends to rise in a fluid, the bubble rises to the top and center of the vial when it is truly horizontal (level), vertical (plumb), or at a 45-degree angle off vertical and plumb. Levels with paired vials that have more pronounced curves are easier to use. Always read the top vial of a pair.

The spirit levels you'll need most are the *carpenter's* level and the *torpedo* level:

- ✔ A lightweight, aluminum-body 2-foot *carpenter's level* is a handy size that's suited to large and small tasks. If you need a longer level to get more accurate readings, you can "stretch" a 2-foot level by pairing it with any long straightedge.

- ✔ Like the carpenter's level, a magnetic *torpedo level* has a level, plumb, and 45-degree vials. But its 9-inch length makes it handier for leveling over short distances or when a 2-foot level won't fit where it needs to be positioned.

Of course, a level will do more harm than good if it gets out of whack. Here's how to check the accuracy of a spirit level: Mark a level line and a plumb line on a wall. Then flip the level over or end for end, as shown in Figure 4-3. It should again read level or plumb. If not, the vials are no longer in the correct position. The vials in some levels are adjustable, and some expensive levels may be worth having repaired. But in most cases, you probably just need to buy a new level if yours no longer gives an accurate reading. Buy a hard plastic case for a carpenter's level and take care not to bang or drop a level.

Figure 4-3: Verifying the accuracy of a level is easy.

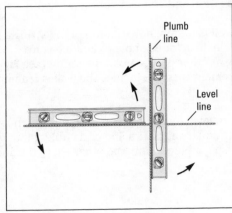

Plumb line

Level line

When you need to check level across a long distance a *water level* is the way to go. A *water level* is simply a clear tube partially filled with water and capped on one end. Extend the tube in a U-shape between any two points, and the top of each column of water will always be level because Isaac Newton said so. Of course, he's also the guy who sat under an apple tree while fruit was bouncing off his noggin. Although you may need a water level only once or twice in your second career as an independent homeowner, it's the easiest, most low-tech way to check level when, say, you want to be sure that each post for a deck or fence is cut off at the same height as the first one you cut. And here's how you do it: Hold an end of the tube against each post, and move the ends up or down the posts until the top of the water column is at the top of the first post; then mark the second post at the top of the other water column. Although you can buy a water level, you can also make one by filling any length of clear tubing with water. Add food coloring to make the water more visible.

When you need to make sure something is straight up and down (wallpaper, wall framing, and so on), a *plumb bob* is the tool for you. A plumb bob is a precision-engineered, balanced weight that hangs perfectly straight from a string so that its point lies directly below the spot where the top of the string is positioned.

To find out where to, say, put the top and bottom of a new wall-framing member, suspend the plumb from a high point and have a helper steady the plumb initially but then allow it to come to a standstill with its point just above the surface being marked.

To draw a plumb line on the wall, you need to do an extra step (the bob does not allow the string to sit against the wall). So, to transfer the location of the string to the wall, hold a square against the wall and move it so that the other blade just touches the string. Then mark the wall at the edge of the blade. Repeat this in a second location and connect your marks with a straightedge.

To determine whether a wall is plumb, hold the top of the string a known distance from the wall — 1 ½ inches, for example — and measure the distance from the wall to the string at other points along the string (see Figure 4-4). If you get any other measurement than 1 ½ inches, the wall is leaning in or out by the difference.

You can use a plumb bob to level by using it with a square, such as a framing square. With one leg of the square against a line or an object that you have determined is plumb by using a plumb bob, the other leg of the square will necessarily be level.

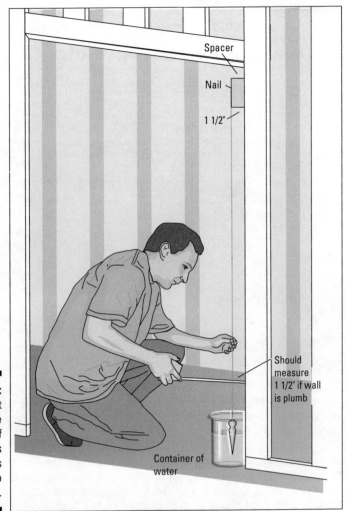

Spacer

Nail

1 1/2"

Should measure 1 1/2" if wall is plumb

Container of water

Figure 4-4:
You can't beat the accuracy of a plumb (as long as it's not too windy).

How to Be Square

If you've ever tried to "eyeball" a cut across a 2x6, a sheet of plywood or even a 2x4, you know that the result is almost always crooked. That's why the ancient carpenters invented the square, and why carpenters through time have used it to mark square cuts, then check their cuts after they were made. Today, as much as it was yesterday, a square is an essential tool, one that makes the difference between trash and tremendous.

A *combination square* should be in every would-be carpenter's toolbox. This multipurpose measuring/marking/leveling has a lockable, sliding 1-foot ruler that's square to one face of the body and at a 45-degree angle to the other. Figure 4-5 illustrates some of the many uses of a combination square.

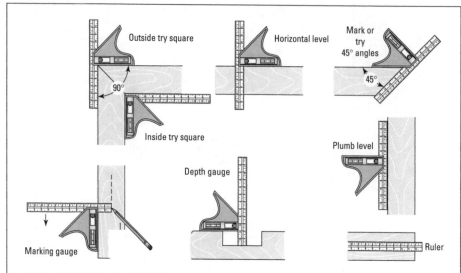

Figure 4-5:
The versatile combination square belongs in every do-it-yourselfer's toolbox.

Professional carpenters use a *framing square,* also called a *rafter square,* to lay out roofs and stairs — its two legs are conveniently sized to match standard stud spacing (no measuring required!).

Homeowners usually use a framing square, shown in Figure 4-6, to test, set, or mark a square corner. Its long legs make it a reliable straightedge, too: Held against anything, it shows whether the object is straight or flat or can be used to guide a straight pencil line. Imprinted on the blades are tables and formulas for a variety of building-related calculations. A little booklet comes with the square that describes how to use the tool and its tables.

A *speed square* and a *protractor guide* are two handy tools that you use to guide a circular saw making crosscuts on boards. Hold the guide against the edge of a board with one hand, as shown in Figure 4-7, and make the cut with the saw shoe against the other edge of the guide. The speed square guides 45- and 90-degree cuts. The protractor can be set to any angle between 45 and 90 degrees.

Figure 4-6:
The framing square has the long legs necessary to test whether two surfaces are truly square, such as the doorframe being installed here.

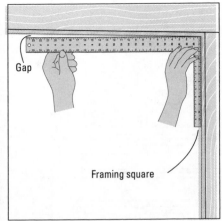

Figure 4-7:
Use a speed square and protractor guide for marking; you can also use them to guide crosscuts with a circular saw.

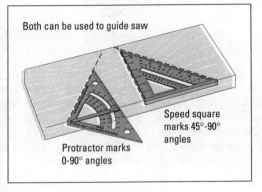

An inexpensive stationery-store compass marks circles, but carpenters use it more often to mark a *scribe*. A scribe is a cut made on the edge of one material to make it conform to the irregular shape of another. If you were paneling a wall up to a stone or brick chimney, as shown in Figure 4-8 for example, you would scribe the edge of the paneling so it would fit neatly against the stone. If you draw a scribe's metal point against an irregular surface and hold the pencil point against the material to be marked for cutting, the pattern will be transferred.

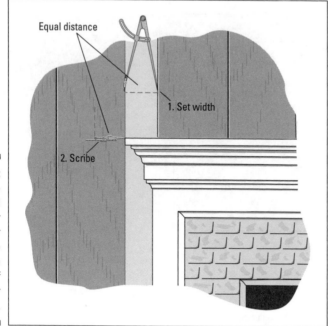

Equal distance

1. Set width

2. Scribe

Figure 4-8:
Use a scribe
to mark and
cut wood or
another
material so
it will match
the profile of
an irregular
surface.

You must maintain a consistent angle relative to the surface or your penciled line will not accurately reflect the profile of the surface. More often than not, you must make more than one scribe cut to get a perfect fit, so whenever possible make sure that the piece being scribed is large enough to allow that. Only when the scribe is perfect do you then cut the opposite side (a straight cut) to length. If this is not possible, you can make a template by scribing a piece of plywood, for example, and, once it's right, trace the irregular line onto the other material.

A *sliding T-bevel* may sound like a wrestling move, but it's a valuable tool when you must duplicate an angle that is neither 90 nor 45 degrees. The T-bevel has a blade that slides and pivots at any angle in relation to the handle, and it features a thumbscrew lock to hold a measured angle. Be aware that the T-bevel has no markings, so you won't know the actual value of the angle, but you will be able to measure an existing angle and transfer that precise angle to another piece of material. To gauge the existing angle, set the handle of the tool against one plane, and the blade against the other plane, and tighten the thumbscrew. To transfer the angle, position the bevel in the same relative position against the material to be cut and pencil a line against the blade, as shown in Figure 4-9. If you do want to know the angle, hold the T-bevel square against a protractor.

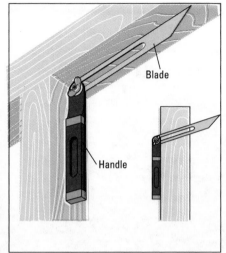

Figure 4-9:
Transfer
angles from
one object
to another
with a
sliding
T-bevel.

Blade

Handle

How to Make Your Mark

Measuring is just part of the process. Most of the time you also have to make a mark so you know where to cut, where to attach something, or where to start. A pencil will do the job in most cases, but sometimes you need something else.

A *butt marker* isn't a leaky pen in your back pocket. It's a metal jig that serves only one specialized function: It marks the outline of the area that you must cut out (called a *mortise*) to accommodate the leaf of a butt hinge on a door-jamb and on the edge of the door. Butt markers are available in several sizes.

To use the butt marker, place the device at the desired distance from the top of the door (or from the top of a jamb) with its two guide tabs against the face of the door (or the edge of the jamb). Then strike the butt marker with a couple of sharp blows from a hammer, as shown in Figure 4-10. The sharpened edges of the butt marker will cut into the wood, marking the outline of the mortise.

A *chalk line* or *chalk reel* contains a spool of string in a chalk-filled cavity that can be extended from one point to another to mark a straight line between them. Carpenters usually use the tool to snap a line on plywood, drywall, or other panel materials to mark them for cutting. But you can also use a chalk line to mark a straight guideline against which things, such as flooring tiles, are positioned.

To use a chalk line, hook the string end over the edge of an object, such as a piece of plywood or drywall (or have a helper hold the string at that point) and extend the string taut to a second point. Lift the string straight up a few inches above the surface with your other hand and snap it against the surface *once*. On very long lines, have a helper press down on the taut string at roughly its midpoint, and then snap each half of the line separately.

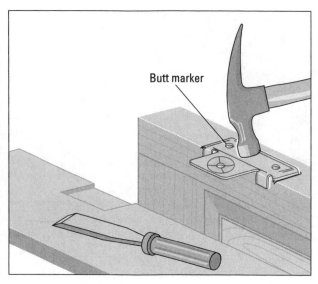

Butt marker

Figure 4-10:
A butt marker marks the precise location and size of the mortise for the two halves of a butt hinge on a door and the doorjamb.

Although a chalk line is not as accurate as a plumb bob (see the section "Keep Your Spirits Up"), the chalk line can double as one.

How to Find Studs

A *stud finder* is a handy tool to have when you need to attach heavy things to the walls or ceilings, and want to make sure you get the fasteners into solid wood instead of wallboard. Plain and simple, a stud finder helps you locate and mark the position of framing members. So, no, it isn't a tool for finding hunks in a bar (unless they're trapped in the walls!).

The electronic models "sense" the mass of a framing member, such as a wall stud or ceiling joist, behind drywall or plaster. You place the battery-operated device against the wall (or ceiling) and slide it left or right until an array of lights and/or beeping sounds signals that the tool is centered over or at the edge of the framing. Only the high-end models do well on plaster, tile, or double-thick drywall walls and ceilings. An inexpensive magnetic model locates framing behind drywall by finding the metal fasteners that secure it to the framing. With the tool against the wall, search around until the magnetic needle pivots over the point where the head of a nail or screw attracts it.

Chapter 5

Cutting, Shaping, and Smoothing

. . . .

In This Chapter

▶ Planes, knives, chisels, and saws

▶ Get on the cutting edge with power saws

▶ Tips that make tricky cuts easier and safer

▶ Sanders that get the job done faster

. . . .

*T*his chapter is about cutting, shaping, and finishing wood, not your hands, legs, fingers, and toes. Obviously, a tool that can cut wood has the potential to really do a number on skin and bones. With the increased availability of affordable good-quality power tools, comes increased risk for do-it-yourselfers. The bottom line: A handsaw can *cut* your hand, but a portable circular saw can *cut off* your hand. Do-it-yourselfers generally do not learn proper tool use in a school or as an apprentice to a carpenter. Some read the tool manual (as everyone should), but most learn by trial-and-error (and injury).

Don't forget these important general safety tips when using cutting, shaping, and sanding tools:

✔ **Wear eye protection** for cutting operations and a dust mask for sanding work. Ear plugs or muffs protect your hearing.

✔ **Store tools safely.** If you have very young children, safe storage may mean placing them in a locked or out-of-reach cabinet.

✔ **Never turn off a power tool by disconnecting the plug,** particularly with power tools that have a lock-on option, such as a saber saw (they already could be on the next time you plug them in!). As an added precaution, never plug in a power tool unless the tool is in your hand or somewhere it could do no damage if its switch is in the on position.

✔ **Cover, retract, remove, or otherwise store cutting tools** and accessories to protect yourself from accidental contact when you reach into a toolbox or inadvertently power up a tool.

✔ **Cut away from, not toward your body or hand** when using knives, chisels, and similar cutting tools; use clamps, not your hand, to hold the piece.

- ✔ **Don't overreach.** Maintaining full control over a heavy power saw or sander is hard enough when it's at your side and held with two hands. Overreaching results in reduced control of the tool. You increase the chance of making an error, having the tool kick back, damaging the work, or injuring yourself.

- ✔ **Use sharp cutting tools.** Using a sharp tool is safer than using a dull one. A not-so-sharp chisel blade, for example, will tend to skip out of the cutting area, making a nasty gouge in the wood or your hand. With a sharp tool you need to exert less force and therefore can maintain greater control. You also get better results with less work.

- ✔ **Place a fire extinguisher in a clear and prominent place.** Read the owner's manual and know how to use the device. For fast access, have more than one fire extinguisher in different parts of your work area.

- ✔ **Do not wear jewelry or loose clothing.** A ring, watch, or neck chain can get caught easily in the equipment. Baggy clothes are also a hazard. If you have long hair, tie it back.

Some tools and blades can be sharpened, but others are considered throwaway items by the pros. Of course, what is expedient for a contractor may be expensive for the DIYer. You'll need to weigh the cost of buying a new tool against the time and trouble of sharpening it.

Handy Saws

Roy was on his first carpentry job and, being practically tool-less, he asked to borrow a handsaw from the trim carpenter on the job. With a straight face the carpenter asked, "What's that?" Easily intimidated, Roy could respond only with "Huh?" Roy got the joke when the carpenter smiled and explained that he used one so rarely that he didn't carry one in his toolbox. "There might be one buried in my truck," he added. (Roy didn't find one.)

Although power saws have all but replaced the handsaw and other non-powered saws for most cutting operations, there are still times when using a hand tool is more efficient or better.

While technically a *handsaw* is any non-powered saw that cuts wood, most people think of a handsaw as the familiar crosscut saw. But there's more to the "standard" saw. *Crosscut saws* are designed to cut across the grain, *ripsaws* for cutting with the grain, and *combination saws* for doing both.

In fact, hand saws come in dozens of types. A basic toolkit should include a small combination saw and a *hacksaw*. You can buy a *coping saw* (looks like a "C") and *compass saw* (looks like a swordfish) or a similar *keyhole saw* (looks like a skinny sword) or *drywall saw* (a keyhole saw with a thicker, coarser-toothed blade) as needed.

Toolbox handsaw

The relatively short toolbox handsaw is a particularly aggressive type of combination ripsaw and crosscut saw that works well for cutting lumber along its length (*ripping*) and across its width (*crosscutting*). You may see a toolbox handsaw advertised as "fast cutting" or by various trade names that suggest that feature, but you can easily recognize one by its short length and its tooth configuration. This saw has very many teeth of varying sizes set at a steep angle, sometimes referred to as "shark teeth."

Contrary to what you might think, handsaws such as the toolbox saw take considerably more skill and experience to use efficiently and accurately than a power saw. Here are the basics:

- ✔ **Support the work** at a convenient height that allows you to hold the work in place with your knee and the weight of your body. Otherwise, secure the work with a clamp to prevent it from chattering around during the cut. Clamping also permits a two-handed grip, which gives you more control and makes the task easier.

- ✔ **Start the cut** by holding the saw nearly upright, and place the midpoint of the blade on the waste side of your cut line. With your other hand, grip the work and rest the side of your pointed index finger or thumb against the blade to guide the start of your cut. Make a few short, slow pulling strokes to start the cut and a couple of full-length backstrokes until the *kerf* (the channel left by a saw blade) is about ½-inch deep.

- ✔ **Complete the cut** by using push-and-pull strokes. When the blade is contained in the kerf, you can move your hand out of harm's way.

- ✔ **Support the waste piece** as needed to prevent it from sagging or breaking off near the end of the cut. You may be able to reach with your other hand to support a short cutoff; but if the cutoff is long, it's best to have a helper support the waste end. Or, if you're alone, you can reverse the board when you're halfway through so that the longer waste end is fully supported and the work end is hanging over your support. Switch your position to the other side, and start sawing. As you complete the cut, use slow, gentle, vertical strokes, and support the waste.

This tool can help you cope

The *coping saw* is the hand-operated version of the *scroll saw*. The blade, which is not much bigger than a piece of string, and the tool's large, C-shaped frame enable you to make very tight (sharp) curves in relatively thin materials (under ¾-inch). The blade is normally mounted to the frame with the teeth facing out so they cut on the downstroke. You can easily switch it so the teeth face inward, flip it upside down to cut on the upstroke, or turn it so the teeth face sideways, if required.

The primary application for the coping saw is for interior and exterior trim. (Woodworking hobbyists also use it for some fancy joinery work, but we won't get into that here.) *Coping a joint,* as the process is called, is a trim joinery technique where two pieces of molding meet at an inside corner. Although cutting 45-degree angles on two pieces of molding that meet at an inside corner (called a *miter joint*) is possible, the *coped joint* (in which one piece is cut to fit the curves of the other) is less likely to open up and more tolerant of out-of-square corners.

To cope a joint, using baseboard trim as an example, follow these steps.

1. **Extend a piece of baseboard on one wall all the way to the corner. The end should be cut square.**

2. **Cut an open miter on the end of another baseboard, just as you might if you were planning a mitered joint (in which two 45-degree angles meet to form the 90-degree inside corner).**

   Use a pencil to trace a line where the bevel surface meets the face of the first baseboard (as shown in Figure 5-1a).

3. **Place the second baseboard face up and overhanging the edge of a sawhorse. Use a coping saw (see Figure 5-1b) to cut the line you traced.**

   If possible, clamp your workpiece or kneel on it so you can hold the saw by the handle with one hand and by the forward end of the saw frame with the other hand.

4. **Starting at the top edge of the trim, make your cut perpendicular to the face of the board. Then immediately change the blade angle so that you will cut more off the back of the board than the front (called *back cutting*) and complete the cut following your line. (See Figure 5-1c.)**

   While baseboard and other moldings that are installed flat against the wall require only slight back-cutting, coped joints on crown molding or other moldings that are installed at an angle, require much greater back-cutting.

   To avoid splintering the wood as you start the cut, use very light pressure until the kerf forms; as you complete the cut, support the waste and use very slow, controlled stokes with minimal pressure.

If you are working with trim that has a wide flat surface and is only molded at the top, such as base molding, you may want to use another saw to make the straight portion of the cut and use the coping saw for the molded portion only.

More handy saws

While rarely used in carpentry per se, you often need a *hacksaw* for cutting metals and other nonwood materials for "carpentry" projects, such as installing wire-shelving units.

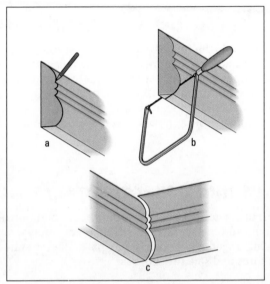

Figure 5-1:
Coping a
joint.

A special-purpose *mini-hacksaw* is very compact — virtually no more than a blade and a small holder/handle. Because the blade is unsupported at the front end, you can insert it into a crack to cut fasteners or in other similar situations where the frame of a full-size hacksaw prevents its use.

Several other saws are very similar in that they each have pointed blades ranging from about 6 to 12 inches long. You can insert the blades into relatively small holes or slots to make an internal cut as a saber saw might. And like the mini-hacksaw, you can insert it into a crack to cut a troublesome screw or nail. The *compass saw* and the *keyhole saw* have traditional pistol-grip handles and are used primarily in woodcutting. The more versatile *nesting saw* has interchangeable blades that fit into the plastic handle, including ones for fine and coarse wood and metal-cutting.

The *drywall saw* has an extra-thick blade and very coarse teeth; it cuts internal holes in drywall without any need for a starter hole, such as making cutouts for electric outlet boxes. Hold the tool with one hand with the point on your cut line and give the handle a sharp blow with the palm of your other hand. Then, continue using a sawing motion.

The *holesaw* is a cup-shaped drill accessory with saw-like teeth that fits into a drill. You use it to bore holes in wood, metal, and other materials.

Cutting with a Portable Circular Saw

The portable circular saw is the tool of choice for most rough carpentry, and is versatile enough to handle many more demanding finish carpentry tasks when used with the proper guides. (See the section titled, "Making guided and unguided cuts" later in this chapter.) Although you might find a handsaw on a remodeling or homebuilding job, it is rarely used for more than finishing off cuts that a circular saw or other power saw may not be able to handle for some reason.

Maintenance and general safety

Before you use a circular saw, make sure it is in proper condition. In addition to the general cleaning and maintenance tasks that may apply to any power tool, such as replacing frayed power cords, pay particular attention to the following safety features and safe procedures:

✔ **Never use a saw with the *safety guard* removed, tied back, or otherwise disabled.** The guard, under most circumstances, protects the blade (and therefore you and anything it might otherwise accidentally come in contact with). Periodically check the guard to make sure it moves up and down easily — a heavy build up of resin-hardened sawdust can cause it to stick open. Most circular saws also have an automatic brake that stops the blade when you release the trigger. If this safety mechanism fails to operate, take your tool in for repair or replace it.

✔ **Make sure to use the correct blade, and that it is properly and securely mounted.** There's a right way and wrong way to install a toothed blade. In most cases, you can see an arrow on the blade that must face out and match a similar arrow that's imprinted on the saw housing or blade guard. The arrows indicate the direction the blade will spin. If you were to put the blade in backwards, the teeth would bite into the top surface of the wood and might rip the saw right out of your hand. When the blade is properly mounted, it enters the wood on the underside and exits from the top.

✔ **Always use a sharp blade appropriate for the material you are cutting.** The wrong blade can produce poor results and may cause injury. A dull blade similarly produces less-than-desirable results and puts undue strain on the saw motor. Most importantly, a dull blade forces you to push harder and therefore increases the risk of injury.

✔ **Whenever possible, place the wide part of the saw shoe on the workpiece so it is fully supported and does not rock from side to side.** If only the narrow side of the shoe will fit on the workpiece, place a block of wood the same thickness as your workpiece under the wide portion of the shoe to support it.

✔ **Make a habit of not setting the saw down until the blade has stopped spinning.** The blade guard can fail to close over the blade. For the same reason, never rest a circular saw on your leg, even if the blade has stopped spinning.

✔ **Don't force a cut.** If you have to push hard, you are probably using a dull blade or trying to cut too much stock too quickly for the power of your tool. Or maybe you forgot to plug in the saw!

✔ **Set the proper depth of cut.** Ideally, to allow proper clearing of sawdust, the blade should penetrate the wood until the gullets (the gaps between the teeth of the blade) just clear the material. Setting the blade deeper than this increases risk as you expose more blade; and with greater contact between the blade and the wood, there is more friction and that increases the chance of dangerous kickback.

If a circular saw becomes twisted in the workpiece, or if the wood pinches the saw blade for any other reason, the force of the spinning blade throws the saw up and backward (the *kickback*) out of the wood toward the user. For this reason do not stand directly behind the saw, and if your second hand is not either holding onto the saw or needed to hold a guide in place, keep it behind your back.

✔ **Start the saw and let it reach full speed before advancing it into the wood.** Release the trigger as you reach the end of your cut and follow through until the blade is clear of the workpiece. If you must stop with the blade in the work, allow the blade to come to a full stop before you lift the saw out.

Making guided and unguided cuts

Whether you are cutting along the length of a board (ripping) or across its narrow dimension (crosscutting), an *edge guide* can improve accuracy and safety. A guide is any straight edge that the saw shoe rides against. You hold some guides, such as the Speed Square, in place for making relatively short crosscuts. For long cuts, quick-clamping metal guides come in several varieties, but you can make one or just clamp or tack a straight board to your workpiece.

Even when cuts don't require great precision and can be made freehand, making guided cuts is safer because you're less likely to twist the blade, which can cause kickback.

When you want to make an unguided cut, just follow these steps:

1. **Mark your cut line with a sharp pencil.**

   A dull pencil produces a wide line, and that makes it hard to know where to cut. A thin line leaves no room for debate, and allows you to cut where you want to — just on the waste side.

The secret to an accurate unguided cut is to keep your eye on the point where the blade is cutting. Makes sense, right? But with most sidewinder saws, which have the blade mounted on the right side, this means standing over the saw to look back at the blade. Here's a tip: You can see the cut line through the open gullets of the spinning blade.

2. **Start by aligning the guide on the nose of the shoe with the cut line.**

3. **Shift your attention to the edge of the blade, turn on the saw, and slowly push it toward the workpiece until the blade just nicks the wood.**

4. **Fine-tune your position so that the edge of the blade cuts on the waste side of your line.**

Cutting bevels

To cut a bevel, release the locking lever and tilt the saw shoe in relation to the blade. Most saws have a positive lock or stop at 45 and 90 degrees. Check periodically to be sure that these stops are accurate with guided cuts through a thick workpiece; and make sure to keep the shoe flat on the work. Check the result with a combination square.

Bevel cuts are difficult to make accurately and safely. Because more of the blade surface is in contact with the wood there is more friction and greater chance of kickback. It's also more difficult to see your line. For these reasons it is even more important to use a guide, and you should not attempt to reach as far as you might when making a square cut.

When making bevel cuts, the blade guard (which normally retracts automatically as the cut is made) may hang up on the edge of the board, especially when you are cutting a small amount off the end of a board. To avoid this situation, you need to manually retract the blade guard and hold it back with your thumb before you start the saw and begin the cut. This is the one situation in which you need to saw without having the guard to protect you. So be very cautious when working with the blade exposed in this manner. You'll have both hands on the saw, so your workpiece must be clamped or otherwise held in place.

If you forget to retract the guard and it does hang up, don't attempt to retract it with the blade spinning. That's very dangerous. Instead, release the trigger and hold the saw in place until the blade stops. Then, reposition the saw — with the guard retracted — to complete the cut.

Making crosscuts

To make a safe, accurate crosscut, always support your workpiece and whenever possible, use a clamp or a stop block against the far edge of it to prevent the workpiece from moving as you push against it during the cut. This will enable you to keep two hands on the saw in most circumstances.

If you are right-handed, stand so that your cut will be made on the right end of the board. That way, the wide part of the saw shoe (and therefore, the bulk of the weight) rides on the workpiece.

If you are cutting a small amount off the end of a board, you can usually allow the waste to overhang and let the cutoff fall to the floor. If the cutoff is long and you were to just let it fall, it might break off under its own weight and splinter the workpiece before you fully complete the cut. In this case, you need to support the waste. Have a helper lightly support the end on open palms. (Open palms are preferred so that the helper doesn't inadvertently exert pressure that might cause binding.) If you're on your own, support the workpiece and cutoff. You can support the entire length on scrap lumber; or support it on numerous short lengths of wood placed perpendicular to the work. Ensure that you have at least two supports under the workpiece and two supports under the waste.

Never make a crosscut in the middle of a board that is supported only at the ends such as one resting on a pair of saw horses or wall stud that's secured at the top and bottom. Doing so can cause the most violent kickback.

Because the spinning blade enters the underside and exits from the top, it may cause splintering, especially when you are cutting across the grain. Veneered products, such as plywood and some doors, are particularly vulnerable.

You can minimize splintering several ways:

✔ **Use blades with more teeth or finer teeth,** and make sure the blade is sharp. Score the surface with a razor knife guided by a straightedge, and then make your cut just slightly to the waste side of the line. This approach is more effective with laminated products than with solid wood.

✔ **Apply tape to the work and cut through it.**

✔ **Put the good side of the workpiece face down** when cutting so that any splintering occurs on the other side.

Using hand-held guides

For crosscutting narrow stock such as 2x lumber, use a speed square, which guides a 90- or 45-degree cut, or an adjustable protractor/saw guide. Position the guide with its lip against the far side of your board. Doing so tends to hold the guide tighter against the work as you counteract the pushing force of the saw. For longer cuts or for sharp angle cuts beyond the range of your guide, tack or clamp a straightedge onto the workpiece.

Making rips

To cut a board or panel along its length (called *ripping*), use a guide if possible, especially if the cut requires a long reach. For cabinetwork and other projects that require precision, always use a full-length guide.

If you're ripping a relatively small amount off a board and precision is not critical, you can use an accessory *rip fence* designed for your saw. The long leg of this T-shaped adjustable guide locks onto the saw shoe, and the top of the T rides against the edge of your workpiece. Because the top of the T is short, you can easily twist the saw (if you're not careful), but not as easily as you can without a guide.

In most cases, you either need precision and would use a full-length guide or can make a freehand cut; so most carpenters have long since lost their never-used accessory guide.

Ripping seems to release pent-up forces within board lumber and even plywood, which is more stable as a rule. As a result the kerf (the channel left by a saw blade) may close up behind the cut and pinch the blade. This increases the risk of kickback and strains the motor. If kickback does start to happen, stop and insert a *kerf keeper* in the channel. (You may need to reposition it during a long cut.) The keeper can be as simple as a shingle tip or other wedge, or a block of wood with a ⅛-inch fin that protrudes below the surface.

Taking a plunge

When you need to start a cut in the middle of a workpiece rather than at an edge, you can make what is called a *plunge cut*. There are two approaches to a plunge cut; use the one that feels safer for you.

In the most commonly used approach (see Figure 5-2), you rest the saw on its nose on the workpiece and then lower it to check that the blade will contact the wood on the waste side of your line. If everything looks OK, raise the saw back up, pull the switch and slowly lower it until the blade just nicks the work on your line. Continue to lower the saw until the shoe is in full contact before continuing the cut.

Figure 5-2:
Making a
plunge cut.

It's important to position the saw far enough forward so that you can lower it fully before moving it forward. Unless you've guessed perfectly, you'll need to extend the cut behind the saw. *Never* move the saw backward to make that cut. The teeth may bite into the wood and rip the saw uncontrollably right out of the wood. Instead, back up the saw a bit to repeat the plunge; turn the saw around to cut in the other direction; or use another saw, such as a saber saw or handsaw to complete the cut. You often need a second saw anyway, to square the corners that a circular blade cannot.

You can improve accuracy and safety by using a guide. A thick board, such as a 2x4 tacked onto the waste will guide the edge of the saw shoe before the blade ever hits the wood. You can set the proper depth-of-cut, which offers the added advantage of allowing more of the edge of the shoe to contact the guide before the blade contacts the wood.

In lieu of a guide, we find it's easier to see the blade with it set at maximum cutting depth for the initial, lowering phase of the plunge cut. Once the shoe is in full contact with the surface, the cut will be nearly as long as the diameter of the blade. Release the switch, and when the blade stops lift the saw out to set the proper depth before lowering it back into the workpiece to complete the cut. Since the initial cut is longer than the now exposed portion of the blade, you can lower the saw into the kerf with less chance of hitting the back edge.

While it may be possible to reposition the saw in a kerf before turning it on, doing so increases the risk of kickback. If the blade is slightly twisted in the cut, or if torque caused by starting the saw twists it in the cut, it can bind or jump out of the kerf.

Cutting dadoes

Not to be confused with the extinct bird with a similar goofy name, a *dado* is a channel or groove cut across the wood grain to provide a secure joint between it and a second perpendicular board. An example would be the ends of a shelf that fits into a dado cut into the side of a bookcase.

To make a dado without a special dado head, follow these steps:

1. **Mark the outlines of the dado.**
2. **Adjust the saw to the required dado depth and make guided cuts on the waste side of each line.**
3. **Make a series of unguided cuts, spaced about ¹⁄₁₆-inch apart, all across the dado.**
4. **Clean out the remaining thin strips with a hammer and chisel.**

Cutting plywood and other panels

Support the entire sheet of plywood on two or more boards placed perpendicular to your cut on sawhorses or a large worktable. Set the cutting depth to just over the thickness of the panel and make a guided cut.

While you may have the skill necessary to make a reasonably accurate unguided cut in situations that do not require reaching, such a cut across the full 4-foot width of a panel can be very dangerous. A slight twist can cause the saw to bind and result in dangerous kickback. So use a guide, such as the one shown in Figures 5-3. To further limit the risks involved, keep your second hand on the saw or behind your back during such cuts.

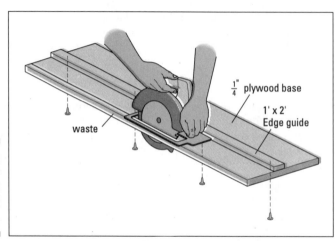

Figure 5-3:
A properly supported and guided cut.

Doing the Saber Dance

While it may not be the best saw for every cut, the *saber saw* (a portable jigsaw) is certainly one of the most versatile power tools. In fact, it was Roy's first power saw. He purchased it for a basement paneling job that involved cutting furring strips to length; ripping straight lines the full length of 4x8-foot panels; making cutouts for windows, and square and round cutouts for electrical outlets; making scribe cuts on paneling that abutted a brick fireplace; and trimming sandwiches down to size.

Second only to the electric drill in power tool popularity, a good saber saw with variable speed control and the right blade can cut just about any material, including steel or 2x lumber. Variable-speed models are much better than a single-speed or multiple-speed tools. While a saber saw can make irregular cuts, it cannot match the work of a scroll saw when the workpiece calls for very fine, intricate cutting. A saber saw can't match the power of a circular saw; but then again, it can cut right up to a vertical obstruction and can (literally) cut circles around the circular saw.

There are two saber saw body styles — the barrel-grip and the top-handle. Choose whichever one feels more comfortable for you. With some "scrolling" models, you can rotate a knob to steer the blade (360 degrees) while others you have to steer the saw. One of life's great mysteries is why you can make sharper turns with the scroller-models, but you can. A scrolling model also can get into places that a fixed-blade model cannot. For example, say you were trying to cut a circular hole in a cabinet floor near the back of the cabinet with a fixed-blade model. The back end of the saw would bump into the back of the cabinet as you rounded the back of the circle, stopping you dead in your tracks. Critics say (and most manufacturers agree) that you give up a little quality with a scroller, but we like the added versatility.

Choosing the right blade

Use the correct, sharp blade for the material. Blades vary primarily according to the blade length and width, and the number of teeth and their *set* (angle). Choose the shortest blade that will cut through the material. Generally speaking, the more coarse or aggressive the blade, the faster you will be able to cut. If you require a fine cut, one that does not splinter and leaves a smooth surface that may not even require sanding, use a fine-tooth blade or even a tungsten-carbide toothless blade, but be patient. Keep in mind that the finer the blade, the slower the feed-rate needs to be. To cut sheet metal, heavy metals, tile or stone, use a "toothless" carbide abrasive-grit blade. Following the directions for your particular saw, make sure the blade is securely locked in the tool before you start cutting, and check it occasionally to be sure that vibration has not caused it to loosen. To prevent burning your fingers, do not grab the blade barehanded immediately after making a cut. The blade will be very hot from friction.

Using the saber saw

Many saws offer the option of adding a degree of orbital action to the normal straight up-and-down blade movement. Orbital action clears debris more quickly and results in faster cuts, a cooler blade, less blade wear and improved cornering ability. The higher the orbital setting, the more aggressive and faster the cut. Don't use orbital action for thick and/or hard materials such as metal, tile, or dense hardwoods — stick to a straight up-and-down cutting action.

Use an orbital setting for:

- Work requiring sharp turns
- Thick softwoods to help clear the materials and increase speed
- Plastics to clear the cut material more quickly and keep the blade cooler

Be careful with the orbital action when you cut veneered materials such as plywood, because you may tend to make the cut quickly. Rushing the cut increases the likelihood of chipping the top surface.

Keep these other hints in mind as you exploit the power of the saber saw:

- **Adjust the saw speed to suit the blade and the material.** Generally, use slow speeds with coarse blades, which are usually heavier (thicker, wider), and higher speeds with fine blades. This is just the opposite requirement for the feed rate, which describes how fast you move the saw through the material.

- **Secure your work.** The reciprocating motion creates considerable vibration if the work is not held fast to a solid base and if the saw is not held tight to the work. Secure the work with a clamp, if possible, and use two hands to press the saw firmly against the surface.

- **Try to place your work with the good or most visible face (if any) down, to avoid splintering it.** As with the circular saw, the saber saw cuts on the upstroke. If you can't lay the good side down, then use a fine blade or a toothless one, which will not splinter the surface. Some saws include a clear plastic insert designed to limit splintering by extending the base of the saw right up to the sides of the blade — they work with limited success.

- **To prevent splintering, apply masking tape to the surface, draw your cut line on the tape and complete the cut.** You can also draw your cut line first and then apply a clear packing tape over it before making the cut.

- **Be your own guide.** You have a great deal of control when guiding the saw, so most cuts are unguided. Use the edge guide accessory to guide straight cuts that run parallel to an edge and are within the capacity of the guide (several inches wide). Outside that range, use any of the guides described for circular saws in the previous section, such as a straightedge clamped to the workpiece.

One weakness of a saber saw is the tendency for the blade, which is secured only at one end, to twist or bend off perpendicularly. This tendency is most noticeable when sawing thicker materials; when making bevel cuts, which means cutting through more material due to the angle; or when entering thick materials at an angle. The farther off perpendicular your approach (or the sharper the angle), the greater the tendency for the blade to bend out at the lower end. Enter the work slowly, and don't force the cut. To minimize the problem, use the proper blade, make sure that it's sharp, and let the blade do the work. If you need to push or hear the motor strain, you are likely using a dull blade or the wrong one for the task.

To prevent a blade from bending as it enters thick material at a sharp angle, clamp a scrap onto the edge of your workpiece. Cut into the scrap head-on; when the blade is entirely within the material, angle over toward the cut line on your workpiece. Voilà! No bending at that point now.

Making internal cuts with a saber saw

An _internal cut_ is one that does not start from the edge of a material (that type of cut is a _lead-in_ cut). The best approach to an internal cut is to drill one or more starter holes with a diameter at least as wide as the blade. (See Figure 5-4.) Drill the hole anywhere within the waste area. If you are cutting a square, drill a starter hole at each of the four corners to make turning easier at these points. If you are cutting a circle, one hole anywhere along the circumference will do.

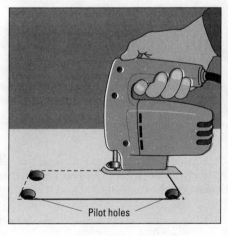
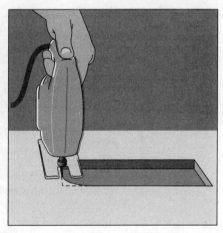

Figure 5-4:
Making an
internal cut.

Pilot holes

Do you want your cutouts to have rounded corners? Draw your cutout on the workpiece. Next, choose a drill bit that will produce the desired radius (a 1-inch diameter bit produces a ½-inch radius) and drill the four corners.

You can eyeball the spot to drill, but try to go for precision:

1. **Beginning at one side of a corner, measure an amount that is equal to the radius of the bit. At that point, pencil in a short line that is parallel to the opposite side.**

2. **Repeat this for the other side of the corner.**

3. **Drill where the two lines intersect.**

If it is not possible to drill a starter hole, use the saw to make a *plunge* (*pocket*) cut. The general idea is to tilt the tool forward so you can rest the nose of the base plate on the surface and then turn on the tool and *very slowly* pivot the saw so the blade enters the work. Keep lowering the saw until the base is in full contact before you start forward motion.

Not surprisingly, the harder the wood the more difficult it is to make a plunge cut. If your saw has orbital action (see the section, "Using the saber saw" in this chapter), use it. It will help. If the saw moves the slightest bit backward in the process, the tip of the blade jabs into the uncut area. This action can break the blade or easily damage the surface as the saw bounces out of the work and off its line. So make sure that you have a firm grip on the tool with two hands; and be conscious of not letting the nose move backward. To make it easier to keep from moving or twisting the saw, clamp, tack or tape a guide block on the surface perpendicular to cut line and at the nose of the saw base. To further minimize the risk of damaging your workpiece, make plunge cuts in the waste area rather than right on your line.

Cutting thin materials

To prevent splintering or creating jagged edges on sheet metal or other thin materials such as plastic laminate, take in these tips:

- ✔ Lay the thin material on a solid base, such as a scrap of plywood, and cut through both materials simultaneously.

- ✔ For the ultimate control, sandwich the work between two layers of plywood.

- ✔ If you can't back the material for whatever reason, feed the blade through the work very slowly or use a toothless carbide-grit blade to minimize splintering or burring the material.

Shaping and Smoothing Tools

After you finish the preliminary cutting, many projects require additional shaping, smoothing, and final sanding. (Is this going to be fun, or what?) An incredible variety of tools and materials are available for every conceivable task in this area but really only a few that need to be part of your tool arsenal:

- ✔ Block plane
- ✔ Butt chisel
- ✔ Hand and machine sanders and accessories
- ✔ Surface-forming tool (often called *Surform*, a trade name), rasps, and files

While a number of planes are indispensable for the serious woodworker, the homeowner can get by with just one — the 20-degree *block plane*. This tool is intended primarily for smoothing end grain, but it can do a serviceable job with the grain, such as when tapering the edges of boards or taking off sharp edges from corners. On occasion, you may need a plane to pare some wood from the edge of a door that's too big for its opening, or to true the edges of two boards that you wish to glue up to make a wider board (called *jointing*). A longer bench or smoothing plane or even the very long jointer plane yields a straighter edge; however, using one only occasionally doesn't warrant buying one.

Adjusting a plane

Install the blade in the plane with the bevel side up. If you install it upside down, the tool will chatter so much that your hair will fall out. Use the depth-adjustment knob to adjust the blade until it just barely projects below the face of the plane. (This is a trial-and-error process. Test the plane and readjust the setting until the tool produces a very fine cut.) Use the lateral adjustment lever to adjust the blade so that it is parallel to the mouth. If your plane has a mouth-adjustment lever (and we recommend only this type), make sure the opening at the mouth is wide enough to allow shavings to pass through easily.

Planing techniques

The block plane (see Figure 5-5) fits in your hand like it was made for it. (It was.) The rounded heel fits the hollow in your palm and indentations on the side of the body suit your thumb and pinky, and there's just enough room on top for your three middle fingers. In case you're counting, that's five fingers per hand. You can push or pull to plane. Before you begin, it's important to look at the board from the side to see which direction the grain travels. You want to move the plane in the "uphill" direction. If you go the opposite way, the blade will dive down into the wood, gouging it and getting stuck, instead of shaving off a paper-thin sliver.

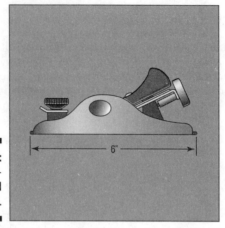

If you use a plane to smooth the end grain and plane all the way to the edge, you'll likely split the wood at the edge. An example is when you plane the bottom of a solid wood door. As you approach the edge, you contact the end grain of the stiles (the vertical members of a paneled door). To avoid splintering the edge, clamp a block of wood on the edge so that it's flush with the edge you are smoothing.

If you need to take an even amount off the edge of a board or door, for example, pencil a line along the full length on both sides of the work and plane to the line. To plane a taper, divide the work up into sections. Take one stroke beginning at the end where you need to remove the most material doing only that first section. Go back to the beginning and this time plane two sections. Go back to the beginning and plane three sections, and so on. Peer down the edge of the work looking for any high spots.

Getting a perfectly straight edge on a long edge by using a block plane is difficult, so when you are close, get out a belt sander (if you own one) to even out any irregularities.

In the event that you need to do extensive amount of door planing, consider renting a power plane. This tool has a fence that helps you keep the plane from rocking, and when you need to do a bevel (as required on the edges of many doors), you can tilt the fence at an angle to cut the necessary bevel.

Working with a Utility Knife — Indispensable and Aptly Named

Retractable utility knives are one of the best tool values out there. If you buy a good knife, it will last forever through countless uses. In fact, you're likely to lose it long before you wear it out. Use this tool to trim, carve, score, scrape, and cut wood, drywall, and other panel goods, plastics, vinyl siding, and even thin sheet metal.

Do not buy plastic utility knives. These plastic versions are cheap, but can be unsafe and unreliable for many tasks; and they may not last more than a single use. Choose, instead, an "industrial" or "heavy duty" model that has a retractable blade. (You'll appreciate that feature the first time you squat down with the knife in your pocket — ouch!) Light-duty, pencil-size cutters with breakaway blades are not strong enough (and therefore not safe enough) for cardboard box cutting, let alone most carpentry projects. Save them for wallpapering, craft projects, and opening tortilla chip bags.

Paring Wood with a Chisel

By far the most common (and perhaps sole) application that the handyperson/carpenter has for a chisel is cutting mortises, such as for hinges and other door hardware. The basic bench or butt chisel, which has a fairly short blade with beveled sides and a beveled working end, is the type to buy. You can buy these chisels individually, but sets containing ¼-, ½-, ¾-, and 1-inch sizes, are cheaper on a per-tool basis and include a protective case.

Care and sharpening

While some drill bits, saw blades, and even handsaws, are virtually disposable, chisels are not, and must be sharpened. Take these important steps to properly care for your chisels:

- ✔ Protect chisels from damage when they are not in use. They should not be loose in your drawer or toolbox, and the tips should be covered.

- ✔ Don't use a wood chisel for any material other than wood or in situations likely to involve embedded nails or penetration through the wood into a surface that might damage the chisel. For example, do not use a chisel to pry up rocks in the garden.

✔ Maintain (sharpen and hone) the cutting edge. The primary bevel will rarely need grinding if the above precautions are taken. Grinding is probably worth having done professionally unless you have other uses for a grinding wheel setup. You should, however, purchase a guide that will hold the blade at the proper angle and a bench-style diamond whetstone to maintain the secondary bevel.

If you look at the cutting end, the primary bevel is immediately obvious. You achieve this bevel on a grindstone. Look more closely, and you'll see a $\frac{1}{16}$-inch wide secondary bevel, which is best honed by using a diamond whetstone.

Using a chisel

Maintaining a sharp tool and securing your work are the two primary safety precautions you should take before you start to chisel. Hold a chisel in one hand and push it with the other, or hold it with one hand and tap the end of the handle with a mallet. (You're not supposed to use a nail hammer, but who's looking? Plastic-handled chisels with metal caps on the ends hold up just fine.)

To cut a shallow mortise for a hinge or similar hardware, just follow these steps and Figure 5-6:

1. **Mark out the perimeter of the mortise with a combination square and pencil or with a butt-marking gauge.**

2. **Using a chisel as close to the full width of your mortise as possible, chisel out a small V-shaped notch anywhere within the mortise.**

3. **Starting ¼ inch back from the notch, make numerous cuts that are spaced ¼-inch or less apart.**

   With the bevel edge facing up, have the chisel at a 45-to-60-degree angle to the surface. Tap the heel of the chisel with a mallet.

4. **Stop the levering cuts about $\frac{1}{16}$ inch shy of the end. Turn the work around (or change your position) so you face the other end of the work and repeat the procedure working back to the other end of the mortise.**

5. **Finish the end with a single sharp blow with the chisel held vertically and the bevel facing into the mortise.**

6. **Turn the chisel over (bevel facing down) and carefully scrape out all the chips.**

7. **Clean up the side(s) of the mortise.**

   Grip the chisel (beveled side facing into the mortise) with two hands. Insert the corner of the chisel into your line and press down as you pivot the chisel into the wood. Doing so makes vertical cuts in a very controlled fashion, leaving a clean, straight edge.

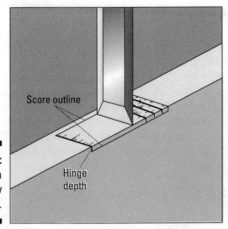
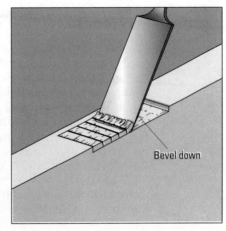

Score outline

Bevel down

Hinge depth

Figure 5-6:
Chiseling a shallow mortise.

If you find that you need to go back over your work to deepen the mortise, that's good. Most novices err on the too-deep side, which is harder to remedy. With practice, you'll get the "feel" for how hard you need to strike the chisel to make a cut that equals the desired depth of the mortise.

For deep mortises, use a drill to bore a series of adjacent holes along the length of the mortise, as shown in Figure 5-7. (The bit diameter should equal or be just a bit smaller than the width of the mortise.) Then, clean up all four edges with the chisel held as described in Steps 5 and 7, above; and clean the bottom as described in Step 6, above.

When cutting a deep mortise in relatively thin stock, sandwich the work between two boards and clamp the assembly to prevent accidentally splitting the workpiece.

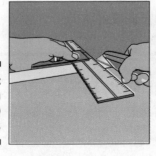
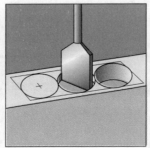
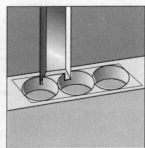

Figure 5-7:
Cutting a deep mortise.

Using Rasps and Files

Files are flat metal bars with shallow sharp-edged grooves that form teeth used from abrading or smoothing metal, wood and plastics. When you cut or drill metal, you usually create a sharp edge or leave burrs that may cause damage or injury. Metal files will quickly take the sharp edge off and remove burrs. These files are also useful for sharpening the edges of scrapers, putty knives, and other tools. These durable little guys have proven to be unaffected by exposure to flour, milk, and eggs — even when baked at 350 degrees for two hours and then festively decorated with greetings like, "Happy Birthday! See you in 12–25 years."

Rasps are coarse files with individual points as teeth and are used for abrading wood only, and therefore, won't work in a cake recipe.

In general, use files with more widely spaced teeth on softer materials. If a file doesn't come with a handle (and most don't), it usually has a tapered end, called a *tang,* which is intended to fit into a handle. Don't use the tang as a handle — it's hard on your hand. Insert the tang into the handle and, with the file pointed upward, tap the handle on a solid surface. Never strike the file with a hammer.

When using any file it's very important to secure the work in a clamp, vise, or by other means — between your knees is a very bad idea. Securing the workpiece makes the task safer and easier because you can use two hands. Grasp the handle with one hand and tip with the other (usually with two fingers and the thumb on top).

Use moderate pressure. Too light or too heavy, and the file won't cut well and dulls more quickly.

How much pressure you exert is largely a question of "look and feel" — adjust pressure until you can see that you are producing the greatest quantity of filings and notice how the file feels when it's cutting well.

Make room for a nifty hybrid

Surform is a commonly used trade name for a surface-forming tool that is a cross between a plane and a rasp. It won't cut as quickly as a plane, but its hundreds of little teeth make it very easy to use to shave and shape wood, and it does the job without all the finicky adjustments and sharpening that a plane requires. The tool is available in a variety of shapes, including one that's similar to the block plane. One of the best uses that we've found for the tool is smoothing polyester-resin wood filler. A Surform is also great for easing the bottom edges of a door after it gets cut, or for similar splinter or fuzzy wood smoothing.

Metal files themselves are relatively harmless, but sharp metal edges and fil-ings are not. To minimize danger use moderate pressure and moderate speed on the push strokes and don't rush to reposition the file after each stroke. Keep your attention focused on the work. One slip and you'll wish you had not just done such a good job sharpening that scraper! Heavy leather gloves offer added protection in case of a slip.

Hold the file at a 30-degree angle to the work. Push away from yourself and toward the point of the file simultaneously. Files cut on the push stroke, and it's good to lift the file off the work between strokes.

Keep your file clean. A clogged file doesn't cut as well and dulls more quickly. The best way to clean a file is by brushing it with a *file card*. This device has very short, fine, and closely spaced wire bristles to get into all the of the file's tight grooves and channels.

Sanding: By Hand and Machine

Sanding is usually required to give wood projects a smooth, unblemished look and feel. Sanding levels uneven surfaces and removes milling imperfec-tions, splinters, and other "fuzzies," such as the "raised grain" that often occurs when wood gets wet or gets its first coat of finish. Sanding is also an effective approach to removing old finishes. Sanding often makes a finish, such as paint, bond better to the base material and may be required between finish coats to give the underlying finish the proper texture (called "tooth").

If you're like most people, you are anxious to lay on the finish on a just-completed woodworking project and are looking for the most efficient way to get the job done. Start with the right abrasive. In addition to the familiar abrasive-coated paper and cloth sheets, people generally understand the term *sandpaper* to include sanding belts and precut disks used on power sanders. Other abrasive products include abrasive-coated rubber and foam; steel and bronze wool; and the familiar green, nonwoven abrasive pads.

Sandpaper, other abrasives, and accessories

Despite its name, "sandpaper" no longer contains sand (alert the media), and paper may be only one of the backing materials of these *coated abrasive sheets*. You can choose from dozens of types of sandpaper, but *closed-coat aluminum oxide* sheets are the most popular for woodworking. This type provides the best overall balance of hardness, durability, and sharpness.

Buy sandpaper in familiar 9x11-inch sheets or in precut sizes for specialty hand-sanding blocks and power sanders. Grits range from super-coarse to paper so smooth that you wonder how it can ever have any impact on a finish. The paper usually is identified with descriptive terms (coarse, medium fine, very fine, and super fine) or with numbers ranging from 12-grit to superfine 600-grit (and higher). Most often, you'll stay within the 60-to-220 range.

Precut sheets are convenient but costly. To cut sandpaper sheets to fit your tool or sanding block, do one of the following:

- ✔ Fold and crease the sandpaper (abrasive side in) and unfold it to tear it along the crease
- ✔ Cut the sheet through the backside with a utility knife, guided with a straightedge

General techniques

When you use the right sanding tools the right way, you get a professional-looking finish. Start by matching the shape of your sanding block or pad to the contour of the surface. The standard power sanders (belt, random orbit, and finishing) should be used only for flat work or for rounding over edges and corners. For a flat surface, you can simply wrap and staple sandpaper to a block of wood, but hard rubber sanding blocks work better. Wrap sandpaper around wood dowels, thin scraps of wood, or custom-shaped rigid foam, wood, or rubber blocks that match the surface contour. Relatively soft foam sanding blocks conform well to curved surfaces.

Start off with an abrasive paper only as coarse as it needs to be and step up in stages to as fine a paper as the project requires. Removing very fine scratches requires only very fine paper, while leveling an uneven surface may require starting with a very coarse paper. With woodworking projects involving planed lumber, start with 80-grit and end with a minimum of 120-grit paper — preferably 220-grit or even 400-grit.

In general, sand with the grain (along the length of a board or panel). When more aggressive removal is necessary, you can sand across the grain or at a 45-degree angle to the grain. This method works fast but creates scratches that remove with a final sanding that goes with the grain and using the same grit paper. Before stepping up to the next grit, always sand with the grain until there are no cross-grain scratches or other imperfections.

Take a look at these other techniques as you fine-tune your sanding skills:

- ✔ Avoid the tendency to sand in a concentrated area to remove a local imperfection. Doing so creates visible depressions or differences in texture.
- ✔ Don't tilt the sanding pad so that all the sanding is done on one corner of the pad. Use the entire surface of the pad.

✔ Keep moving — don't sand in one area for long.

✔ Consider doing a preliminary sanding *before* assembling a project. This way, you don't have to do so much hand sanding in corners or other tight spaces where the power sander can't go.

✔ Evenly sand a large, flat surface by first drawing numerous *light* pencil lines across the entire surface. Sand until all the marks are gone (and no fair concentrating on the pencil marks!). Repeat the procedure at every grit stage.

✔ Locate fine scratches. Fine scratches may be difficult to see on a freshly sanded board — until you apply the first coat of paint or stain. Wipe the surface with a cloth dampened with mineral spirits to reveal any fine scratches, especially if you plan to apply a stain.

Power sanding

If you have more than a small area to sand, it's time to turn to power sanders. (Yay!) The four principal types are the *belt sander*, the *random orbit sander*, the *pad sander,* and the *palm sander.*

The big, bad belt sander

The belt sander's 3- or 4-inch-wide abrasive-coated belt (available in *coarse* to *very fine* grits) spins rapidly under the relatively heavy tool. Use this sander on fairly large and flat surfaces. Without restraint, the belt sander will beat a Porsche off the line and erase it simultaneously. Similarly, if you don't restrain your workpiece, the force of the spinning belt can send it flying. To prevent being surprised when you plug in the sander with its switch locked on, never turn off a belt sander by removing the plug and don't plug a sander in that is resting on its belt. If the trigger switch is locked on, the tool will shoot across the room with surprising speed and force. Let the belt come to a full stop before you set it down.

In most applications your hands and fingers are at a safe distance from the spinning belt. Make sure that you are not wearing loose clothing that might get caught in the belt. For example, don't belt-sand while wearing a necktie or a toga. If you want to bring work to the sander (that is, use it as a stationary sander), then mount the tool in an accessory stand. Feeding work to the sander by hand, especially small pieces, can be dangerous, and can result in permanent manicures.

Always secure your work. Typically, the best approach is to butt the back end of the workpiece up against a thinner block that is clamped or tacked to your workbench. On long boards, you can also clamp your work at one end while working on the other. Contain very small or irregularly shaped pieces with blocks on two or more sides as needed.

Because the tool is so aggressive you must keep full control:

- ✔ Grip the sander firmly with two hands.
- ✔ Start the tool before you contact the surface.
- ✔ Keep the tool flat. If you rock onto one side or the other or put more weight on the nose than the heel, you'll gouge the wood. If you let it roll down as it leaves the front or back edge of a surface, you'll round over the edge.

To eliminate any chance of rounding over, extend the front and back ends of your board with scraps of equal thickness, and then sand them together. The tool will be fully supported while it is on the workpiece and any rounding-over will be limited to the scraps.

- ✔ Keep the tool moving at all times.
- ✔ Don't overreach. If you do, you tend to put more weight on the heel of the tool.

When you need to remove a lot of material fast, you can break the sand-with-the-grain rule. (See "General sanding techniques," above.) Sand either directly across the grain and then with the grain before changing to the next-finer belt. Alternately, sand on a diagonal, first one way and then the next, to assure the most even removal. Then sand with the grain before switching belts.

If you need to sand the edges of several boards, clamp them all together. You're less likely to rock from side to side on the wide surface and ensure that all the boards will be exactly the same width when you are done.

The nice, neat finish sander

Finish sanders include two-handed models with pads as large as 4½x9¼ (half-sheet of sandpaper), and the one-handed palm sander (which accepts ¼ sheet of sandpaper). Finish sanders are very easy to control and are suitable for all flat surfaces. These sanders may have an in-line (forward and back) motion only, orbital (tiny circles) motion or both. The orbital action works a little faster but does not produce quite as smooth a finish as in-line sanding. The finish sander is the least aggressive type sander but still far more efficient than hand sanding.

Another type of sander (and the one we'd recommend if you were buying only one) is called the *random-orbit* sander. It falls between the belt sander and the pad sander in sanding efficiency and ease of handling, and yet it can sand as fine and smooth as any pad sander.

Using a pad sander in the orbital mode or a random-orbit sander makes no difference as far as the grain goes. (A boon for disoriented woodworkers.) With an inline sander you can remove more material if you sand directly across the grain but must always end by sanding with the grain. (See "General sanding techniques," earlier in this chapter.)

Let the sander do the work. You can't leave the room, but apply only light pressure as you guide the sander back and forth across the work. If you are using a two-handed model with one hand, don't exert any pressure at all since it is bound to be greater on the back end.

Many of the tips and techniques described in previous sections on general sanding, hand sanding, and other power sanding also apply to finish sanding, so be sure to refer to those sections for additional information.

If you are sanding the edge of boards with a pad sander it may be difficult to avoid rounding over the corners. Part of the problem is that the pad is relatively soft and tends to wrap over the edge when you exert any pressure. To minimize the problem, use minimal pressure. To avoid it altogether, sandwich the work between two pieces of scrap wood so the edges are all flush. You may find that it's easier to just wrap some sandpaper around a hard block of wood — it won't wrap over the edge — and hand-sand board edges.

Chapter 6

Drilling, Driving, and Fastening

● ●

In This Chapter

▶ Finding the best drill to buy . . . and some to rent

▶ Figuring out which hammer is right for the job

▶ Exploring basic wrenches, pliers, and other gripping tools for carpenters

▶ Creating a tight hold with clamps and glue

▶ Looking down the barrels of stapling and caulking guns

● ●

C arpentry and related work, such as hardware installation, inevitably involves assembly and, one way or another, attaching things together. In this chapter, you find out about the tools and techniques involved in this work — and how to use them safely without gluing your fingers together or nailing your shoes to the floor.

Trial Assembly Pays Off

You may have heard the old tip, "Measure twice, and cut once." The extra moment it takes to double-check your measurements often prevents disasters, or at least saves the time required to correct problems that arise from an error in measuring. The same principle applies to the assembly stage of the work. Double-check your cut, positioning, or fit before final assembly. Make a habit of doing a *trial assembly* or *dry fit* before you nail, glue, or screw parts together.

If you are nailing, a dry fit can be as simple as holding the work, such as a piece of trim or length of siding, in place to make sure it fits well before driving any nails. In other situations you may need to *tack* the piece in place, which is what carpenters call it when they secure a workpiece with a minimum number of nails, driven just deep enough to hold the work in place but shallow enough that they can be easily removed if the piece must be repositioned or recut.

Trial fitting is especially important when glue and adhesive are involved. Once you apply glue or adhesive, you are, well, stuck if the work doesn't fit. At best, you'd have glue all over a piece you need to recut. At worst, you'd be dripping glue all over the place and then tracking it through the house. *Always* trial fit before assembling with contact cement (which sets instantly) and other fast-drying glues. Disassembly without damaging the work would be difficult or impossible.

Don't think you're home free just because you are using screws. Sure, you can easily remove them, but you've still got the holes you made in the process. Even if you can recut a too-long board or use a too-short board, the holes may not be where they need to be. Similarly, if the piece needs to be moved slightly, the holes in the base material may need to be plugged and redrilled. So hold, tack, brace, or clamp the work before you drill pilot holes or drive screws.

Drilling and Power Driving

Today's ⅜-inch variable-speed reversible drill/driver, available in plug-in or cordless models, uses steel screw-driving tips to drive in or remove screws, and various bits and accessories to drill holes, sand wood, mix piña coladas, and other important carpentry tasks.

The electric drill has for decades been the top-selling power tool and the first power tool that the majority of people buy. Then, variable-speed triggers and reversing motors were added to the drill. This new tool, called a *drill/driver,* was more versatile. One tool could perform both high-speed and low-speed drilling operations and, most significantly, it could drive and remove screws easily.

More recent improvements have put the drill/driver at the top of everyone's power tool wish list. Batteries replace cumbersome and inconvenient electric cords, adjustable clutches let you control the *torque* (the driving force), and with a keyless chuck you can change bits or accessories in a flash. You'll never again ask that age-old question, "Hey, where's my chuck key?" Simply grasp the keyless chuck with one hand and activate the tool with the other, in forward or reverse depending on whether you are installing or removing a bit.

With the ability to drive screws almost as easily as pounding nails, the drill/driver brought on a parallel change in screw design and a dramatic reduction in swollen thumbs. Tapered, slotted-head wood screws have been widely replaced by straight-shank, Phillips-head screws. The changes also have spawned a line of screw-driving accessories, the most significant of which is the magnetic bit holder.

You may want or need to purchase or rent other drills for a particular task. The *hammer drill,* for example, adds a high-speed pounding force to the rotary action for drilling in concrete, tile, your mother-in-law's meat loaf, and other hard materials. The *right-angle drill* fits in tight places that a standard drill won't go because the shaft (and therefore the bit) is perpendicular to the body.

Accessories for your drill/driver

You can find more accessories available for the drill than skeletons in a politician's closet. Accessories can turn this hole-drilling tool into a grinder, a sander, a carving tool, and even a fluids pump. Explore the possibilities, but start with these essentials:

- ✔ **An index of high-speed steel twist bits.** Buy a large *index* (a metal box with labeled slots for various size bits). Then, depending on your budget and the amount of use you anticipate, either buy a small set of bits and add to them as needed, or bite the bullet and go for a full 64-bit set. If you own a ⅜-inch drill (the size we'd recommend) and buy twist bits that are over ⅜-inch diameter, make sure that the chucked portion of the shaft is ⅜ inch in diameter or smaller.

- ✔ **A set of spade bits.** These flat, wood-boring bits are required for deeper holes and holes with diameters larger than ½ inch. These bits work better at high speeds.

- ✔ **A set of multibore or screw pilot bits.** Although many situations allow you to drive screws without the necessity of drilling pilot holes, most often you try to avoid those loveliest of sounds — wood splitting and screw heads snapping off. These multi-duty combination drill bits eliminate the need to change bits because one bit bores the *clearance* (or *shank*) hole and the *pilot* (or *lead*) hole, and when called for, the *countersink* and *counterbore,* all in one easy step.

- ✔ **An assortment of Phillips and standard bits and a magnetic bit holder.** Start with the following five bits: Phillips (#1 & #2) and slotted (¼, ³⁄₁₆, and ½₂). Buy bits for more exotic screws such as the Pozidrive, square-drive, and Torx, as needed. The purpose of the magnet (duh) is to hold the screw and free up your other hand for more important things such as holding the work, digging for the next screw, or scratching your, uh, nose.

- ✔ **A set of carbide-tipped masonry bits.** Buy bits ranging from ⅛ inch to at least ⅜ inch. These bits usually come in a handy plastic storage box. Use masonry bits for concrete, brick, and other masonry products, plaster, and tile. (Never use steel twist bits, which will quickly become dull and produce more smoke than a cheap cigar.)

In addition to the above accessories, following are some you may well need some day, but we'd suggest that you purchase them as the need arises:

- ✔ **Holesaw.** The holesaw is primarily used to cut large holes in metal or wood. (If you thought that a holesaw was twice as big as a "half saw," please put down this book before you hurt yourself.) One type has a cup-shaped cutter with teeth along the rim. Another has band-type blades. Each type of cutter fits on a spindle, called a *mandrel,* which also holds a pilot bit that enters the work and holds the holesaw in position as the large cutter enters the work. Holesaws come in several sizes, up to 5 inches or more, but the only application you are likely to need one for is to bore a 2⅛-inch-diameter hole in a door for a lockset. It is the only practical, affordable tool to make that size hole.

- ✔ **Doweling jig.** In many woodworking projects, wooden dowels reinforce joints. Holes are drilled in the mating pieces, and a dowel is inserted. The doweling jig precisely locates the holes and sets the depth, so when the pieces are joined they align perfectly. Today, professionals favor the *biscuit jointer.* This joiner is worth the investment if you do a lot of woodworking, but doweling is fine for the occasional woodworker.

- ✔ **Sanding, grinding, and other abrading tools.** Take advantage of the drill's versatility with these accessories that enable you to shape and smooth wood, clean and debur metal, remove paint, and a host of other tasks.

- ✔ **Portable drill stand.** Precision or repetitive drilling is ideally done on a drill press, a heavy piece of stationary equipment that few remodeling professionals even own. If you don't have a drill press, then lock your drill into one of these handy, portable stands for easier and more accurate drilling.

- ✔ **Bit-extension tool.** Lock a twist drill or spade bit into the end of an extension shaft to extend the reach or to drill very deep holes. This tool gets a lot of work when rewiring an old house. To fish wires from one place to another, you often need to drill holes at an angle through a wall, into a stud cavity, through a floor or ceiling joist bay to the floor below or above — a distance of 12 inches or more.

- ✔ **Flexible shaft.** You can literally drill around corners by securing your drill bit in the end of a flexible shaft. Okay, so it's not something you'll use everyday, but it's still great to own.

Watch your speed!

After you determine the proper bit to use, it's time to put on safety goggles and, if required, a dust mask. Then figure out the speed that you want that bit to turn and the amount of pressure to exert (called *feed pressure*). We suppose you could memorize a chart full of specs on the optimal speed for drilling holes in dozens of common materials (yeah, right), but all you really need is one general rule, a little common sense, and some trial-and-error drilling. In general, the larger the hole and the harder the material is, the slower the speed you want to use; and if your drill can't spin as fast as it should, ease up on the feed pressure and take a little more time.

In some cases, you may find it easier to start slow and pick up speed once the location is established. Similarly, stepping up from smaller diameter bits until you reach the desired hole diameter is a very useful trick when drilling in concrete, masonry, metal, and other hard materials. Lubrication — oil for metal drilling or water for concrete/masonry drilling — cools the bits and improves the efficiency of the cutter, too.

When drilling into masonry always use a carbide-tipped masonry bit. Start with a ⅛-inch diameter bit and step up the bit size ⅛ inch at a time until the hole is the desired diameter. Your bits will work more efficiently and more accurately and will last longer with this method.

Assuming that you are using the proper bit/cutter and that it is sharp and properly secured in the tool, adjust your drilling speed and feed pressure if any of the following warning signs pop up:

- ✔ The bit or other cutter fails to do its job.
- ✔ The bit or cutter jams or turns too slowly.
- ✔ The bit or cutter overheats, as evidenced by smoke or blackening of the workpiece or bit.
- ✔ The drill motor strains or overheats.

As long as you can maintain control, you can often drive screws at a drill/driver's maximum speed. Indeed, screw guns, a single-purpose professional tool designed exclusively for driving screws, operate at speeds two or three times faster than the fastest drill/driver. However, if a screw is going in at a bazillion miles a second, you certainly can't rely on the reaction of your trigger finger to stop the bit at just the right point. You'd likely drive the screw too deep, strip the screw head, snap the screw in half, or damage your workpiece . . . or all the above. Better drill/drivers have an adjustable clutch, which limits the torque (turning force) to set levels. Basically, when the screw is seated, the bit stops turning.

Slow down if you're not sure. Use your head. Do you really want to drive a brass slotted-screw into an expensive piece of hardware at high speed? (This question does not require a whole lot of thought.) Of course not.

Drilling techniques

To accurately locate a hole, called *spotting*, it's often helpful to create a small indentation to guide the bit's initial cut and prevent it from spinning out of control like a drunken figure skater. The harder the surface and the greater the accuracy required, the more advisable it is to spot a hole before drilling. In softwood, this step can be as simple as pressing the bit or a sharp pencil point into the wood. In hardwood you might want to use an awl. In metal, it is virtually required that you use a hammer and center punch. To further prevent the bit from wandering off course, hold the tool perpendicular to the surface. If you do need to drill at an angle, tilt the drill after the bit has started to penetrate or clamp an *angle-guide block* onto your work.

To make an angle-guide block, drill a hole through a block of wood with the bit you intend to use. Then cut the bottom of the block at an angle that equals the angle of the hole you want to drill. If, for example, you want a hole angled 30 degrees off vertical, then cut a 30-degree angle on the bottom of the block.

Grip the drill firmly, with two hands if possible, for better control. Heavy drills have higher torque and may even include a side handle so that you can control the tool if the bit jams in the work and the drill keeps turning. Whenever possible, clamp workpieces that may not be heavy enough to stay put under a drilling load.

A drill tends to splinter the exit hole. To prevent this from happening, ease up on the pressure so the drill is doing all the work. Or even better, take time to back up your workpiece with a piece of wood scrap before you start drilling. Any splintering will occur on the scrap, not the workpiece.

The Nail Hammer: The Quintessential Carpentry Tool

Nail hammers come in two basic types: the one you bought, and the one you borrowed from your neighbor three years ago. Just kidding. Actually, there's the curved-claw hammer, which has a curved nail-pulling claw, and the ripping-claw hammer, which has a straight claw.

For general use, we recommend a 16-ounce, curved-claw hammer with a fiberglass handle. Like wood, fiberglass will cushion the vibrations to your hand and arm, but has the added advantage that it won't break under tough nail-pulling conditions.

The curved claw on this hammer gives you good nail-pulling leverage (see the section "Pulling nails," below). It is also heavy enough for most nailing projects, including framing work, as long as the project is modest in scope — such as studding a basement wall. For a big framing project, you'll want a heavier hammer. Although it is heavier to hold, the added weight (and usually a somewhat longer handle) of a 20-ounce ripping hammer does more of the work for you, whether driving large nails, banging things apart or just fine-tuning a dented fender. When a project involves demolition, you can easily force the claw of a ripping hammer in between two materials that are fastened or glued together.

Some precautions

When you want to bang on something other than a nail, always think twice before reaching for your nail hammer. When you need to "persuade" something into position but might damage it by using a metal hammer, reach for a rubber mallet.

Never, never, never strike one hammer against another. The hardened steel can chip off a small piece of metal and send it flying at such great speed that the shard can embed itself deep into your body and can present a particularly great danger to your eyes. Plus, you'll never get through an airport metal detector without setting off the alarms.

For the same reason, don't use a nail hammer to strike cold chisels, masonry chisels, punches, or other hard metal objects, with the exception of nail sets, which are designed to be struck with a nail hammer. Avoid using a nail hammer on concrete, stone, or masonry, too. As a general rule, don't strike anything harder than a nail with a nail hammer.

Plus, such abuse ruins the face of a nail hammer. If you look closely at the face of a hammer, you'll see that it is not just flat and round. A quality nail hammer has a shiny, slightly convex face with beveled edges to minimize surface denting. Some ripping or framing hammers have a milled face (checkered or waffled) to make it less likely to slip off the head of a nail that you don't strike squarely.

For cold chisels and center punches use an *engineer's hammer* (also called a *ball peen hammer*). For masonry chisels, concrete and masonry, use a *lump hammer* (also called a *hand-drilling hammer* or simple a mini-sledge). See Figure 6-1.

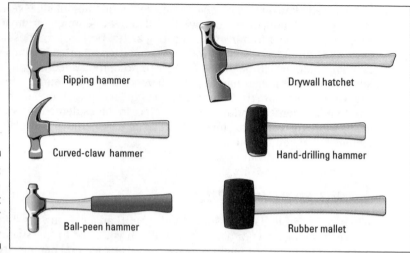

Ripping hammer

Drywall hatchet

Curved-claw hammer

Hand-drilling hammer

Figure 6-1:
Use the
right
hammer for
the job.

Ball-peen hammer

Rubber mallet

Driving nails (into wood, not from the store)

Like all carpenters, we've had our share of smashed fingers and bent nails. But you can avoid them most of the time by driving nails the right way. Whether you're nailing a hook for a picture or nailing a 2x4 to the garage wall, follow these basic steps for ouch-free installation:

1. **To have proper grip, grasp a claw hammer almost at the end of the handle and with your thumb wrapped around the handle.**

   Thinking that they might gain more control, beginners often make the mistake of lining up their thumb on the handle. Not only does this grip fail to improve accuracy, it is inefficient and may cause injury to your thumb. The one exception to this rule is when you are nailing sideways across your body, in a technique called *nailing out*.

2. **Start the nail by tilting it slightly away from you and giving it one or two light taps. Then move your fingers and toes out of harm's way and drive the nail with increasingly forceful blows.**

   The handle should be parallel to the surface at the point that it strikes the nail. For rough work, drive the nail home, that is, until the nail draws the pieces tight and is set slightly below the surface. For finish work, stop when the nail is just above the surface. Finish the task with a *nail set* so that you don't risk damaging the wood. (See "Finishing touches," in this chapter.)

The rules are a little different for a 20-ounce ripping or framing hammer. Unlike a claw hammer, grasp the handle a little higher — about ¼ up from the end, and keep a little looser grip. Also, take a bigger backswing and use a more forceful downswing. With the heavier hammer and added driving force, it becomes imperative to keep your other hand well out of harm's way, preferably behind your back.

If a nail driven straight in would penetrate out from the backside of your workpiece and you don't want to use a shorter nail, you may be able to drive the nail in at an angle. Carpenters often use this technique when they are nailing up doubled wall studs or headers over framed door and window openings. Nailing at opposing angles improves the holding power significantly.

Because of their small size, brads and tacks are difficult to hold safely when starting the nail. If you have a tack hammer use it; but if you must use a claw hammer, save your fingers by using long-nose pliers to grasp the nail while you give it the tap or two required to get it started.

Face-nailing and toenailing

Face-nailing and toenailing (shown in Figure 6-2) are not horrible punishments that carpenters inflict on a plumber who cuts too-big holes in their floor joists. Rather, they describe the two common ways of nailing things together.

Most often you will nail through the face of a board and into the backing material. This is called *face-nailing*. As a general rule, nail through the thinner member into the thicker one whenever possible. The deeper that nail goes into the backing, the more holding power it will have.

Here's a good guideline to follow when you need to figure out the proper length of a nail: A nail should penetrate into solid backing material at a depth equal to twice the thickness of the member being attached. For example, if you are nailing a ¾-inch-thick furring strip on a drywall-covered wall, you'd want to use at least a 2-inch nail (2 x ¾, + ½-inch for the drywall).

When one piece of lumber is secured to another at a 90-degree angle, such as a wall stud attached to a sole plate or top plate, you have one or two nailing options, depending on whether you have access to the top of the "T." Typically, if you can face-nail through one board into the end of the mating board, that will be the easiest and preferred technique. If you don't have access, or if the board is so thick that face-nailing through it would be impractical, you must *toenail* through the end of one board into the face of the other board.

Driving the first nail at such an angle tends to push the board off its mark, so as you drive the nail you need to back up the board (typically with your foot). It also helps to drive the nail to where it just penetrates one board, and then reposition it as necessary before driving one sharp blow. In fact, you may want to assume that driving will tend to push the board past its mark and compensate for that by positioning it a little to the opposite side of the marks.

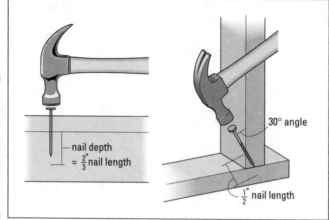

Figure 6-2: Most of the time you'll either face-nail (left) or toenail (right).

nail depth = $\frac{2}{3}$ nail length

30° angle

$\frac{1}{2}$" nail length

Blind-nailing

Blind-nailing may sound dangerous, but it's nothing to worry about. The term describes any nailing technique where the nail is completely hidden from sight without the use of putty or wood fillers. In its most common form, the technique is used to secure tongue-and-groove boards, such as solid wood paneling. Nail into the tongued-edge of the board at a 45-degree angle. When the next board is installed, its groove conceals the nail, and so on across the wall or floor. The first and last boards typically must be face-nailed as described in the previous section.

Finishing touches

In finish work, you generally want to sink the nail head slightly below the surface, as shown in Figure 6-3, and later fill the depression with putty, caulk, or wood filler. For this you'll need a nail set, which comes in sizes ranging from $\frac{1}{32}$ to $\frac{3}{16}$-inch in $\frac{1}{32}$-inch increments to suit various nail head sizes. Buy a set of three and you'll be ready for any nail you're likely to encounter in house carpentry.

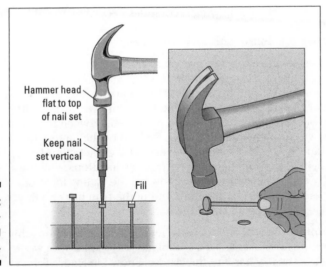

Hammer head
flat to top
of nail set

Keep nail
set vertical

Fill

Figure 6-3:
Two nail-
setting
approaches.

Anytime you need to hold one tool and strike it with another, your fingers are vulnerable. (Theoretically you could ask for nail-holding volunteers, but you won't get much interest.) Generally, holding the nail as you would hammer isn't a problem when setting finish nails because you need a relatively minor blow to drive the nail. Such light hammering is easier to control and does less damage if the blow is off mark.

When nail-setting heavy common nails, such as might be required for face-nailed deck boards, a heavier blow is required. After mashing our fingers a number of times, we adopted an old carpenter's nail-setting trick, and since then it's never happened again. Lay a 16d common nail flat on the surface with its head over the center of the nail head to be countersunk. With your fingers holding the nail a safe couple of inches from the head, strike the edge of the nail head and it will set the nail below. The process tends to mush the nail head, so after rotating the head a couple times and after setting a half dozen nails or so, use a new nail.

Nail Pulling

When it comes to pulling nails, you can choose from many techniques and tools. The ones you choose will depend on whether you need to protect the surface, whether the situation allows you to pry the materials apart, whether you can talk someone else into doing this job, and several other factors. To be prepared for most situations, you need a nail hammer, one or two _cat's paw_-style _nail pullers_ and a couple of _pry bars_.

Try one or more of the following techniques according to your needs:

✔ **Remove the board, and then the nails.**

Most often, the easiest approach to taking things apart is to either bang or pry them apart or give them to a 2-year-old child. Take, for example, trim removal. To do this job while minimizing the damage to either the trim or the surface that it's nailed to requires a pry bar with a straight, wide blade that's thin enough to be driven between the materials — a *trim bar*. (You may want to grind the end of such a tool to an even thinner taper to make it easier to insert.) Drive the tapered end of the trim bar behind the trim between two nailing locations. Pull toward yourself gently and work your way over toward the nailing locations. Then pry it still farther out using the other end of the trim bar or a larger pry bar, working your way all along the board.

To protect the wall and increase leverage, insert a shim (shingle tip), a thin stiff material such as a stiff-blade putty knife, or a wood block between the pry bar and the wall, as shown in Figure 6-4.

Virtually all nailing, demolition and nail-pulling operations require you to wear proper eye protection.

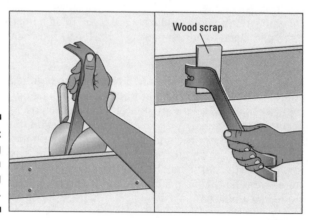

Wood scrap

Figure 6-4:
Minimizing damage to a board being removed.

✔ **Pry nails from removed boards.**

If you have pried a board off a surface and nails remain in the board, tap the pointed ends to drive the heads above the opposite surface, at least enough so they can be pulled from the face with a hammer claw or bent end of a pry bar. If you're trying to avoid damaging the face of the board (as you might for trim that was removed and is being reused), pull the nails through the back side. It's easy for finishing nails, and with enough force (and soft wood such as pine) you can pull common nails out backwards, too.

To pull the nail, use a hammer as described in "Side-to-side technique," below. Alternately, *end-cutting pliers* (sometimes called *nippers*) work well, especially with finishing nails. Grasp the nail shaft with the jaws of the pliers as close to the surface as possible. Roll the pliers over to one side, then the other, but don't grip too hard or you'll cut the nail.

✔ **Pry a little, pull a little.**

If you want to protect the surface and can pry a board a little above the surface, do so. Then drive the board back with a sharp hammer blow. The goal is for the board to go back in place and leave the nails standing proud (or humiliated, if they are shy types). Protect the surface from the hammer blow with a scrap of wood. Then pull the nails with a pry bar.

✔ **Pull nails from the face.**

If you cannot get behind a board to pry it free, you must attack the nails from the face of the board. For this you need a claw-type nail-puller. For rough work, where damage to the surfaces is not a concern, a cat's paw, which has a relatively wide head works well. But to minimize damage, you'll need a puller with a narrower head and sharper jaws that don't need to be driven so deeply into the wood in order to bite into the nail head. This style also has sharper claws that will bite into the shaft of a nail while the wider paw generally needs a head to pull on. There's also a mini version of the same tools for small finish nails.

Position the puller with the points of the claw just behind the nail and drive it down into the wood and under the head of the nail. Pull back on the tool with a steady, controlled motion to pull it at least ½ inch above the surface. Then use one of the following approaches with a hammer or pry bar.

• **Standard approach**

Once the head of a nail is above the surface, hook onto it with a hammer claw (or with the V-notch on the bent end of a pry bar), and pull the handle of the tool toward you to pry out the nail. Making grunting sounds doesn't really help, but they may impress someone in the next room.

Don't jerk a hammer in an attempt to free a nail that's too stubborn to pull out with a steady, smooth motion. With the loss of control comes increase risk of injury. Does "toppling over backwards" sound like fun? The sudden force may break a wooden hammer handle or snap the head off the nail making it harder to remove. Instead, use a pry bar or nail puller that will give you the additional leverage required.

• **Side-to-side technique**

If the nail is long or if you need to protect the surface, slip a scrap of wood under the hammer (as shown in Figure 6-5) to give added leverage and enable you to pull a long nail out entirely. To pull large nails or headless ones, carefully swing the claw into the nail with enough force to make it bite into the shaft as close to the surface as possible. Then push the hammer over sideways and the nail will come out about 1 inch. Reposition it and push sideways in the opposite direction to pull it another inch. If you have a good quality hammer with a sharp claw, it will not slip off the shaft of the nail. When the nail has been sufficiently loosened, use the standard pull-toward-yourself approach to pull it out the rest of the way.

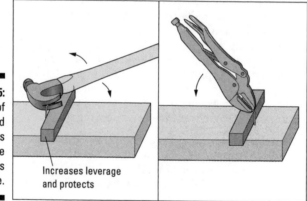

Figure 6-5:
The block of wood increases leverage and protects the surface.

Increases leverage and protects

Fastening with Staples

The staple gun is handy for many projects in remodeling, such as securing insulation, ceiling tile, or plastic sheeting, as well as for household repairs and projects such as recovering a seat cushion or rescreening a porch. (But we don't recommend using a staple gun to keep your hat from blowing off during windy days.) The tool is available in manual and electric models. Each has pros and cons, but given the typical limited use, it probably doesn't matter which you choose.

Most staple guns can be fired into the air so there is a risk of eye injury if they are used improperly or without care. While there may be a safety catch on the trigger of an electric stapler, it is very easy to accidentally fire a staple (too easy, in our opinion). Make a habit of setting the safety lock after every series of shots and when the tool is stored. The temptation to play "guns" with the electric model suggests that you keep it out of the hands of unsupervised children.

A dial on the hand-powered models regulates the force of the blow. The harder the material you are stapling into and the longer the staple, the more force you will need. To make sure that all the force that you set is delivered, press the stapler down firmly as you fire the staple. If an occasional staple stands proud, give it a tap with a hammer — not the stapler.

Driving Screws

Despite the overwhelming popularity of the drill/driver (see "Drilling and Power Driving" in this chapter), screwdrivers are still an essential item for every homeowner. You've probably heard the advice, "Use a tool only for its intended purpose." Generally, that's good, sound advice. Very often you can injure yourself, ruin a tool or damage your work if you fail to heed that advice. However, if using a screwdriver for a task other than driving screws were a crime and the punishment were banishment from hardware stores, the aisles would be empty.

The first rule for driving screws is to use a driver that matches the type and size screw that you are driving. The majority of screws are either *Phillips* screws, which have a cross-shaped recess in the head and require a *Phillips* screwdriver, or *slotted* screws, which have a single slot cut across the diameter of the screw head and require a *standard* driver.

You get the best deal and are prepared for most screwdriving situations if you buy an assortment of screwdrivers. At minimum, your collection should contain two standard drivers, a ⁵⁄₁₆-inch *cabinet* and a ¼-inch *mechanics,* and two Phillips drivers, a 4-inch *#2* and a 3-inch *#1.*

Alternately, buy either a *4-in-1* or *6-in-1* driver. The 4-in-1 has a double-ended shaft, two ⁵⁄₁₆-inch and ³⁄₃₂-inch standard, and #1 and #2 Phillips interchangeable bits (tips). In the 6-in-1 model, the two ends of the shaft serve as a ¼-inch and ⁵⁄₁₆-inch nutdriver. Buy other size screwdrivers as needed. One advantage of these multidrivers is that they accommodate different bits; when you run across screws with square holes, star-like holes, or other tip configurations, you need to buy only the appropriate tip, not another tool.

When it comes to screwdrivers, it's best to avoid the bargain racks. Shop for name brands, and look for tempered (heat-treated) tips.

The way to use a screwdriver is essentially obvious, but we have a few points that are worth mentioning. First, don't hold the tool between your knees or teeth — you'll get lousy torque pressure. Always match the driver to the fastener. Failure to do so will inevitably deform the screwhead, sometimes to the point where it can no longer be twisted out or in. This is particularly true with brass screws (which are easily damaged because the brass is relatively soft) and also when the screw is unusually tight or stuck.

If you are trying to draw and fasten two things together with a flathead screw, say two pieces of wood, join the two pieces together and use one of the following approaches:

1. **Clamp the two pieces together and, using a bit that is a little smaller than the diameter of the screw, drill a *pilot* hole as deep as the screw is long.**

   Finish by using a countersink bit to bore a conical hole that suits the screwhead. Clamping is necessary because the screw tends to force apart the two pieces as it enters the second piece.

2. **Alternately, bore the appropriate *pilot, clearance,* and *countersink* holes before driving the screw.**

   Using a bit that is a little smaller than the diameter of the screw, bore a pilot hole through both pieces that is equal to the screw length. Then, using a bit that is equal to the diameter of the screw, bore a clearance hole through the top piece only. A *screw pilot* or *multibore* accessory bit bores all three holes at once and is available in sets to suit various size screws.

Predrilling for screws is always best and makes driving screws by hand much easier. Predrilling is essential for most finish work (where neatness is important) and to prevent splitting when screwing into hardwoods, plywood, end grain, or near the ends of a board. There are many occasions, however, when you may not need to drill pilot holes or countersinks, especially if you use a drill/driver. The best screws to use in wood without pilot holes have bugle heads (similar to flathead screws), straight shafts, and coarse threads.

Lubricate screws (especially brass ones) with wax to make them easier to drive. (Don't use soap, as it tends to corrode the screw.)

Although you can by a depth-gauge for drill bits, a piece of tape (masking, electrical, duct, whatever) wrapped around the shaft of a bit will tell you when to stop drilling.

Sometimes it's hard for beginners to drill holes at the desired angle (usually perpendicular to the surface). If accuracy is critical, hold a combination square (or a block of wood that you know is cut square) on the surface and against the top of the drill. As long as you keep the drill centered on your guide and in contact with it, the hole will be accurate.

Whenever you need to bore many holes in identical locations in more than one piece of wood, use a template. Take, for example, drilling screw holes to locate knobs on a number of cabinet doors, or a drilling a series of holes in the side of a bookcase for plug-in shelf supports. For knobs, the template might be a board (with a hole drilled in it) that fits over the corner of a cabinet door so that the hole lies precisely over the same spot whatever door it is placed on. For shelf supports, the template might be a 2-foot-long strip of

¼-inch hardboard with a series of holes so that you only need to align the template with front or back edge of the bookcase side to drill holes in the exact same spots every time.

Hinges must be located accurately if one half is to mate well with the other, and to ensure that the door is precisely located in its opening. Pilot holes for hinge screws must be exactly centered or they tend to push the hinge off mark, or the screw head won't sit flush with the hinge. Any irregularity in the wood grain can push an unguided drill or punch off the mark. A *self-centering pilot drill* or a *self-centering punch* has tapered ends that fit into the countersink of a screw hole in the hinge, automatically centering the drill bit or the punch. One size fits all for the punch, but the drill accessory comes in several sizes to suit #6, #8, and #10 screws.

Getting Down to Nuts and Bolts

Nails and screws aren't the only fasteners that the home carpenter encounters. Product installations often involve nuts and bolts, and many carpentry projects make use of lag bolts and a variety of other metal anchors and fasteners. And you'll often find that you need a firm hold on a variety of non-fastener items such as pipes, product and machinery parts, wiring, hardware, and so on. These tasks require one of the following gripping tools.

Pliers: Grippy, grabby, and pointy

Slip-joint pliers have toothed jaws that enable you to grip various sized objects, like a water pipe, the top of a gallon of mineral spirits, or the tape measure you accidentally dropped into the toilet. (One instance when "Fetch boy!" just won't work.) Because its jaws are adjustable, slip-joint pliers give you leverage to firmly grip the object. This tool is on everyone's most basic list of tools, but we can count the times we've used them on our six hands. Instead, we prefer *locking pliers* (commonly known by one brand name, Vise-Grip). Locking pliers easily adjust to lock onto pipes, nuts, screws, and nails that have had their heads broken off, and practically anything that needs to be held in place, twisted, clamped, or crushed.

For occasional minor electrical work and repairs, every tool kit needs a pair of *long-nose pliers* (often mistakenly called needle-nose pliers, which have a much longer, pointier nose). Long-nose pliers cut wire and cable, twist a loop on the end of a conductor to fit under a screw fitting and, turned perpendicular to the wires, do a fair job twisting wires together. If you find yourself doing more than occasional electrical work, pick up a pair of *lineman's pliers,* too. This tool does a better job twisting connections and cutting heavy cable. *End cutting pliers* probably have some real valuable electrical value that has eluded us for many years, but they are invaluable nail pullers and cutters.

Wrenches: A plethora of options

Carpentry work often involves minor plumbing work, primarily the temporary removal of piping connections for work such as cabinet installations and trying to fish Timmy's pet hamster out of the garbage disposal ("Don't touch that switch!"). And all sorts of projects involve nuts and bolts and similar fasteners. Wrenches are the primary tool for this work.

An *adjustable wrench* is included in most basic tool kits because it will accommodate any size nut — metric or standard (Democrat or Republican), and small-to-moderate-size pipe fittings. On the downside, they don't grip as well as fixed-sized wrenches. Even better quality ones are marginal, so don't waste your money on a cheap pair. Get a good automotive-quality tool.

For a better grip choose a wrench that is sized for the fastener or fitting. *Combination wrenches,* which have one open and one closed (boxed) end, are sold in standard or metric sets, or in sets that include both. Standard is still far more common in carpentry work, so buy a standard set first. For most carpentry work, you'll only need a small assortment (6 to 10).

If you find you run across metric bolts only a couple of times a year, you can save the cost of buying a set of metric wrenches by buying one of those self-sizing wrenches like the "Metwrench" sold at Sears stores and on late-night TV infomercials.

For many projects, you can avoid the standard-metric debate altogether by purchasing a nice combination set of *socket wrenches.* Socket wrenches not only are sized for specific fasteners (which helps fight the age-old rounding-off-the-hex-head problem), but they also offer a ratcheted handle that allows you to tighten or loosen a nut without repositioning the tool every half turn or so, as is required for combination wrenches.

Set screws, fittings, and other fasteners have hexagonal-shaped recesses that require an *Allen wrench* (also called a *hex key* or *hex wrench*). They are designed for turning screws or bolts that have hexagonal sockets in their heads. These metal bars come in several shapes — straight, L-shaped, or T-shaped (where the top of the "T" is a handle). The Allen wrench, used to assemble everything from knock-down furniture to bicycles to gas grills and plumbing fittings, was invented by a man named . . . umm, let's see, his name was . . . well, we'll have to get back to you on that one.

Although you can buy Allen wrenches individually — they may even come with a product that requires one for assembly, adjustment, or maintenance — it's best to start with a matching set or two. On the rare occasion that you need one that's not included in a set, then buy it separately. Straight-wrench sets fold into a handle like a pocketknife. L- and T-shaped sets come in a plastic case or other little pouch. The L-shaped ones are the most versatile because the shorter leg of the "L" gets into places that the longer straight or T-shaped ones can't.

Clamping and Gluing

An old carpentry adage states that you can never own enough clamps. And why not? It's like trout fishing — there's no legal limit. In any case, clamping is an essential part of many carpentry projects. Clamps hold your work in place while the workpiece is being tooled with saws, drills, sanders, and other tools. Clamps also hold together two or more objects in precise alignment while you drill pilot holes and install fasteners. In the final stages, clamps hold things together while waiting for glue/adhesives to cure, in some cases reducing the number of fasteners required or eliminating the need for them altogether. The number of clamps required for a project will vary widely but typically you'll need one every 8 inches or so along the joint.

Types of clamps

Because carpentry and woodworking projects assume an endless variety of shapes (flat, square, 90- and 45-degree corners, cylinders) and sizes (very long or very short, very big or very small), you need a variety of clamps and ones that offer the greatest versatility. While there are dozens of types, a few basic clamps have proven their worth. (See Figure 6-6.)

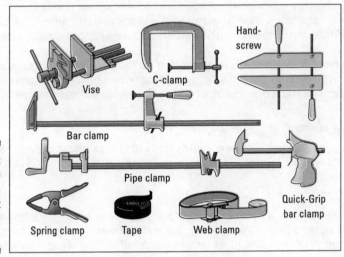

Figure 6-6: Get a grip with the right clamping tools.

Vise

C-clamp

Hand-screw

Bar clamp

Pipe clamp

Quick-Grip bar clamp

Spring clamp

Tape

Web clamp

C-clamps

The *C-clamp* (named for its C-shape — you can't sneak anything past us!) comes in sizes that describe the maximum open capacity of the jaw, from ¾ to 12 inches. It is the primary clamp used for woodworking. Most jobs require a minimum of two clamps, so make a practice of starting out with at least a pair of a particular size, and buy more as needed. C-clamps exert tremendous force. There's never a need to use anything other than your hand to tighten them. Prevent damage to your workpiece by placing a wood scrap between the clamp and the work. Such boards, if heavy enough, can also be used to more evenly distribute the force. A variation on the C-clamp is the *edge C-clamp*. This clamp is designed to hold wood strips against the edge of another board, such as a plywood shelf or a kitchen counter. To use it, lock the "C" onto the board and then tighten the edge screw against the edging strip.

Pipe clamps

Pipe clamps consist of one fixed crank screw (head stock) and one movable jaw (tail stock) mounted on a pipe. The crank screw threads onto the end of the pipe and the movable jaw slides over the pipe. It locks onto the pipe when pressure is exerted. You can use any length pipe and easily move the clamps from one pipe to another to suit the project. *Bar clamps* work like pipe clamps, but the bars are not interchangeable and therefore not as versatile. Both types may be equipped with rubber pads to prevent them from damaging the work.

If you put the movable jaws all on one side of the workpiece, they tend to make the work bow up at the middle. Counter this tendency by alternating the clamps from one side to the other. If that doesn't solve the problem, you can straighten a bowing surface by easing up on the clamp pressure just a bit and inserting a thick block of wood on the workpiece under the pipe at the midpoint and tap a shim in between the block and the pipe. Check for straightness with the edge of a framing square or other straightedge.

If you need to use a pipe clamp for non-rectangular workpieces, such as a round or triangular tabletop, cut a jig that, when clamped against the opposite edges of the work, yields a rectangular shape for the clamps to lock onto.

Spring clamps

Spring clamps work like giant clothespins for quick clamping and releasing of projects where clamping is near the outer edge and not too thick.

Handscrews

The *handscrew* has parallel wooden jaws that won't damage wood workpieces as readily as a steel clamp. It exerts tremendous power with little effort on your part, but most important, it will not apply any twisting force, which tends to move your pieces out of alignment. The jaws can also adjust to accommodate work where the two faces are uneven or not parallel to each other.

Web clamps

Web clamps wrap around irregular surfaces and exert inward pressure. Perhaps the most common application is gluing up chair legs and the spindles that span between them. Loop the web around the work and thread it through a ratcheted metal fixture, much like a belt is put through its buckle. Once the band is pulled hand tight, use a wrench or a large screwdriver to tighten down the ratchet.

When clamping glued work, use just enough pressure to squeeze and hold the parts together. Too much pressure squeezes out too much of the glue, resulting in a weaker bond.

Real sticky stuff

If you are using *contact cement,* the bond between the surfaces occurs — as the name suggests — on contact. This means that the mating surfaces must be perfectly aligned before they are brought together. Depending on the size and shape of the objects, try one of the following tricks to assure correct alignment.

- ✔ Rest the parts on a flat surface with the bonding surfaces facing each other and slide the pieces together. This assures the bottom edges will be in alignment. Tack a fence or guide to the worktable and keep the two pieces against both the guide and the table top as you slide. Then two sides will be perfectly aligned.

- ✔ When the contact cement has dried sufficiently for bonding, lay dowels or other similar spacers on top of one piece. Then place the second piece on the dowels in proper alignment with the piece on the bottom. Then remove the dowels one at a time, allowing the glued faces to touch. With two boards, you might have just two or three dowels, depending on the length of the boards. For flexible material, such as plastic laminate or other veneers, you might need a dowel every 6 inches or so.

- ✔ Sometimes it's possible to glue two things together and then cut, plane, or sand both pieces simultaneously. This approach may eliminate any need for special care during assembly because any misalignment would be corrected.

Guns for Pacifists

Caulk, adhesive, and glue are messy materials; whenever possible, it's best that the containers that hold them also dispense them. Hence, many such materials are available in squeezable containers. Sometimes, dispensing tools (usually called guns of one sort or another) are required.

Hot-melt glue gun

No surprise here. A *hot-melt glue gun* looks like and does what its name suggests. Insert a stick of hard-cool glue in the back end, plug in the gun, wait for it to heat up, and squeeze the trigger. The trigger action forces the hard glue past the heating element, and out the nozzle comes burning-hot, melted glue.

The glue is not only very hot but sticks to your skin — be careful! It would be embarrassing to arrive at work in the morning with a coffee table glued to your knees. The metal tip tends to ooze glue when the unit is hot, so protect whatever surface you rest it on. The metal tip remains very hot for a while after the tool is unplugged, so use care with how and where you set it down. Use this type of glue gun when you need instant gratification or to hold something in place until you get a chance to install fasteners. It's really a lifesaver when you need to glue a very small or thin piece of wood in place that would otherwise crack if you attempted to use a fastener.

Caulking gun

A caulking gun dispenses caulk and adhesives that are packaged in cardboard or plastic cartridges. (For information about adhesive, caulk, and glue, see Chapter 3.) The open-frame style dispenser is easy to clean, but the most important feature to look for is a quick-release button on the back end. Press it with your thumb as you near the end of an application. If you have to fumble with a less convenient or reliable release system, adhesive will ooze out all over the place before you relieve the pressure.

Adhesive from a cartridge is usually applied in straight ribbons, such as when applied to floor joists before plywood subfloor is installed or to studs before drywall is hung. When used on larger surfaces, such as interior paneling being installed over existing drywall, lay down squiggly lines. Just follow the installation instructions for the product.

Cut the tip of the cartridge at a 45-degree angle with a utility knife. How much you cut off depends on how wide a bead you want, but keep in mind that you can always cut off a little more if the bead is too small. There's not much you can do if you cut off too much.

Chapter 7

More Great Tools and Gizmos

. . . .

. . . .

As you may have guessed from the title and the preceding list, this chapter is a catch-all for tools that we don't normally think of as tools (or at least not as carpentry tools). Nevertheless, some tools are just as essential as your hammer and screwdriver and, for certain jobs, they're absolutely indispensable.

Safety Gear

Carpentry, demolition and home repairs often put the unaware and the unprotected do-it-yourselfer at risk. Some risks, such as cuts, falls, and eye injuries are immediate; others, such as lung disease and damaged knee joints may not show up for years. Don't be foolish. Find out how to perform tasks and use tools safely, and buy and use the appropriate protective clothing and equipment.

Protective clothing and accessories

Protect your skin from cuts, abrasions, blisters, punctures, and other injuries, and prevent unnecessary exposure to chemicals and materials that may cause discomfort or do you harm. Depending on the circumstances — tools being used, material being worked on, and other environmental conditions — proper clothing may mean any of the following:

✔ **Long pants and long-sleeve shirt.** The right work clothes will protect you against cuts, scrapes and scratches — the kind of minor (but painful) injuries that will make you crazy.

✔ **Heavy-soled shoes or ones with special gripping soles.** If you've ever dropped a 2-by-4 on your toes or stepped on a board with a nail sticking out, you know why sturdy shoes with strong soles are important. And grippy, sticky soles will prevent nasty falls and slips.

✔ **Heavy work gloves and chemical-resistant gloves.** Leather work gloves will protect your hands against splinters and blisters, and, most important, from cuts caused by sharp, rough materials. Chemical-resistant gloves will keep you from discovering the acute discomfort that can be caused by cleaning fluids, solvents, and such seemingly innocent but caustic materials like tile grout.

✔ **Coveralls.** This one-piece garment protects you from paint splatters, dirt, and drywall dust. Inexpensive, disposable ones are available. Of course, you could wear your old leisure suit, but you would scare little children.

✔ **Kneepads.** These cushioned rubber pads, held in place with elastic strips, protect your knee joints from the inadvertent bumps and constant pressure of kneeling on hard surfaces. (Pretend that you're rollerblading, and you won't feel so silly.) Kneepads are especially important to wear when you're crawling around on hard, debris-strewn surfaces.

✔ **Hard hat.** While you rarely see a DIYer don a hard hat, proper headgear is very important when heavy construction work is going on around you. (If you don't want to buy one, how about using your bike helmet? It's better than cracking your skull!)

Protecting your eyes and ears

Cuts and broken bones may heal, but eye injuries related to carpentry work often are very serious, and may even result in permanent blindness. The worst thing is that the majority of eye injuries are 100 percent preventable. All you need to do is wear proper eye protection — it's just that simple.

Goggles used to be clunky contraptions that only kid chemists wanted to wear, but now they're available in designer styles (well, sort of). Goggles, or safety glasses with side shields, are inexpensive investments that may save your eyesight. Just remember to put them on! A tiny chip of wood, a bit of fiberglass, or a speck of metal or hardened paint can seriously damage your eyes, so protect them at all costs. Make sure the goggles or glasses are well-vented or they may fog over.

If you wear prescription glasses, choose a pair of safety goggles that fits over your glasses or invest in a pair of prescription safety glasses.

Hand tools (especially power tools) are noisier than you think — a day with a circular saw will leave your ears ringing, and the blam!, blam!, blam! of a hammer in an enclosed space will make the TV sound seem softer for a while. No lie: You can permanently damage your hearing doing many of the things at-home carpenters typically do.

Protect your ears!

If you typically use a noisy tool in one location, such as a garage shop, hang a pair of earmuff-style protectors near your workstation so that they are convenient.

More often, you need protection-to-go. We'd be the first to admit that it's often inconvenient at best to put on ear protection every time you pick up a circular saw, especially if you are in the attic and your ear protectors are in the basement! The answer? Little, very soft foam earplugs that mold to your ear canal. You hardly know you have them in, and you can keep a little container full of them in a tool belt or toolbox so you'll have them when you need them.

Dust masks and respirators

You wouldn't eat dirt off the floor, so why would you eat or breathe it out of the air? Wear a dust mask whenever your work raises dust (sawing, sanding, sweeping, insulating, and so on).

Particulate filters are typically rated at 95 percent or 100 percent efficient. For most construction dust, the models that are 95 percent efficient are adequate. If you're dealing with toxic dust from, say, sanded lead paint or pressure-treated wood, or extremely small particles, however, you need the HEPA (high-efficiency particulate air) filter. Filter types also will be designated as "N" (*not* resistant to oil), "R" (*resistant* to oil) and "P" (oil-*proof*). R-type filters are necessary when there is limited exposure (typically less than 8 hours) to contaminants that contain oil.

Particulate filters don't stop vapors and fumes. So if you are applying finishes, paint strippers, or solvents, or working with adhesives or other products that give off fumes — wear a cartridge-style, carbon-filter respirator. Look for what manufacturers call a "multi-gas" filter so you'll be safe from anything these products may contain. Finally, if your work involves both dust and fumes, stack the appropriate combination of filters (in any order).

For the best protection against breathing in dust and fumes, follow these tips:

- ✔ Prevention is key. Start by taking whatever steps you can to limit the amount of dust you create. Try to ventilate or exhaust the dust outdoors. For example, sprinkle a sweeping compound on the floor before you sweep to keep dust from becoming airborne; put an inexpensive, 24-inch fan in a window (see Chapter 5); or use a shop vacuum for dust collection. (See the section titled, "Keeping up with the mess," in this chapter.)

- ✔ A totally effective filter can't protect you if the mask is not well sealed. Pull any adjusting straps tight. Cover the mask with your cupped hands and exhale to detect where air may be escaping.

- ✔ Many so-called nuisance dust masks are virtually useless because they don't seal well around your mouth and nose. The versions with soft metal ribs that you can bend to conform to your nose are better, but don't hesitate to step up to a cartridge-style respirator. These respirators fit much better.

- ✔ Inspect the mask and filters often. If the filters or mask are dirty, either replace the filters, or toss a disposable type.

- ✔ When in doubt, ask! Air filter manufacturers have health and safety technical assistance departments to answer your questions and guide your filter/mask choices.

Keeping Up with the Mess

Most people can't even eat without making a mess, so it's no surprise that home repair and remodeling projects generate an enormous amount of dust, debris, and other trash. Big messes call for big cleanup capabilities, and two tools come immediately to mind for this work:

- ✔ **Shop vacuum or a wet/dry vacuum.** Shop around. All models are noisy, but some are unbearable. Compare any noise ratings or simply try it out before you buy. Some models collect debris in bags, which is more costly, but they can handle fine dust such as the powder that sanding drywall leaves behind. Shop vacuums without bags tend to choke on fine dust and spew more back into the room. The wet pick-up capability is handy for spills and floods that result from leaky pipes or foundation.

Choose a shop vacuum that has hoses and attachments that allow it to be used as a dust-collection system for your power tools that are similarly equipped. You'll stay healthier and your house or work site will stay cleaner.

- ✔ **Push broom.** You don't want to haul out a big vacuum all the time, so keep a sturdy push broom — preferably one that has a reinforcing plate that braces the handle where it joins the head to prevent breakage. And get a good dustpan!

"Now that's a serious dustpan," a friend once said as he eyeballed my large metal industrial-model shop dustpan. "Yep," I responded. "I make serious messes." (Mom must be so proud.)

Climbing to New Heights

Get a sturdy stepladder for interior work and an extension-type ladder for work on siding, exterior trim, roofs, and other outdoor areas. A stepladder should feel solid and not wobble side-to-side when you move on it. If you plan to spend lot of time on a ladder, (ask yourself "why?") then make sure the treads are wide, flat, and comfortable.

Ladders can be made from several materials. Here are some general characteristics:

- **Wood ladders** are solid, heavy, and economical.
- **Aluminum ladders** are lightweight and strong.
- **Fiberglass ladders** are strong, electrically nonconductive, and expensive.

For most home carpenters, a good-quality wood or aluminum ladder is more than adequate. Wood ladders are the least expensive, but they get wobbly with age, heavy use, and abuse. Aluminum ladders cost more, but if you ever lifted your grampa's long, wood extension ladder, you'll appreciate the huge savings in weight and the better maneuverability that aluminum offers. Be aware, however, that aluminum ladders are excellent conductors of electricity, so you won't want to be standing on one when you're putting in that new ceiling fan. Electrical conductivity considerations and durability give fiberglass ladders the edge with some professionals. But unlike the pros, you won't be using your ladder everyday, so why spend the extra dough?

Ladders have four basic duty ratings that define the maximum safe-load capacity of the ladder. This weight includes the person plus the weight of any tools and materials being carried onto the ladder. Translated, it's your weight plus all the stuff you wear and haul up the ladder with you. The bottom line: If you're a big person, you should make sure you get a ladder that will safely hold your weight.

The four duty ratings for ladders are:

- **Type IA.** Extra heavy-duty industrial use, carries a 300-pound duty rating
- **Type I.** Heavy-duty industrial use, has a 250-pound duty rating
- **Type II.** Commercial light-maintenance work, has a 225-pound duty rating
- **Type III.** General light-duty household use, carries a 200-pound duty rating

There's no big mystery to using a ladder, but to be safe there are some important rules to follow:

- Use ladders only for the purpose for which they were designed. They are not meant to be used as a bridge between stepladders, as a sawhorse, or as a place for more than one person to work.

- Inspect your ladder for structural defects, such as broken or missing rungs, and broken or split rails or cross braces.

- Set ladders only on stable and level surfaces to prevent accidental shifting. Many extension ladders have adjustable feet to help you find solid footing on uneven ground. Use them, not a brick or board. If there is any question at all about a ladder's stability, re-set it.

- Position extension ladders at the proper angle. The horizontal distance from the house to the foot of the ladder should be about ¼ of the working length of the ladder (the extended length of the ladder).

- To raise a tall ladder, place the lower end against something solid, walk it up to a vertical position, move it close enough so you can lean the top end against the house, then pull the base away from the wall a distance equal to ¼ of its working length. To put it another way, don't just stick the legs on the ground and let the ladder fall against the siding — it could bounce or slide sideways, breaking a window and/or marring the clapboards. It could also fall over and pound you into the ground like Wile E. Coyote.

- When ascending or descending a ladder, face the ladder and keep at least one hand free to grasp the ladder.

- Don't carry too heavy or awkward objects that might cause you to fall.

- Don't climb or stand on the cross bracing on the rear of stepladders unless the ladder is specifically designed for access from both sides.

- Never stand on either the top of a stepladder or its top step.

- Don't stretch. Keep your belly button within the ladder rails.

- Don't ever attempt to move, shift, or extend a ladder while you are on it. (Although, hopping sideways while on a ladder is a great way to meet people — like doctors and nurses.)

- Make sure tools are secured in a tool belt or proper holder.

- Never stand below an occupied ladder; you may wake up in an ambulance with a dent in your head.

- When you get off a ladder, don't leave any tools on it that might fall on the next user's head. Keep the area around the bottom of a ladder clear, too. Just in case, don't ever move a ladder without looking up.

- When using an aluminum ladder outside, be aware of electrical wires. Look up when moving and placing your ladder — don't let it brush, rest, scrape, touch, or fall against power lines. If you do, this is what you'll hear (briefly): ZZZZZZZzzzzzzzapppp!

By the way, tool rental outlets rent ladders and scaffolding by the day, week, or month and also offer a range of accessories. *Ladder jacks* allow you to extend a platform between two extension ladders. *Stabilizers* allow you to safely reach a wider area. Ask for instructions on proper and safe use of any equipment that you rent.

Very Specialized Tools

Some tools are so specialized or good at what they do that you simply must have them for a particular task, but they are typically useless for anything else. So don't run out and buy such a tool unless the need arises. And if the need does arise, don't try to get away with some other tool.

Here are a few specialized tools that you should know about:

- ✔ **Zip tool.** When installers put vinyl siding on a building, they work from the bottom up, with each successive course overlapping and interlocking with the one below. But what if you need to replace a damaged course? Well, just unzip it! The zip tool is a unique, single-purpose tool that unlocks the course above the damaged one so that you can access and remove the fasteners that secure the damaged piece. When the new piece is nailed on, the zip tool zips up the opening. (See the section on patching and replacing vinyl siding in Chapter 16.)

- ✔ **Window zipper.** When years of carelessly applied paint build up between a double-hung window sash and its channels, the sash becomes difficult or impossible to operate. The problem with many repair approaches is that they rely on brute force or tools, such as a pry bar. These methods often result in a damaged sash, frame, or the glass — and the easy fix turns into a royal pain. The window zipper (or simply a *window tool*) has a blade the lays flat against the sash and a serrated edge that safely cuts the paint bond and cleans out the old paint (see Chapter 14).

- ✔ **Electronic stud finder.** This device works quite well for locating framing behind drywall-covered ceilings and walls. Move the sensor over the surface until lights or beeps indicate that you are over the framing. You get what you pay for in terms of sensitivity. Inexpensive versions work fairly well over ½-inch drywall but not much else.

- ✔ **Electronic calculators.** Units that can calculate in fractions and convert metric/standard dimensions are quite handy and reduce the risk of costly mistakes like buying 1,500 square feet of insulation instead of 150. (Those decimal points are pretty tricky.) Construction calculators are neat, too, but they cost much more and have many advanced functions, which only professionals and advanced DIY builders and remodelers would likely need.

- ✔ **Board stretcher.** Cut a board a little short? This is the tool for you. No carpenter's dream toolbox should be without it.

✔ **Neon circuit tester.** This $2 item can be a lifesaver (literally) whenever you have to work on an electrical switch, receptacle, or power source. Before you begin tinkering with a device, use this circuit tester to make sure that power isn't flowing to it.

Drywall Finishing and Spackling Tools

All simple repairs on drywall involve applying and smoothing a material called *joint compound* or *spackling compound*. The material is a premixed, white plaster-like substance that has the consistency of plain yogurt — but with slightly more flavor. Here are the tools you'll need:

✔ Use a *putty knife* for spackling very small holes, such as those left by removed picture hooks.

✔ Use a 5- or 6-inch *taping knife* for smoothing joint compound over larger holes or over the paper reinforcing tape that covers the joints between pieces of drywall.

✔ If you are planning significant taping (as the finishing process is called), you may also want a longer *smoothing knife*.

✔ You also need either a plastic *mud pan* or a *hawk* to hold an immediate working quantity of compound. The mud pan looks like a bread pan with a metal straightedge built into one long edge. The hawk is simply a large square of textured aluminum with a cylindrical handle mounted on the underside.

To avoid contaminating the compound, never work out of the product bucket. Instead, remove a couple of large scoops of compound with a clean knife and place it into a plastic mud pan (a bread pan will do in a pinch) or onto the hawk. Clean your knife often on the metal edge of the pan or hawk and discard any compound that is contaminated with dirt or dried specks of compound.

✔ The *pole sander* is a soft-rubber sanding pad that swivels on the end of any long, threaded, broom-type handle. The handle and swiveling action enable you to reach walls and ceilings without ladders or stooping, and the handle puts some distance between you and all that dust!

Powering Up!

Typical extension cords range from two-prong, light-duty, 16 AWG (American Wire Gauge) "lamp" cords to three-prong (grounded) 12 AWG "heavy duty" job-site cords. Cords are also rated for indoor or indoor/outdoor use, and some are specifically designed to remain flexible in freezing weather, which is important if it's typically kept in an unheated garage or shop. It's nice to have at least one heavy-duty, *multi-receptacle extension cord* to bring power to your work area for tools or other smaller extension cords. Some cords even incorporate a standard circuit breaker to prevent overloading. (Now if someone can only invent an extension cord that you can't trip over!)

Make sure the cord that you use can handle the amp rating of the tool you are using as described in Table 7-1. The more amperage the tool draws (see its label) and the longer the cord, the heavier the wire gauge requirements.

Table 7-1	Minimum American Wire Gauge (AWG) Requirements for Extension Cords		
Cord length (in feet)	Ampere Rating (A) of AC Tool Up to 12 A	Up to 16 A	Up to 20 A
25	16 AWG	14 AWG	12 AWG
50	16 AWG	14 AWG	12 AWG
75	16 AWG	14 AWG	12 AWG
100	16 AWG	14 AWG	12 AWG

A Gizmo That Actually Works

Multi-tool. There are a lot of multi-purpose tools out there. Many sacrifice quality, design, or function for the overall convenience. Understanding this, there aren't too many we'd run out and buy — but there's one, generally known as a *multi-tool* that we think is a cool tool.

The multi-tool is a big brother to the Swiss army knife. Depending on the model and the maker, it may have various screwdriver bits, pliers, scissors, wire cutters, file, wood saw, and many other handy tools that all fold up into the handle of the pliers. The versatility of this tool makes it a great tool for the kitchen "junk-drawer." Good for the man or woman who has every tool, but equally valuable for the deprived, tool-less members of our society.

Chapter 8

Rough and Finish Carpentry Techniques

··

In This Chapter

▶ Joining and fastening lumber

▶ Tackling rough-framing techniques

▶ Framing nonbearing walls

··

*O*ne way or another, most carpentry — rough or finish — involves connecting lumber together or fastening it to another surface, and doing so according to a plan.

In rough carpentry (framing) the idea is to make a strong structure. Looks generally don't matter because everything will be hidden.

In finish carpentry, the plan is to make trim members (baseboards, crown moldings, window trim, and so on) fit together with nearly invisible joints that stay that way.

In most woodworking projects, the plan is to build a box of one sort or another (for example, a bookcase, toy box, drawer, or cabinet). Its joints, too, should be tight but must also be strong enough to hold together and remain square as forces of one sort or another are applied to it.

As a home handyman, you'll encounter both structural and nonstructural elements. When you're building nonstructural elements (the only kind we deal with in this book) the frame serves mainly as a nailing surface for some finish material. These nonstructural elements may not support significant weight, such as a roof, but the connections must be strong. The same would be true for outdoor projects such as fences. The posts and rails are a support and nailing base for the pickets or boards.

The secret to DIY success is making all those connections correctly. Naturally, the process involves measuring, cutting, fastening, gluing, and other skills that we describe in Chapters 3 through 7, as well as lumber, fasteners, and other building materials covered in Chapter 2.

Making the Right Connections

No matter what you're doing, you need to choose the best way to join the various members that make up your project. And, of course, when you're ready to build the project, you need to know how to make those connections properly. Choosing and making those connections is the topic of this section.

What are you trying to do?

First, decide how you want pieces of lumber that you intend to join will stand in relation to one another. Will they form a corner, butt into one another, overlap or what? Naturally, this depends on what you're building — for example, the boards that make a box will meet to form 90-degree corners.

Second, choose from the many ways to make that connection that meet your needs by determining the relative importance of factors such as strength and appearance. Using our box example, if appearance were not particularly important, you might butt the two boards and secure them with common nails. If appearance and strength were important, you'd *miter* the corner and secure the joint in a more sophisticated, good-looking way.

Making strong connections

In most applications, strength is a high priority; but the joinery or fastener you choose depends on the forces you are trying to overcome or the kind of load you are trying to support. For example a *shearing stress* tends to make two objects slide in relation to one another. An example would be the weight of books on a shelf attached to the sides of a bookcase. In some cases, *tensile* or *pulling stresses* are your concern. An example would be something heavy attached to the ceiling. In many cases, your concern is twofold. If that bookcase, for example, were mounted on a wall, there would be both shear and tensile forces working on the fasteners holding it to the wall.

Determining the direction of the force is also important. While a 2x4 wall frame or a bookcase may be able to support a heavy load, both are easily racked (distorted out of square) if any force is exerted from the side, unless some form of diagonal bracing is present. This is true because a rectangle is a weak construction when compared with, for example, a triangle or a circle. Usually you need to brace a rectangle with a board applied diagonally or a piece of plywood nailed to one face, such as sheathing on wall studs or a back on a bookcase.

The joint and fastener you use, as well as an adhesive, can help stiffen the construction. If you attach a bookshelf to the sides of a bookcase with a *dado* instead of a simple *butt* joint, use screws instead of nails and glue the joints, the shelf will bend or break before the joint at the side fails; and the bookcase will be better resist racking, too. (See the section titled, "Dealing with joints," in this chapter for more detail about joining lumber.)

Moving together vs. separately

The nature of wood is to move as it expands and contracts with changes in temperature and humidity or to flex as it is subjected to forces. When you build with wood you must determine whether to allow connected pieces to move independently (like the boards in a finish floor), or in unison (like the members that make up a cabinet or the trim around a window.

Nails and framing anchors used in house construction and other rough carpentry work generally allow the most independent movement, while screws and similar fasteners allow much less. You achieve the greatest joint strength with glues and adhesives. Some adhesives remain flexible and some do not. (See "Using Adhesives" in this chapter.)

Lookin' good vs. a butt

In finish carpentry it's important that joints look good. For example, a mitered connection is preferable to a butt joint. In a mitered connection, the ends of two boards meet to form a 90-degree corner, which conceals the less attractive and difficult-to-smooth *end-grain* (ends) of the board. In a butt joint, the end of one board is exposed. But more than that, the joinery, itself, can be a design detail and, in the hands of a craftsman, an art.

Quick and dirty vs. slow and beautiful

Time is a consideration when it comes to making joints. Some joints are very easy to make — tack, tack, and you're done. And others can take hours of meticulous cutting and chiseling — throw skill level and tool availability into that formula, too. The less skill you have or the fewer specialized tools you own, the longer it will take for you to complete you work; and the results, therefore, may not justify the effort. This judgment call mainly comes into play when appearance is important and is made on a case-by-case basis.

Using adhesives

Adhesives, a general term that includes glue, cement, mastic, epoxy, and other materials that stick two surfaces together, may be used by themselves but are more often used in conjunction with fasteners. Typically, the adhesive provides significantly more strength than the fastener alone, and in some cases the fastener serves primarily to hold the pieces together while the adhesive cures. Check out Chapter 2 for information of various adhesives.

In house building, construction adhesives significantly increase the strength of various systems, such as floors and built-up beams (headers) over large openings. Construction adhesives remain flexible and can withstand both shock and considerable movement caused by either expansion and contraction or forces such as wind, varying loads on floors, and even earthquakes.

Applying adhesive between flooring layers and between the subfloor and joists also eliminates floor squeaks. When adhesives are used to install drywall to the framing, it prevents a common problem with drywall installation called *nail popping* and significantly reduces the number of fasteners required.

One goal in woodworking is to join two perfectly mated pieces of wood permanently as if they were one. Although there are many other glues and adhesives that will bond wood to wood, polyvinyl-acetate (PVA) adhesive, also called yellow glue or carpenter's glue, is the standard woodworking glue. It is not as flexible as some other adhesives but does not become brittle.

Most trim work joints and cabinetry require glued connections to assure that the joints between the members will not open up as a result of either normal expansion/contraction or day-to-day use. Two other considerable factors to note: Interior wood should not be subjected to extremes in temperature and humidity; and higher quality lumber, which does not move as much as framing lumber or other lesser grade lumber, should be used.

The materials being bonded must be held tightly together with fasteners or clamps for a minimum of one hour and then allowed to cure for four or more hours before use. When fasteners are used, they are generally left in place for added strength as a backup or just because there's no need to remove them.

Dealing with joints

Of the zillions of ways to connect one piece of lumber to another — well, maybe not zillions but lots — there are only about a dozen that are used all the time. (See Figure 8-1.) As nifty as some of the other joinery techniques are, it's just not likely that you'll ever run into many of them. Even with all the extensive remodeling that we've done, we rarely use any but the following basic joinery techniques.

For information on securing joints with nails or screws, or on using clamps to temporarily hold an assembly together while glue dries, see Chapter 6.

Butt joint

The subject of many poor jokes, a butt joint is easy to make. It is used primarily in rough carpentry. Strength and rigidity depend entirely on fasteners, hardware such as framing hardware or angle braces, or wood cleats. Framing hardware, widely used in deck and house framing, makes a stronger joint than nails and won't cause wood splitting as nails often do when driven close to the ends of board lumber. In finish carpentry, you might use connecting *dowels* or *biscuits* with glue to reinforce the connection.

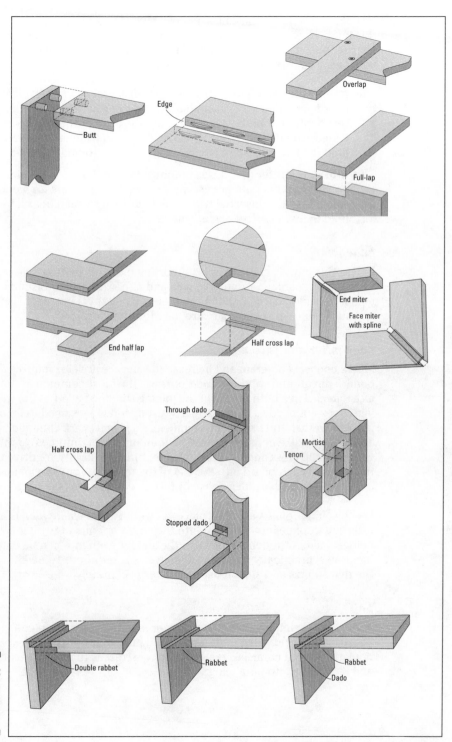

Figure 8-1:
Some of the best joints in town.

Installing dowels and biscuits requires special tools that are not covered in this book. However, both tools are easy to use and come with detailed instructions. If you do get involved in more than occasional cabinetmaking, you'll want to own one tool or the other:

- ✔ **A doweling jig,** used with an electric drill and a twist bit, clamps onto a board and guides a drill so that it makes perfectly vertical holes, the correct depth and in the exact center of the edge of the two boards being joined. The dowels are inserted with glue, halfway into each board, to hold the two in perfect alignment as they are joined together.

- ✔ **A biscuit jointer** (no, it was not invented by Nabisco) is a single-purpose power tool that cuts precisely sized and located slots for wood wafers, called biscuits. Inserted with glue, halfway into each board, the wafers hold them in perfect alignment.

Edge joint

Unless this joint is made over a supporting member such as a floor joist or the edge of a cabinet, it requires glue and either dowels or biscuits. Basically you make wide boards out of narrow ones using this joint, such as when making a tabletop, a cutting board, or wide shelving.

Edge miter and face miter

Miters conceal end-grain and increase the surface area for improved glue bond. Trim around windows and doors are the most common examples of *face miters*. Since both pieces of the joining trim are nailed to the wall, the joint does not need to be particularly strong but glue is used to hold the pieces together and in perfect alignment. *Edge miters* are common in bookcase and other boxlike constructions. The joint must be reinforced, at minimum, with glue and *cross nailing,* also called *lock nailing.* (Nails are driven through the edges of each board into the end of the other board.) Maximum strength is achieved only with a glued *spline* or biscuit connectors (see "Butt joint").

Like biscuits, splines are little pieces of wood, and a *spline joint* is made by inserting a spline into slots cut into the edges or ends of two pieces of wood being joined. Although splines and the slots they fit into can be cut with handsaws, practically speaking, a table saw is required. To be effective, both the thin splines and slots must be cut very accurately.

Lap

A *lap* joint — simple *overlap, half lap,* or *full lap* — is used to connect two boards. In the end, a lap joint looks like a butt joint but is much stronger, particularly when it comes to resisting lateral stresses that tend to turn squares and rectangles into parallelograms.

Dado

A *dado* is a joint in which a groove that is cut across the grain of one board receives another board. A dado is stronger than a butt joint because of the increased gluing surface and the interlocking nature of the joint. It absolutely prevents shearing (lateral movement); and when the second board is held into the groove with screws, the joint resists pullout, too. However, diagonal bracing or plywood must be fastened to the front or back of the project to prevent racking.

You can cut a dado with a backsaw and chisel, or a circular saw. To maximize the joint strength and minimize weakening the grooved board, the optimal groove depth is ⅓ the thickness of the board — ¼-inch deep for a ¾-inch-thick board, for example.

A dado joint is commonly used in woodworking projects involving shelves because a shelf set into the sides can hold a great deal of weight. If the groove extends the full width of the board it is called a *through dado*. If the groove stops before it reaches the front edge of a board, it is called a *stopped dado*. When stopped on both edges it is called a *blind dado*. In effect, the last portion of the joint is a butt joint. This generally looks better than a through dado joint, and without sacrificing any measurable strength. A notch, corresponding to the depth of the dado and the length of the ungrooved portion of the receiving board, must be cut in the end of the mating board.

When working with plywood that will be edge-banded with veneer or faced with a frame, use a through-dado joint, which is easier to make. Then apply the veneer or frame to conceal the dado.

Rabbet

Like a dado but cut on the edge of a board either along its length or across the end, a rabbet serves the same function as the dado but at a corner. However, one of the most common applications for this prolific little rabbet is to provide a recess for a back on a cabinet or bookcase. When a precisely fit back is glued and nailed into the recess, it automatically squares the case and is not visible from the sides or top, as it would be it if were just nailed to the back edge using a butt joint. While a table saw or router are the preferred tools for cutting rabbets, you also can use a portable circular saw. In this example, the rabbet cuts would need to be made before assembling the case.

Tongue and groove

Some siding, board paneling, and most wood flooring products are milled with tongues on one edge and grooves on the other. When installed, the tongues interlock with the grooves. In both cases joint itself is not nailed but rather, each board is *toenailed* through its tongue into the framing, forcing the groove on the opposite side over the tongue of the previously nailed board. The first board is usually face-nailed along the tongue edge and if the flooring or siding stops at an inside corner, such as where a floor meets a wall, the last board is also face-nailed.

Mortise and tenon

A mortise-and-tenon joint is very strong and resists racking. It is usually used where there can be no hardware or bracing. The most common applications are connecting the vertical (stiles) and horizontal (rails) members in raised-panel-door construction and joining the various parts of tables, chairs, and other furniture. As a beginning woodworker, therefore, you're not likely to ever make one, but you may need to deal with one if you do furniture repair.

Rough-Framing Techniques

If you know how to swing a hammer, use a tape measure, cut lumber, and fasten things together, the only challenge standing between you and your first basic framing tasks is understanding the requirements. For an overview of house framing, and a clarification of much of the italicized terminology that appears in this section, refer to Chapter 1.

We limit our discussion in this book to framing things within an existing structure and not modifying the original structure. Our discussion of wall building (or removal), for example, is limited to *nonbearing* walls, which are those that don't support the load of a roof or floor above. They include interior partition walls, closet walls, knee walls in attics, and perimeter walls against a basement foundation.

Doing the layout

Whether you are framing a stud wall, installing furring strips on a basement wall for paneling, laying down sleepers over a concrete slab for a plywood floor, or any other house framing, the first step is to determine exactly where each member will go — a process called *layout*.

We describe the layout process in detail in the next few sections on wall building, but the same principles apply for other framing applications that follow later in this chapter.

Knowing studs and headers

Stud walls provide nailing surfaces for finish materials such as drywall or paneling (on the inside) or sheathing and siding (on the outside). A standard wall is 8 feet ¾ inch tall and is composed of *precut studs* (92-¼ inch), sitting on a bottom plate (called a *sole plate*) and topped with two more plates (called a *double top plate*). The studs are spaced on either 16- or 24-inch centers to accommodate standard sized drywall, paneling, or exterior sheathing. When you're building a wall in an existing structure that may already have finished floors or ceilings or heights other than 8 feet ¾ inches, it is more likely that you will use 8-foot 2x4s and cut them to suit your needs. Also, *nonbearing walls* such as partitions or basement perimeter walls do not require a second top plate.

When a wall is built under a sloped roof, such as in rooms with sloped ceilings, it is called a *rake* wall. Each stud is cut to a different length and with an angle at the top. The easiest way to build such a wall, by the way, is to snap chalk lines on the floor to indicate the exact dimensions of the space and then lay the studs in place to mark them for cutting where they cross the chalk lines.

Openings

Openings in walls for doors and windows are located without regard for the position of the regularly spaced studs. Each opening consists of a header across the top, and two studs ("king" and "trimmer") nailed together at the sides. The header is a horizontal timber that carries the load of the vertical studs cut to make the opening. The *king stud* is a stud that frames the sides of the opening. It runs from the bottom plate to the top plate, and is nailed directly to the end of the header. The trimmer (also called a *cripple stud* or *jack stud*) is cut to fit between the bottom plate and the underside of the header — it supports the header and carries its load downward to the sill.

This *rough opening (R.O.)* should be 2 inches wider and 2¼ inches taller than the nominal dimensions of the door or window. To achieve the correct rough-opening width, cut the header 5 inches wider than the nominal door width. To achieve the correct height, cut the king studs the same length as other studs and cut the trimmer studs so the top will be 82¼ inches above the floor. This height allows room for a standard 6 foot-8 inch doorframe. (For door-frame installations, see Chapter 10.) Pocket doors — the kind that slide into a wall — usually require a taller R.O.

The opening for a window or a pass-though is framed the same way as the opening for a door, except that the bottom is filled in with a *rough sill*, a flat 2x, supported by short studs called *sill jacks*. The sill jacks are installed according to the initial 16-inch on-center layout, without regard for the window location.

Where wall meets wall

When walls intersect they must be secured to each other at the top, bottom and at least two other points in between. You must also provide a nailing base for finish materials applied to the intersected wall. At intersecting corners, this is done by providing an assembly of two backing studs separated by 2x4 spacers. At midwall intersections the spacers must be about 3½ inches wide and, therefore, 2x4 spacers are installed on the flat.

Building a nonbearing wall

In most cases it is easier to frame a wall on the floor and tilt it up into place. If you are building more than one wall, do all the layout work at once. That way, if any problems arise, you can correct them before you have built the wall. For information on the nailing techniques described here refer to Chapter 6.

Follow these steps and Figures 8-2 and 8-3 to build a wall:

1. **Map out the wall locations on the floor (see Figure 8-2a).**

   To determine placement, measure off the two ends of an existing wall that is parallel to the wall you want to build; and snap a chalk line between the two marks. Now verify that your chalk line is perpendicular to the wall or walls it intersects by using a framing square for short walls or, for longer walls, the 3-4-5 triangle rule described in Chapter 1.

2. **Cut the plates and mark for openings and intersecting walls as shown in Figure 8-2b.**

   Cut the plates for one wall the same length and lay them together on the floor. Mark the header widths for any door or window openings, as well as the locations of any intersecting walls or corners. Mark these on the face and edge of the plates. Finally, mark the stud locations.

   One important difference between new-construction wall building and framing a wall into an existing space is that the length of the opening for a wall at the ceiling might be a little different if the existing walls are not plumb. If that is the case, cut both plates to the shorter dimension.

   When laying out for framing members, always make a single line indicating where one edge of a framing member should go and place an X on one side of the line or the other to indicate the stud location.

3. **Mark remaining stud locations (see Figure 8-2c).**

   The remaining studs are spaced exactly 16 inches OC (or 24 inches OC) with two exceptions. First, assuming the edge of any wall panel would start right in a corner (not ¾ inch away as it would be if it were in the center of the stud), the distance between the first and second stud must be 15¼ inches. Second, the last stud will likely fall less than 16 inches on center (OC) from the second to last stud.

   Allow for one other complication when framing two walls that intersect. Decide which wall will be finished first and then allow for that thickness when locating the second stud in the other wall. If you are using ½-inch drywall, for example, the near edge of the second stud would be 15¾ inches from the end of the wall.

   Double check your layout after you have marked the first four stud locations: Measure out from the end of a wall where you started the layout, and your 4-foot mark should be in the middle of a stud (or ¾ inch past its layout line).

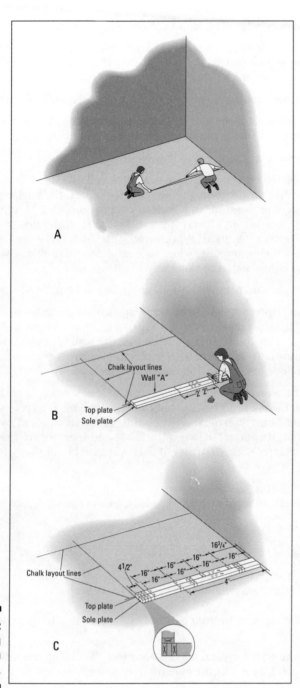

Figure 8-2:
Getting
started with
your wall.

4. **Assemble rough-opening members (see Figure 8-3).**

   Nail a trimmer to each king stud with the bottom edges aligned; nail up the header, which consists of two flat 2x4s in a nonbearing wall; and nail the header between the king studs and on top of the trimmers.

5. **Nail together backing assemblies for intersecting walls or corners.**

   For a corner, nail three short 2x4 blocks flat between two studs. For an intersecting wall, nail a full-length stud on edge between two studs.

6. **Build the wall on the floor, as shown in Figure 8-3a.**

   Turn the plates on edge with one against a wall and the other about 8 feet away. Place framed rough opening assemblies, the backing stud assemblies, and the studs in position. Working one stud at a time, carefully align the stud with its layout mark — the stud should cover the X — and nail through the plate into the stud with three 16d common nails. When one side is complete, slide the complete end against a wall and nail on the other plate the same way.

7. **Raise, plumb, and secure the wall as shown in Figures 8-3a and b.**

   Tilt the wall up and align the bottom edge with the chalk line on the floor. Nail the sole plate to the floor by using 10d common nails, preferably driven into floor framing. Check that the wall is plumb, in-and-out and left-and-right. When the wall is plumb, nail the top plate into the ceiling or floor joists with 10d common nails.

   If the partition wall is parallel to the ceiling joists and falls between two joists, you have a problem: Nothing you can nail into. To give yourself an attachment point, you must open up the ceiling and insert 2x4 nailers (an appropriate name!) between the joists and then secure the top plate to those nailers. Locate a nailer at each end and about every four feet in between.

   If you are building a wall on a concrete slab floor, use masonry screws (see Chapters 2 and 6) instead of nails to secure the sole plate to the floor.

Framing a wall in place

If there is not enough floor space, or if the presence of other obstacles would preclude raising a preassembled wall, follow these steps:

1. **Lay out the top and bottom plates. See "Building a nonbearing wall, Step 2."**

2. **Map out the wall location on the floor (see "Building a nonbearing wall, Step 1"), and nail the sole plate in place.**

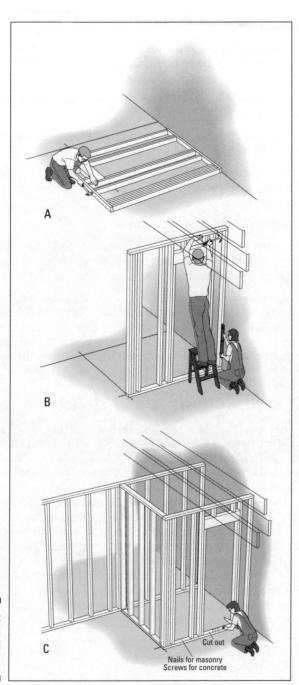

A

B

C

Cut out

Nails for masonry
Screws for concrete

Figure 8-3:
Putting
the wall
together.

3. **Extend the wall location to the ceiling.**

   Plumb or level up from the two ends of the sole plate to the ceiling and mark the two points on the ceiling. Snap a chalk line on the ceiling between the marks.

4. **Secure the top plate to the ceiling joists. See "Building a nonbearing wall, Step 7."**

5. **Nail up any rough-opening or backer-stud assemblies (see "Building a nonbearing wall, Step 5"), and precut the studs.**

   If you later find that some studs are too short because of ceiling or floor irregularities, you can drive shims between the top plate and the ceiling to straighten the top plate.

6. **Toenail the studs in place one at a time.**

   Align a stud with its mark on the sole plate and toenail the stud to the plate by using five 8d common nails – two on each side and one into the front edge. Then toenail the top of the stud to the top plate the same way.

   To help keep studs in place as they are toenailed, cut a length of 2x4 14½ inches long. Lay on the plate with an end against an already secured stud. Then push the next stud against it and drive the nails (toenailing). Remove the block to toenail the other side. Tap one side of the stud or the other to fine tune the placement until the edge is on the layout line.

Building a kneewall in an attic

To convert an attic to a finished room (and keep it from being real small and pointy on two sides), you need to build short walls up to the underside of the sloped roof rafters. To build these *kneewalls,* generally follow the same procedures described in "Building a nonbearing wall," in the previous section, but with a few differences. After you have mapped out the wall on the floor, extend the wall location from the floor to the rafters at each end of the wall. On these short walls, the easiest way is to cut a 2x4 stud about 6 inches long, stand it in position, check that it is plumb by using a level, and trace a line on the rafter along the front edge of the stud. Then temporarily tack the stud to the rafter. Repeat this at the other end of the proposed wall. Stretch a string from the face of one stud to the face of the other about 1 inch below the rafters. (The reason you do this is that some rafters may stick down a bit more than others and would prevent the string from being straight.) Make note of which rafter is closest to the string and plan to build the wall to that height.

To determine the stud length, follow these steps:

1. **Lay a short scrap of 2x4 — a temporary sole plate — on the floor directly before that low rafter.**

2. **Tack 2-to-3 foot 2x4 to the face of two adjacent rafters above it.**

   The front corner of this temporary top plate must extend out to, but not past, the string.

3. **Finally, measure from the top front edge of the sole plate to the front corner of the top plate.**

   This will be the long point of the angle-cut studs. (See Chapter 5 for information on the tools and techniques for making multiple miter cuts.)

After you cut all the studs, preassemble the wall on the floor. Then raise the wall and nail it to the rafters. As you do, use a level to check that the wall is plumb. Wherever there is a gap between the rafter and the top plate insert a shim before you nail.

Part III
Interior Home Improvements

The 5th Wave   By Rich Tennant

"To preserve the beauty and durability of the dental molding, we put fluoride in the trim paint."

In this part . . .

Stand in your house and look around at the walls, doors, windows, floors, and all that woodwork and trim. That's what this part of the book is about: the basic elements of a room. If you haven't given any of them much thought, that's okay, but if you're looking to replace or improve them, well, that's what you'll find here. We'll take you through the process of installing and finishing a wall and hanging shelving on them. You'll get the inside story about doors and windows and what's involved and the skills required to trim them with woodwork. It's a wannabe-carpenter's dream come true.

Chapter 9

Wall Finishing

● ●

In This Chapter

▶ Understanding drywalling basics

▶ Hanging drywall

▶ Finishing a drywall job

▶ Installing solid-wood paneling

▶ Putting up sheet paneling

● ●

*I*f a little remodeling or a lot of damage has put you in the position of having to install drywall or wood paneling, you've come to the right place, because we do walls. More precisely, we tell people how to do walls. And you're in luck — the work is pretty straightforward and well suited for do-it-yourselfers, and even novices who are tackling their very first renovation project.

When it comes to drywall, however, the scale of the job often becomes an issue when deciding between doing the work yourself or hiring a pro. It really pays to do a small drywall project (a small room or less) because a small job requires the same three trips that a large one does. This means you'll usually have to pay a disproportionately higher price for a small job such as a closet, a partition wall or even a small room. The economies of scale really kick in for larger jobs, however, and for ones involving installations on cathedral ceilings. Even professional remodelers who won't bat an eye at the prospect of drywalling one room, usually get in a specialist for bigger jobs. So before you take on a big drywalling job, get a couple of bids and evaluate whether you might better spend your time on another aspect of the work, such as installing trim (see Chapter 12) — or working on your putting game.

Putting Up Drywall

Drywall is inexpensive, requires limited skills to cut and hang, and is forgiving (or at least easily fixed) if you make a mistake. Two drywalling processes are a bit more challenging:

✔ Finishing the joints, a process called *taping* because it involves embedding a paper or mesh tape in compound over the joints

✔ *Spotting*, which is spackling over the fasteners

Although these two processes require more skill and experience, they are still within reach for an average do-it-yourselfer. (The problem is, there's never an average do-it-yourselfer around when you need one!)

The basics

Drywall, also called wallboard, gypsum board, or *Sheetrock* (a brand name), is a panel made of gypsum (a chalky mineral) laminated between paper facing. In addition to standard drywall, there is a version that offers higher fire resistance (Type Firecode "C") for use in garages and kitchens, and around fireplaces and furnaces, and another "blue" or "green" water-retardant type designed for use under tile in bathrooms and kitchens ("blueboard" or Type "W/R").

Sizes

The most commonly used thickness is ½ inch, but ⅝-inch drywall provides extra rigidity on widely spaced framing, especially insulated ceilings, and ⅜-inch and ¼-inch panels are used for resurfacing damaged walls. Drywall comes in 4-foot wide panels that are commonly available in 8, 10, 12, and 14 feet long. You can even find elevator-size 5-foot panels. (You may need to go to a drywall supply company to get sizes other than 4x8.) Drywall usually is fastened directly to wall studs, but may also be applied over cracked plaster walls or ceilings or over existing drywall.

Fastening

Drywall is best fastened with screws and a high-speed screw gun. (This tool, available for rent, differs from the enormously popular cordless drill/drivers in that it operates at only one speed — warp speed — and has a special tip that enables the user to control the exact countersink depth.) Using screws and a screw gun eliminates two common problems with drywall installation: nail pops and improper dimpling of the surface when countersinking a nail with a hammer.

If you're careful, you can get away with using a drill/driver for small jobs. (If you don't want to be careful, you can pound in the screws with a croquet mallet.) Drive the screw below the surface but be careful not to tear the paper facing in the process. Space screws no more than 12 inches apart on every joist or stud. If you apply *drywall adhesive* to the framing, increase fastener spacing to 16 inches on ceilings and 24 inches on walls.

Getting oriented

Drywall has tapered edges along its long sides. When two tapered edges abut, they form a slight recess that extends a couple of inches on each side of the joint. This recess makes it possible to install tape and compound perfectly flat on the wall. When two factory- or site-cut ends adjoin, called a *butt joint*, there is no recess and the joint treatment must be crowned, which is both harder to do and more noticeable when it's done.

To eliminate (or at least minimize) the number of butt joints — and to make the wall stronger — install the panels perpendicular to the framing and, if possible, use panels long enough to span the full length of a wall or width of a ceiling. (Just make sure you can get these extra-long panels in the room and have the extra help needed to handle them safely.)

Installation, step-by-step

If you are drywalling the ceiling, do it before you apply drywall or another finish material on the walls. Then you won't risk damaging the walls; and when the walls are done, you will be able to butt a nice factory drywall edge or paneling trim to the ceiling. Get some tall helpers and make one or two T-braces (see Step 2 below) to hold the drywall in place while you fasten it. (Don't have any tall friends? Try stacking a couple of short ones!)

To install drywall, take the following steps:

1. **Mark the location of ceiling joists on the walls, and mark stud and electrical receptacle locations on the floor.**

2. **Cut and install the first piece of drywall on the ceiling.**

   Cut the panel to length, as shown in Figure 9-1, so that it ends over the middle of a joist. If you plan to use adhesive, raise the panel in position and wedge T-braces (see Figure 9-2) under it to hold it while you fasten it. (Go back to "Fastening" and take a look at "The finish" in this chapter for adhesive and fastening guidelines.)

3. **Cut and install remaining pieces, butting each panel loosely against adjoining panels or the walls.**

4. **Cut and install the upper wall panels.**

   Cut each of the upper panels to length and install them horizontally with a finished edge pushed up to the ceiling.

5. **Cut and install lower panels.**

   Use a large pry bar as a lever and a block of wood as a fulcrum to lift and hold the panel tightly against the upper panel while you secure it.

6. **Allow the panels to run past outside corner and door and window openings and cut them in place.**

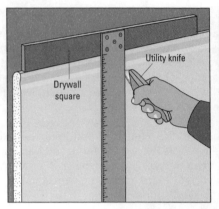

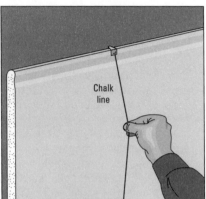

Figure 9-1:
Use a drywall square and score the cutting line with a sharp drywall knife; or use a chalk line to guide a freehand scoring cut. Snap the panel to break it along the line and cut the back paper side.

Figure 9-2:
A T-brace supports drywall while you fasten it to a ceiling.

Dealing with obstacles

When a panel will cover an electrical outlet, you have two options. If you position the panel and bang the panel with the flat of your hand over the outlet location (assuming you have marked the location on the floor), the outlet will make an impression on the back of the panel that you can use to guide your cut. (Put a little lipstick on the edge of the box and you can't miss it! Mascara is optional.) Alternately, measure down and across to the outlet from the panels already installed to locate and transfer those measurements onto the face of the uninstalled panel. Double-check your measurements and cut out the hole with a drywall saw. (Drive the point of the saw through the drywall by hitting the handle end with your palm.)

Similarly measure and precut panels where they will cross into window and door openings.

Protecting outside corners

To give outside corners a sharp, clean, and damage-resistant edge, install metal *corner bead* on all outside corners, such as a vertical corner at the end of a wall or the vertical and horizontal corners at a recessed window or untrimmed passageway. Use metal shears or aviation snips to cut through the two flanges toward the bead at the corner; and then bend the strip back-and-forth to break the uncut bead.

Position the center of the bead over the corner; screw or nail it in place every 9 inches at the outside edges of the flanges. If two corner beads will meet, as they would at the corners of a recessed window, position the two pieces so that the beads meet precisely and are on exactly the same plane.

Before you begin to nail, place a straightedge against the wall horizontally and extending over the corner. Verify that the bead is slightly above the wall plane. Repeat this procedure on the adjacent wall, adjusting the corner bead, toward one wall or the other, until both sides are the same. Repeat this procedure every couple of feet, then fill in with additional fasteners.

The finish

Go over the installation carefully with a utility knife, a 6-inch taping knife (a wide scraper-like thingy), and a Philips screwdriver in hand. Run the taping knife over the fasteners and listen for a telltale "click." That sound indicates that you need to countersink the screw a bit more. Ignore any clicks emanating from your knees and elbows. Use the knives as needed to cut off any frayed edges or loose materials that protrude above the surface. If one corner bead sticks slightly above the other where the two meet, try to tap it flush with a hammer or run a file over it. (Any little bump creates a ridge as you apply the compound in subsequent steps.)

Now you're ready to perform the *three-coat finishing process,* shown in Figure 9-3. Complete one step for the entire project before moving on to the next one. For each coat, do flat joints first, then inside corners, and finish with outside corners. Perform the following steps:

1. **Apply a light coating of drywall compound over the joint.**

2. **Embed the paper tape in the drywall compound and scrape a 6-inch knife along the joint to remove excess drywall compound.**

3. **Immediately apply a thin coat of drywall compound over the tape and smooth it with a 6-inch taping knife.**

   This step reduces wrinkling and makes the tape easier to conceal with subsequent coats. Let the first coat dry completely — it'll be a uniform, bright white color. When the taping coat is dry, give the surface a quick scrape with your taping knife to knock off any high spots or bits of dried compound.

4. **Apply a 10- or 12-inch-wide second coat.**

   A 10-inch smoothing knife is best but you can make two passes with a 6-inch knife, too. This application is intended to conceal the tape and widen the joint treatment. Don't pile drywall compound in a thick coat over the tape; you're not decorating a cake. Let the second coat dry completely and scrape off the high points. While pros will usually hold off on any sanding until after the final coat, we often find it helpful to lightly sand before proceeding with the third and final coat.

5. **Apply a still-wider, thinner third coat, again using a 10-inch smoothing knife (if you own one) or a 6-inch taping knife.**

   The final coat should fill only tiny holes and feather the edges. If you are still filling larger depressions, the material will shrink, and a fourth coat may be necessary.

6. **When the final coat is completely dry, sand the repair area with 150-grit paper on a large sanding pad.**

   Be careful not to sand the face paper — doing so leaves a rough, fuzzy spot that will be difficult to hide when it's time to prime/paint.

Apply a coat of drywall primer/sealer to create a surface that will uniformly absorb paint, wallpaper adhesives, and other finishes. Then you're ready for decorating.

Inside corners

Inside corners are taped much the same way as flat joints (see previous section). Fold the tape at a 90-degree angle along its length. It has a convenient crease at the center line (don't we all!) — that makes this easy to do. Embed the tape in compound as described above. Here there are two approaches you can take for the second and third coats:

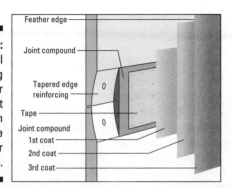

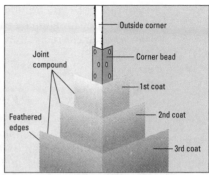

Figure 9-3: The drywall finishing process for a flat joint (left) and an outside corner (right).

✔ Apply joint compound to both surfaces with a taping knife and then smooth both surfaces at the same time with a cornering tool. Use one pass starting at the very top and extending to within a foot of the floor; and a second pass from the floor up about 2 feet. (You may need to repeat this once or twice more until the entire length is smooth on both sides.)

✔ Or use a taping knife to apply and smooth the compound on just one surface at a time. This adds at least another day (and sometimes two) to the time it takes to complete the project because you must wait for each coat to dry. However it is much easier, especially for the do-it-yourselfer or novice taper.

Outside corners

Apply the first coat of compound over one side of a corner at a time. Apply the compound on the wall and smooth it with a 6-inch taping knife by riding one side of the blade along the corner bead and the other against the wall. When that coat dries, scrape off any bumps and apply a second and third coat, each extending at least a couple of inches beyond the previous coat. As with inside corners, stop your long stroke a little above the floor and take a second short stroke from the floor up. (Refer to Figure 9-3.)

Paneling Walls

Fashions come and go (remember leisure suits?) but the warmth, look, and feel of real wood makes it an all-time favorite interior wall surface. If you can afford it, go for solid wood. Lumberyards stock only a few types but can show you samples of many more that can be special-ordered. In addition to the most obvious benefit — the look and feel of real wood — board paneling offers more design flexibility than 4x8 panels.

Both types of wall surface are available prefinished and unfinished in a range of styles, from the most rustic, rough-sawn textures to trendy "pickled" pastels. You can also use prefinished flooring on walls. With all the choices available you're sure to find a suitable one — beautifully finished solid wood wainscoting for a dining room or inexpensive 4x8 plywood paneling for a basement recreation room.

Solid wood paneling

Easy-to-maintain wood looks great the day it's installed and many decades later. Solid wood paneling often is the same material as used for exterior siding but of a higher grade. A wide variety of profiles in various widths are typically either ½- or ¾-inch thick. Many of the boards can face either side out but the patterned side determines the grade. Chief among the many installation options is the orientation — vertical, horizontal, diagonal, and chevron (two not-necessarily-45-degree diagonals meet to form a "V," usually in the center of a wall).

Vertical paneling is by far the most popular style, especially in traditional-style homes but don't limit your choices. (After all, one of the advantages of choosing board over sheet paneling is the design flexibility it affords.) Horizontal paneling tends to lower ceilings visually as it lengthens walls. It is very effective when done on the lower portion of a wall, capped by a chair rail molding. Diagonal and chevron designs are used in many contemporary-style homes but are not out of place in traditional homes, especially on walls with angled ceiling lines. You can mix styles and panel only parts of walls.

Before you make your decision be sure to check with your local building department regarding any requirements related to adequate fire protection. They will tell you how far wood paneling must be from fireplaces and wood stoves. And if you're paneling over foam insulation, for example, it should first be covered with a fire-rated material, such as drywall. If you are paneling an outside wall, you should also be sure to provide a vapor retarder when it's called for. Your inspector can advise you here, too.

To glue or not to glue — installation options

Installation methods vary according to the orientation and the surface it is being applied to — studs, masonry, or an existing finished wall. The easiest way to install over an existing finished wall, such as drywall, plaster, or paneling, is to use an adhesive. Spread the adhesive according to the adhesive-maker's instructions. Typically, you apply it and then spread it uniformly with a notched trowel, but you can also apply it in ribbons with a caulking gun. To draw the joints tight and to hold the panels in place until the adhesive sets up and cures, use braces and a minimal amount of face nailing (right through the face of the panel) or blind nailing (hidden on the edges) as needed.

When you are nailing directly to framing or to furring strips (as shown in Figure 9-4), make sure that you have provided nailing at the ends of boards and every 48 inches in between for ¾-inch-thick boards or 24 inches for ½-inch-thick boards.

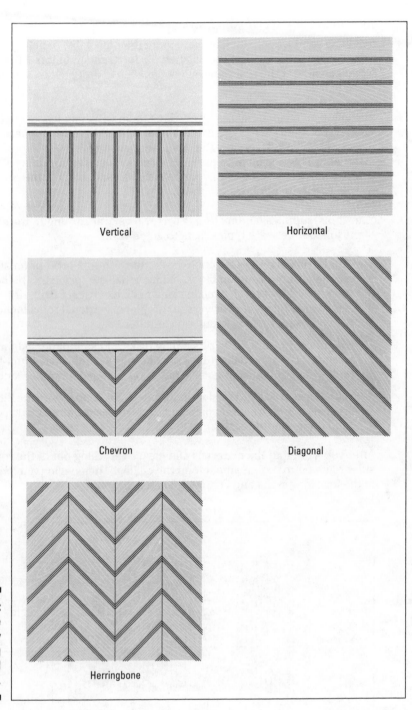

Vertical

Horizontal

Chevron

Diagonal

Herringbone

Figure 9-4:
A few of the
many
paneling
profiles and
styles.

Installing solid wood paneling

Installing solid wood paneling costs more than most 4x8 paneling, and it takes longer to install, but the finished job looks much better. After all, solid wood paneling is the real thing; sheet paneling is designed to imitate solid wood paneling.

Acclimate unfinished boards by stacking them with ⅜-inch spacers (called *stickers*) between them in a heated/air-conditioned room for at least a week prior to installation. (Follow the manufacturer's guidelines for prefinished materials.) This acclimation period prevents excessive shrinking after installation, which causes joints to open. Whenever possible, cut the acclimated boards to length and pre-stain them.

Your tools, supplies, and materials lists will vary according to the specifics of the job, but here are typical lists to guide you:

- ✔ **Tools.** Handsaw, jigsaw, compass/scribe, random-orbit or finishing sander, rubber sanding block, hammer, nail set, pry bars, 16-foot tape measure, 2-foot level, caulking gun, neon electrical tester, drill/driver with wood bits, screwdrivers, block plane. Optional tools include: Circular saw, table saw, and power miter saw

- ✔ **Supplies.** 120- and 220-grit sanding disks and sandpaper, 6d finishing nails, 8d common nails, tubes of construction adhesive, blunt-tip 6d siding nails, 6d finishing nails, outlet-box extension frames, and screws

- ✔ **Lumber materials.** 1x2 clear pine extension jambs; 1x4 and 1x6 furring strips or 2x4 for nailers; paneling; and trim as required (base, ceiling and door/window casing)

After you gather all the materials and clear everything out of the room, consider rolling a coat of fresh paint on the ceiling. Then begin paneling as listed in the following steps and Figures 9-5 and 9-6.

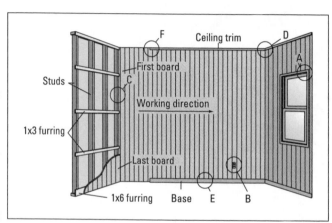

Figure 9-5:
A vertical installation over horizontal furring strips.

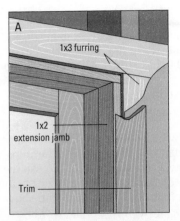

A

1x3 furring

1x2 extension jamb

Trim

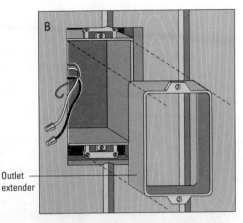

B

Outlet extender

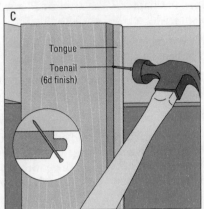

C

Tongue

Toenail (6d finish)

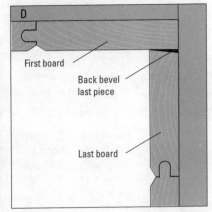

D

First board

Back bevel last piece

Last board

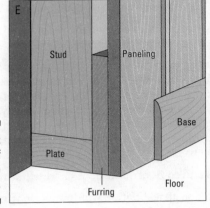

E

Stud

Paneling

Base

Plate

Furring

Floor

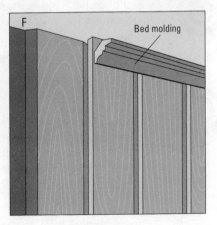

F

Bed molding

Figure 9-6: Close-ups of what you're doing.

1. **Prepare the walls.**

   Remove any existing trim, including base and ceiling trim, and window and door casing. Turn off the power to the room at the circuit breaker and remove any wall-mounted light fixtures. Also remove all outlet covers, and unscrew the devices and install frames that will extend wiring boxes to the face of the paneling.

2. **Provide nailing.**

   If the framing is exposed, nail block between studs or *let in* a horizontal 2x4 into the studs. To cut 2x4 blocking to fit between the studs, measure for each bay at the bottom plate. Predrill clearance holes in the cut boards at a 45-degree angle for toenailing. To let-in a 2x4, position the 2x4 against the face of the studs, level it, and mark each stud above and below the 2x4. Notch between the lines by using a circular saw to cut 1½ inches deep and chisel as described in Chapter 8. Fasten the nailer with screws to avoid damaging the finished wall on the opposite side.

   If you're paneling over an existing finished wall, nail a horizontal 1x6 furring strip at the floor and 1x4s at the midpoint and ceiling.

   Use masonry screws and construction adhesive to secure furring strips to concrete or masonry walls.

3. **Scribe and install first board.**

   Place the first board in a corner with its grooved edge in the corner. Adjust the board until it is plumb. Use a compass to scribe the board to the wall. (See Chapter 7.) Plan to cut off at least the entire groove. Then face-nail the board at the corner and blind-nail through the tongue into each furring strip.

   If you are right-handed, start in a left-hand corner and work to the right; if you are left-handed, start in a right corner and work to the left; and if you are ambidextrous, start at our house. (Hey, you can't blame us for trying!)

4. **Blind-nail the remaining boards at each bearing point, driving the nails at a 45-degree angle just above the tongue.**

   Use a short block of paneling with the tongue cut off as a tapping block: Insert the groove of the block over the tongue of the piece being installed and tap the block with a hammer until the joint is tight. Then drive nails flush with a nail set so the next board will fit tightly. Never hammer directly on an exposed tongue; you'll damage the tongue and then you'll never get the groove of the next board to fit over it, no matter how many profanities you use.

5. **Make cutouts for outlets and to fit around doors and windows.**

   Measure the location of an electrical outlet, window, or doorframe when you are less than one board-width from it. Transfer measurements onto your next board. Use a combination square to mark your cut lines (see Chapter 7) and a jigsaw to make the cuts. For internal cuts, bore a starter hole in at least two opposite corners and cut the opening with a jigsaw (see Chapter 8).

6. **Measure and rip (cut lengthwise) the last board on this wall so that it extends all the way to the corner.**

7. **Start and complete subsequent walls as you did in Steps 3–6.**

8. **Install the final board.**

    After you work all the way around to your starting point, stop one board shy of the wall and measure the gap between it and the first board you installed at numerous locations along the board. If the measurements are all the same, just rip the board to width. Otherwise, scribe the board to fit (see Chapter 7). After cutting with a saw (as opposed to using a food processor), test fit, and then use a block plane to fine-tune the fit.

    Cut (or plane) the board at a 10-degree bevel, called *back beveling,* so that you can insert the groove over the last tongue and pivot the other edge of it into place without damaging the adjacent wall.

9. **Extend window and door jambs.**

    These frames must be flush with the face of the new paneling (see the section on extending jambs).

10. **Trim out the room and apply a finish (or touch up prefinished paneling).**

    Install baseboard, ceiling trim and window and door casing to suit the new paneling (see Chapter 12). Touch up any stain, and apply two or three protective coats of polyurethane. Reinstall outlet covers and any light fixtures before you restore power at the circuit breaker.

Sheet paneling

Acclimate the paneling in the room in which it is to be installed. The best bet is to lay the panels flat with furring strips between the panels to let air circulate. You can also lean them against the walls or anything in the room that will support them — excluding Uncle Al.

Your tool, supply, and material lists will vary according to the specifics of the job, but here are typical lists to guide you:

✔ **Tools.** Jigsaw, compass/scribe, hammer, nail set, 16-foot tape measure, 2-foot (minimum) level, caulking gun, neon electrical tester, drill/driver with wood bits, screwdrivers, utility knife, block plane. Optional tools include circular saw, table saw, power miter saw, or the guy-next-door's saw

✔ **Supplies.** Color-matched paneling nails, tubes of paneling adhesive, outlet-box extension frames with screws, masonry screws (for masonry applications)

✔ **Lumber materials.** Clear pine extension jambs,1x4 and 1x6 furring strips (for masonry applications), paneling; trim as required (base, ceiling, and door/window casing)

With all your tools and materials at hand, and a weekend (and the room) cleared for the project, follow these steps and Figure 9-7:

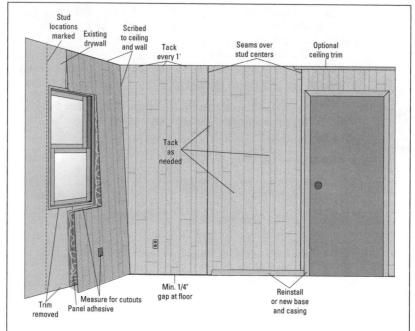

Figure 9-7:
Installing
sheet
paneling.

1. **Prepare the walls.**

   Remove any existing trim, including base and ceiling trim, and window and door casing. If you plan to reuse the trim, mark each piece's location on the backside. Turn off the power to the room at the circuit breaker and remove any wall-mounted light fixtures. Also remove all outlet covers, unscrew the devices, and install frames that will extend wiring boxes to the face of the paneling.

2. **Locate studs and pencil plumb lines at their centers. Mark their position with light pencil marks on the floor and ceiling, too.**

   Don't worry too much if you don't have one of those nifty stud finders — you can also use a nail to probe suspected locations to pinpoint the stud, because you'll be covering up the holes soon enough.

3. If you are installing paneling over a masonry wall, fasten furring strip nailers with adhesive and masonry screws.

You need horizontal nailers at the top, the bottom, and about every 2 feet in between them. Provide vertical nailing at all inside and outside corners, and on 4-foot centers so the vertical edges of all sheets will fall over solid nailing.

4. Cut the first sheet to length.

Measure floor-to-ceiling height, subtract ¼ inch and cut the first sheet to that length. Cut the bottom edge of the sheet, which will be concealed with trim. (See the circular-saw cutting guide in Chapter 5.)

5. Rip first sheet to width.

Measure from the corner to the first plumb line 4 feet or less from the corner. Add 1 inch to this dimension and cut the first sheet to that width. Cut the edge that will go into the corner so one vertical edge will touch the corner and the other will fall over the plumb line.

Apply a 1-inch wide band of wood stain or ink from a marking pen to color the wall the approximate color of the grooves in the paneling. Then, the small seasonal gaps between the sheets won't show white wall or the colored chalk.

6. Scribe the sheet.

Place the sheet against the wall and shim the bottom until the vertical edge is perfectly plumb and the sheet touches the ceiling and the corner wall. If you do not plan to install ceiling molding, scribe the paneling to the ceiling (see Chapter 7). Set your scribe to the widest gap, scribe the top edge. Cut your line and reposition the piece to test the fit. To scribe to the corner, set the compass/scribe to the 1-inch extra that you allowed when ripping the sheet and scribe the edge to the corner wall.

Always score crosscuts that will show to prevent the saw from splintering. In fact some paneling is so thin and soft you can make the entire cut with several firm passes with a utility knife guided by a straightedge.

Stain all cut edges to match the color of the paneling grooves by using a wood stain or a marking pen.

7. Adhere the first sheet to the wall.

Put ribbons of adhesive on the wall at the sheet perimeter and along every stud. Position the paneling and shim under the bottom edge to hold it tight to the ceiling and press it into the adhesive. Then nail it to the wall across the top of the sheet at 8- to 10-inch intervals by using color-matched nails or 4d finishing nails. Then put the bottom of the sheet about 1 foot from the wall and put something on the floor (don't use the cat) to hold it away from the wall for a few minutes to let the adhesive become tacky before you press it back into place.

8. **Cut and install each subsequent sheet the same way, scribing at the ceiling, if necessary.**

   Provide a ¹⁄₁₆-inch gap between sheets so that they won't buckle if they swell in damp weather. (If your wood paneling swells, you need a better air conditioner or a good dehumidifier. If you swell in damp weather, drink more water and use a little talcum powder to prevent chafing.)

9. **If any sheet will pass over any opening in a wall, such as an electrical outlet or doorway, mark and cut the opening; test for final fit before you apply any adhesive (Step 6).**

   Just like for drywall panels, you can transfer the location of an outlet box by applying lipstick or chalk to the edge of the box, position the sheet, and tap it at the box location with the palm of your hand. For windows and doors, just overlap them and mark the sheet in place. Before you cut, double-check your cutting lines by comparing wall measurements with those taken from the edge of the paneling to your cutting lines.

10. **Install the final sheet.**

    Much as you did for the first sheet, measure and rip the last sheet so that it measures about 1 inch wider at the widest gap to allow for a scribe. Then position the panel, shim it level and scribe it to the ceiling (if necessary). Reposition the panel tight against the ceiling, plumb, and touching the corner. Open your scribe to equal the amount that the left side of the final panel overlaps the right side of the one behind it. Then scribe and cut the panel.

11. **Trim out the room.**

    Install baseboard, ceiling trim, window and door casing to suit the new paneling (see Chapter 12). Color-matched trim is often available for pre-finished paneling. Touch up any stain and apply two or three protective coats of polyurethane. Reinstall outlet covers and any light fixtures before you restore power at the circuit breaker.

Chapter 10

The Ins and Outs of Doors

· ·

In This Chapter

▶ Making the right choices for new or replacement doors

▶ Discovering the standards

▶ Replacing a door only

▶ Step-by-step installations of hinged, sliding, and bifold doors

▶ Installing door locksets

· ·

T
he right doors and door hardware can make a world of difference in the quality and feel of a home. And when you're talking exterior doors, add security, comfort, and energy savings to the list. Need three more reasons to appreciate doors? How about: burglars, raccoons, and Uncle Fred.

Hanging doors, as the installation is called, used to require considerable skill, but *prehung* doors, new developments on weather stripping, and the wider availability (and affordability) of power tools have simplified the process.

Even hardware installation is easier. At one time most doors had *mortise locks*, which you needed to fit into a recess in the edge of the door. They're still around (and still a pain to install), but most doors today feature predrilled holes for locksets, dead bolts, or interlocking lockset/deadbolt units. As a result modern doors require little hammer-and-chisel work (only to recess the latch and strike plates) for installation. And of course, the predrilled holes make installing a new lockset or swapping out an old one a piece of cake.

If you're shopping for a new door or door hardware and want to install it yourself, this is the chapter for you. If you're not, this chapter is still worth reading — unless you live in a tent. And if your primary concern is repair, check out the section on doors and drawers in Chapter 10 first, but come on back if you don't get the answer you need there. Familiarizing yourself with new installation methods helps you resolve problems, too.

What's Behind Door No. 1?

You don't have to be Monty Hall to know that you have a lot of options when it comes to choosing a door. Therefore, know what's available before you make your final choices, unless, of course, you're just replacing or adding a door that you want to match your existing doors.

Swinging, bifold, and bypass

The terms swinging, bypass, and bifold seem vaguely risqué, but they're actually the three principal types of doors, as defined by the way they operate and whether they are suited for interior or exterior installation:

- ✔ **Hinged (swinging) door (interior/exterior).** This door swings open and closed on hinges (usually two or more) and is what most people think of when they hear the word "door." The standard type of hinge used is called a *full-mortise butt hinge,* but there are many specialty hinges and pivots that, for example, enable a door to swing both ways or swing completely out of an opening.

  French doors (interior/exterior). French doors are really just two swinging doors that meet in the middle of a large opening. One door has a molding, called an *astragal,* which extends beyond the edge of the door to act as a stop. This door can usually be held closed with sliding bolts to act as a latching point for the other door. A patio door looks like a French door but has a fixed, heavy-duty astragal in the center that a door or doors can be hinged to or lock against. In multipanel exterior models, one door is often permanently fixed (nonoperable) both for added security and to take less interior space when swinging. The second door may be hinged at the side or at the center. Traditional French doors swing open into the room, but outswinging models are also available.

- ✔ **Bifold (interior only).** One or two sets of doors pivot open to provide a wide opening without taking as much interior "swing" space as a larger swinging door would. One panel in a set is fitted with top and bottom pivots instead of hinges and attaches to the other panel with hinges. A roller guide in a track across the top of the opening guides the second panel. Bifold doors are sometimes referred to as *accordion doors* because of the way they fold, not (thankfully) for the way they sound. Multipanel doors operate on basically the same principle and can be used for extra-wide openings, such as for a movable room divider.

- ✔ **Bypass (sliding) doors (interior/exterior).** A pair of doors slides on two parallel tracks. Because they remain within the doorframe when operated, they are great for tight spaces. However, for the same reason, half the opening is always closed. Three or more panels can be used for extra-wide exterior opening with one of more of the panels usually *fixed* (inoperable).

A door is a door?

Both interior and exterior doors are made in a variety of materials to give you the look and performance you need for any application. Doors are either flush (flat), paneled, or flush with an applied molding. Glass can be incorporated in each type and is referred to as a *light* or *lite*. Louvered doors (wood or metal) are available in swinging, sliding, and bifold styles. Louvers are used in lieu of solid panels to provide ventilation for clothes closets, laundry rooms/closets, or any confined area in a basement or other high-humidity area that might get musty without good ventilation.

Solid wood raised-panel doors are available in a variety of species (fir, pine, and oak are common) but aside from these three, they are available by special order only. The wood stiles and rails, which are the vertical and horizontal members, respectively, that frame the panels, are often made of thinner boards that are laminated together with the grain oriented at opposite angles to counteract the evil forces that tend to warp wood. Then the door is veneered with fir, pine, oak, cherry, or some other wood valued for its appearance.

By far the most common interior door is the lightweight, hollow-core door, which has a wood or hardboard (fiberboard) veneer. Lauan mahogany and birch are the two standard veneers. Birch is very smooth and therefore a better choice than lauan for a painted door. Hardboard, often referred to by the trade name of one manufacturer, *Masonite,* is either textured with a wood-like grain or smooth.

Mirrored doors, available in swinging, bypass, or bifold styles, are available in frameless models — you see just mirror — or in steel-, aluminum-, and wood-framed models. Although typically used for wardrobes, mirrored doors can be used creatively in kitchens, dining rooms, and other locations.

While real wood is valued for its appearance, exterior doors increasingly are made of steel, hardboard, or fiberglass over an insulated core because of the energy efficiency they offer. Fiberglass has a woodlike texture and can be stained to look like wood (well, almost). Glass lights, plain or fancy, are optional. Exterior sliding (gliding) glass doors are widely available with solid-wood, vinyl- or aluminum-clad wood, or aluminum frames.

In certain situations, such as between a garage and the interior of a home, building codes require that doors have a 1-hour fire-resistance rating. These fire doors are metal or solid-core wood.

Prehung or separate components

A prehung door is mounted in a frame, called a jamb, and may be predrilled for a lockset and trimmed on one side. Exterior prehung door systems usually include a sill, weatherstripping, and exterior casing. You can also buy separate components. Precut jamb sets and trim packs save time. Bypass and bifold door systems, also available as prehung units, are considerably easier to install and may be installed in untrimmed openings.

One thing seems clear to us (and since this happens so infrequently, you might want to pay close attention): If a prehung door is universally recognized as the easiest way to go, and you can buy or order the door you want prehung, then do so. This is particularly true for exterior doors because of the importance of a perfect fit for a good weather seal. If you don't like the standard *brickmold* casing that usually comes with an exterior door, order it without trim or with the trim of your choice.

Standards to Know

To make everyone's life a little easier, the industry — fabricators, architects, and builders — follow certain standards when it comes to door dimensions and lockset and hinge location. That way, doors and door frames can come predrilled, partially assembled, and ready for installation. Without these standards, every door job would be a DIY nightmare requiring hours of hammer and chisel work.

You're still going to need a chisel and hammer (and a bunch of other tools) to install a door, but standardization makes the job much easier than it was in the old days. Figure 10-1 shows a door's components.

Dimensions

Interior doors typically are 1⅜ inches thick, except folding doors and some sliders, which usually are 1⅛-inch thick. The "economy," ⅞-inch folding doors are too flimsy. Exterior doors are either 1⅜ or 1¾ inches thick. Standard door widths vary in 2-inch increments, from 12 inches up to 36 inches. A 30-inch wide door is called a *2-foot 6-inch by 6-foot 8-inch* door, or simply *2-6* door. The standard height for a residential door is 6 feet 8 inches, but you can special-order a 6½-, 7-, and 8-foot door.

Table 10-1 shows the minimum recommended door widths for various situations.

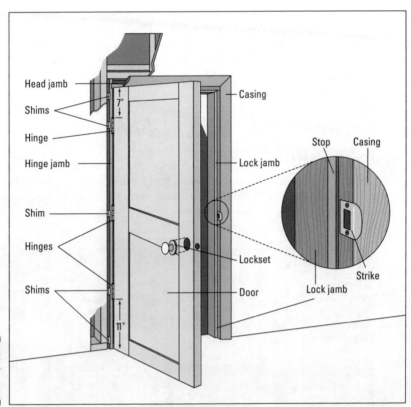

Figure 10-1:
Hinged-door
components.

Table 10-1	Minimum Recommended Door Widths
Door Location	*Minimum recommended width*
Primary entrance	3 feet
Secondary entrance	2 feet 8 inches
Interior hallway	3 feet
Bedroom	2 feet 6 inches
Bathroom	2 feet 4 inches
Walk-in closet	2 feet 4 inches
Small clothes closets and linen closets	2 feet

Doorjambs are also a standard ¾-inch thick, and either about 4⅞₆ or 6⅞₆ inches wide for standard 2x4 or 2x6 walls. (This assumes either ½-inch drywall on each side or ½ drywall on the inside and ½ sheathing on the outside). If you have plaster walls, you must either order custom-width jambs or rip down an over-wide jamb set. The rough opening (R.O.) for a door should be between 2 and 2½ inches wider and taller than the door. A door measuring 2' 6" x 6' 8" would require a minimum R.O. of 2' 8" x 6' 11" R.O. Key rule: R.O.s are always larger than the door.

Left-handed vs. right-handed doors and locksets

If you're wondering why any door wouldn't work for both left-handed people and right-handed ones, don't. The "hand" here refers to the door (see Figure 10-2), not the people who use them.

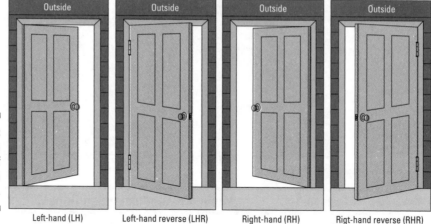

Figure 10-2: Make a diagram of your door in its opening.

Left-hand (LH)   Left-hand reverse (LHR)   Right-hand (RH)   Rigt-hand reverse (RHR)

The *hand* of a door describes the way it opens. To determine the hand, stand on the *outside* of the door (the room side of a closet door, the hall side of a room door, or the outdoor side of an entry door). If the hinges are on the left and the door swings away from you, the door, and lockset are *left-hand*. If the door swings toward you, it is a *left-hand reverse*. Similarly, if the hinges are on the right, it will either be a *right-hand* or *right-hand reverse*. If it slides up and down, you're standing in front of a window.

Some locksets can be reversed to work whether a door swings in or out by simply rotating the latch so the bevel faces the other direction and by installing the keyed side of the handle on the appropriate side. However, some locksets, such as lever-handle and full-mortised locksets, are *handed,* and can be installed only one way. (Locksets are described in the next section.)

To eliminate any possible confusion when buying or ordering prehung doors or handed locksets, bring with you a diagram that shows the swing and location of the door.

Whenever possible, an entry door should open or swing *into* the room, preferably against a blank wall. For obvious safety reasons, doors should *never* swing into a stairwell.

Locks and hinges

The terms *lock* and *lockset* describe all doorknob and latching assemblies, whether they lock or not. *Cylindrical locksets* are keyed in the handle and may interconnect with a second locking mechanism, called a *deadbolt*. Some *interconnected locksets* require that you turn the key in both locks to operate the door and others only one.

Interior locksets are called *tubular locks* and are available in the following models:

- ✔ **Passage.** Has no locking mechanism
- ✔ **Privacy.** Locks from one side with a mechanism such as a push button
- ✔ **Bathroom.** Has a privacy lock with a knob and chrome trim on one side

Both interior and exterior door locks are available in full-mortise styles but are infrequently used. Full-mortise locks are installed into a deep mortise drilled and chiseled in the edge of the door. It's not only a pain to do (drill, chop, and carve) but also weakens the door, making it less secure than a good cylindrical lock.

Cylindrical and tubular locks are somewhat standardized. Most require a 2⅛-inch-diameter hole in the door face. The latch-bolt hole in the edge of the door is usually ⅞-inch diameter. The *backset,* which is the distance from the face of the latch bolt to the center of the lock usually is 2⅜ inches, which means that the center of your 2⅛-inch hole will be 2⅜ inches back from the edge of the door. Other backsets are available, however, from 2 inches for doors with unusually narrow stiles to 18 inches for doors where the knob is centered in the door rather than in the latch stile. Locksets are typically installed 36 to 38 inches above the finished floor.

Hinges are sized according to door thickness and type (see Table 10-2). Three hinges are always better than two. You can get away with two on a hollow-core interior door (and virtually all prehung hollow-core units are sold that way) but always use three hinges on a solid wood or solid-core door whether it is an interior or exterior door. The standard locations for hinges are as follows: The top of the upper hinge should be 7 inches below the top of the door. The bottom of the lower hinge should be 11 inches above the floor. The middle hinge is centered between the top and bottom hinge.

Table 10-2	Selecting the Right Hinge	
Door Thickness/Type	*Hinge Height*	*Number of Hinges*
⅞" to 1⅛" /Solid or hollow core	3"	2 or 3
1⅜" / Solid	3½"	3
1⅜" / Hollow core	3½"	2 or 3
1¾" / Solid	4"	3

Hanging Interior Doors

It seems that there are as many approaches to installing a door as there are carpenters who hang them. In this section, we describe what we believe are the simplest procedures to hanging the three principal door types with professional results. Check out "Installing a Cylindrical Lock," later in this chapter; and for tips on trimming out a room, including doors, see Chapter 12.

Installing a prehung, interior, hinged door

A prehung swinging door comes assembled with the door on its hinges and a *spreader* holding the bottom of the jambs the proper distance apart. Some come with casing already installed on one side just waiting to be installed. Remove the hinge pins to take the door off, remove the spreader, and carefully pry off the side stops before you begin the installation. Then, referring to Figure 10-3, follow these steps:

1. **Level the jambs.**

   Position the doorframe in the opening if you can. Place a 2-foot level on the *head jamb* and shim underneath one of the side jambs as necessary to level the head jamb. When it's perfectly level, measure the amount that you needed to shim and remove the jamb to cut exactly that much off the other jamb.

   If the jamb is too tall for the opening, place a level on the floor, across the opening. Shim the level as needed until it reads level. Then measure the amount you shimmed it and cut that much more off the opposite jamb. If the jamb is ½-inch too tall for the opening, for example, cut ¾ inch off the one leg and ¾ inch plus the thickness of the shim off the other leg. Measure carefully; if you cut the jambs too short you end up with prehung kindling.

2. **Secure the hinge jamb.**

    Center the jamb in the opening and install shims behind the top hinge location. Always install two shims from opposite directions so as not to twist the jamb. Drive an 8d finish nail through the jamb (where it will be covered by the doorstop), through the shims, and about an inch into the framing.

    Then move to the next hinge. This time, use a level to plumb the jamb as you insert the shims. Nail as before, leaving the head of the nail well above the surface in case you need to remove it. Repeat for the third hinge location.

3. **Verify that the hinge jamb is square to the plane of the wall and precisely centered within the wall.**

    The best tool for this is a framing square. Place the long blade against the wall and the inside edge of the short blade against the jamb at each hinge location. Looking at the short blade, adjust the shims as necessary until the blade is flat against the jamb. Looking at the long blade, the edge of the jamb should be flush with (or just slightly above) the plane of the wall on both sides. Use a tapping block and hammer to tap the jamb (at nailing locations) in or out of the opening as needed to center it.

    If the jamb is too narrow for the opening, as it would be if there is more than ½ inch of wall material on either side of the opening, make it flush on the hinge side and plan on adding an extension jamb to the other side. An *extension jamb* is simply a strip of wood ripped to the exact width required to "extend" a door or window jamb out to the wall surface. Usually it is ripped from ¾-inch clear pine to match the doorjamb and attached about ¹⁄₁₆ to ⅛ inch in from the face of the jamb rather than flush with it. This offset is called a *reveal* because the extension jamb is positioned to reveal some of the jamb edge below.

4. **Hang the door on its hinges and use it as a guide to adjust the head and latch jambs.**

    Adjust the head jamb until you see an equal gap between the jamb and the door at the top. Shim and nail the latch jamb as you did the hinge jamb. Start just below the head jamb. (Have we used the word, jamb, enough?) Then shim behind where the strike plate will be and again a few inches above the floor. Check for square as in Step 3.

    To cut off the protruding shims, use a utility knife to score them repeatedly at the edge of the jamb and then break them; or just cut all the way through the soft wood with the knife.

5. **Close the door to check final fit.**

    Hold your breath: Gently close the door. Without any undue pressure, the door should be even with the edge of the jamb all along its length. If it is not, then you can adjust the jambs. Instead of just tapping the latch jamb in or out, split the difference by tapping it only half the required distance. Then tap the hinge jamb to account for the other half. Reinstall the stops.

6. **Install the lock hardware.**

   Typically, the holes already will have been drilled and mortises already cut in the doorjamb, so all you need to do is assemble and fasten the components using a Phillips screwdriver. See "Installing a Cylindrical Lock," later in this chapter.

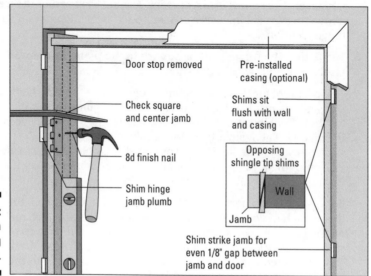

Door stop removed

Pre-installed casing (optional)

Check square and center jamb

Shims sit flush with wall and casing

8d finish nail

Opposing shingle tip shims

Shim hinge jamb plumb

Wall

Jamb

Shim strike jamb for even 1/8" gap between jamb and door

Figure 10-3: Installing a prehung door.

Hanging an interior hinged door from scratch

Installing a new door frame and door combines the skills and procedures discussed in the previous two sections. Buy a door, precut jamb set, and stop and casing moldings. Then make a prehung door unit (without casings installed and without drilling the holes in the door) and install it as described in the previous section.

Here's how to go about hanging a door from scratch:

1. **Install the hinges.**

   Measure and mark the hinge locations on the hinge jamb (see "Locks and hinges" earlier in this chapter). Then position the door against the hinge jamb with the top of the door ⅛ inch below the rabbet for the head jamb and transfer the locations to the door. Mortise the jamb and door and install the hinges as described in "Replacing a door" and the section on chisels in Chapter 5.

2. **Assemble the jamb.**

    Assemble the precut jamb set by nailing the sides into the head with 6d box nails.

3. **Install the jamb as described in the previous section.**

Replacing a hinged door

Measure the existing door or opening and purchase a suitable size door. Use the steps below to guide your installation:

1. **Remove the hinge pins from the existing door and take down the door.**

    If you are reusing the hinges and lock, then remove them. Now might also be a good time to clean them up and lubricate them.

2. **Fit the new door to the opening.**

    Ideally, there should be an even ⅛-inch gap on the top and latch side and a ¹⁄₁₆-inch gap on the hinge side. Place the new door in the opening against the hinge jamb. Wedge the bottom until the top makes contact with the head jamb. If the fit at the top is full and even, then drop the door ⅛ inch. If you see an uneven gap, then lay a pencil flat on the head jamb and scribe the top of the door. The pencil will produce about a ⅛-inch scribe. If the uneven gap at the top is greater than ⅛ inch, place a thin strip of something (don't use bologna) under the pencil to increase the size of the scribe, as needed.

3. **Remove the door and support it so that you can plane the door. See Figure 10-4.**

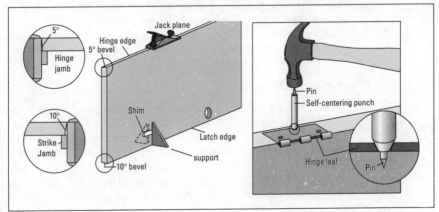

Figure 10-4: New door in an old frame.

Plane the top of the door to your scribe line. When planing across the top of the door, plane from the edges toward the center to avoid splintering the stiles at the corners, and plan to remove ½ your pencil line. Plane the sides just shy of the lines. (Two full ⅛-inch scribes are 1/16 inch more than you want.)

Although it is not necessary to bevel the edges of a 1⅜-inch thick door it is necessary to do so with a thicker door and does not hurt to do so on the 1⅜-inch door. Beveling the hinge side prevents a door from binding on its own sharp corner, while beveling the latch side helps it open and close smoother.

4. **Reposition the door to check the fit and transfer the exact location of the existing hinge mortises on the jamb to the door.**

   Remove the door and double-check the hinge locations. If the new hinges don't align with the old mortises, even Don Corleone from *The Godfather* couldn't persuade the door to fit. Carefully measure from the top of the jamb to the top of each hinge location. Then measure from the top of the door to each hinge location. These measurements should be ⅛ inch less than the first set, because of the ⅛ inch top clearance between the door and the head jamb.

   Use a combination square to measure the width of the hinge mortise in the jamb, locking the blade at that point. Transfer the measurements to the edge of the door. Alternately, check the existing mortise with a butt marker; and if it matches — and it usually will — use it to mark the hinge mortise on the door.

5. **Chisel out the mortise so the hinge sits perfectly flat and its face is flush with the edge of the door. (See "Chisels" in Chapter 8.)**

6. **Install the hinges.**

   Install the hinges on the doorjamb and door. With the hinge correctly positioned on the door, carefully mark and drill a pilot hole for each screw location. A self-centering punch or a self-centering drill (called a *Vix bit*) will guarantee a perfectly centered pilot hole and are worth the few dollars they cost.

7. **Reinstall the door.**

   Position the door at an angle to the opening and lift it to join the hinges. If a slight misalignment prevents them all from joining together, use a hammer to tap the jamb hinge and the mating door hinge in the opposite directions. If that doesn't do the trick, then you need to remove the hinge from the door, plug the holes, chisel to lengthen the mortise, bore new pilot holes, reinstall the hinge, and try again. (You can see why it's better to be very precise and double-check your position the first time around!)

8. **Mark for the lock.**

   With the door closed, transfer the exact vertical center of the latch hole onto the edge of the door to mark the exact height you will need to drill the face and edge holes for the lockset. (See "Installing a lockset," later in this chapter.)

9. **Finish the door.**

   After you have installed the hardware and checked for proper operation, remove the door to seal the bottom edge. Then remove the hardware and finish the rest of the door. Or reinstall it, mask the hinges, and remove the door handle to finish it in place.

Installing bifold doors

Bifold doors are not hinged to a jamb (otherwise, they'd be called bi-hinged) so they don't require a jamb and can be installed in any finished opening 2 feet or wider. Just purchase bifolding hardware and the doors. If you have a rough opening that you want to trim and outfit with bifolding doors, order a prehung unit. All you need to do is secure it in the opening by shimming behind the jambs so the head jamb is level and the side jambs are plumb.

If you want to install it in an existing trimmed or untrimmed opening, buy the appropriate bifolding hardware and doors and you're ready to start the installation. All bifolding doors come with detailed installation instructions, which we encourage even the most adventurous homeowners to read carefully.

Figure 10-5 and the following step-by-step instructions show what you can expect, using a four-panel door as an example:

1. **Size the doors according to the manufacturer's instructions.**

   To determine the width of each door, divide the total opening width by the number of doors and subtract the recommended amount for clearance. If you need to cut down the doors to make them fit, plane an equal amount from both sides of each door. In other words, don't take it all off of one door or one side of one door — that would result in a sloppy, uneven look. If you need to shorten a door, cut the bottom. Use a guided circular saw. (Check out Chapter 14.) If you are crosscutting a veneered door, score your cut line with a utility knife first to prevent the saw blade from splintering the veneer.

2. **Install the hinges.**

   Clamp a pair of doors together with a ⁵⁄₁₆-inch-thick spacer between them and stand them on edge to install non-mortise hinges supplied with the kit.

3. **Install pivots, guides, and alignment brackets (4-door installs) on the doors as directed. (If you're not directed, do it anyway.)**

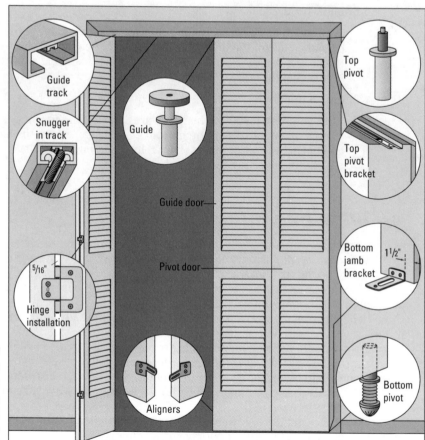

Figure 10-5:
Installing a
four-panel,
bifolding
door.

4. Cut and install the track and jamb brackets.

Use a fine-tooth hacksaw to cut the metal track about ⅛ inch shorter
than the width of the opening. Fasten the track as close to the front of
the opening as possible to maximize the closet depth. If you plan to
install wood trim to hide the track, allow for the thickness of the wood
and a small reveal. Install the jamb brackets by screwing them into the
wall and floor. Their center should be set back the same distance as the
center of the track.

5. Install and adjust doors.

Place the bottom pivot into the jamb bracket and tip the door into the
guide in the track. Then slide the guide toward the jamb and tighten the
locking screw. Repeat for the other door. Adjust both doors so there is
an even ⅛-inch gap between them and so they are the same height.

6. **Install pulls.**

   The most efficient, easy-to-operate position for the pulls (handles) is in
   the center of the guide doors about 36 inches above the floor. Drill a
   clearance hole through the face of the door and place a scrap of wood
   against the backside to prevent the drill from splintering the wood as it
   exits the backside.

Just sliding by: Installing bypass doors

Installing bypass (sliding) doors in an existing trimmed opening is little more
than attaching the hardware to the doors and the track to the opening, and
hanging the doors on the track. If you need to install a jamb, follow the procedures outlined in "Hanging an interior hinged door from scratch," earlier in
this chapter. Because the doors need to overlap 1 inch, plan the jamb opening so that it is 2 times the door width less ½ inch. For example, if you plan to
buy two 2'0" doors, buy a 4'0" jamb kit and cut 1 inch off the head jamb
before you assemble it.

To install bypassing doors in a trimmed opening follow these steps and refer
to Figure 10-6:

1. **Cut the doors to length.**

   To make room for track hardware the door must be cut down as specified by the hardware maker. (See "Installing bifolding doors, Step 1" in
   the previous section.)

2. **Cut and install the track.**

   Use a hacksaw to cut the metal track to fit the opening. Position the
   track in the jamb as directed, mark and drill pilot holes for the mounting
   screws, and secure the track. Be sure the screw heads are flush, otherwise they'll interfere with the doors.

3. **Attach the hangers to the doors with screws as directed.**

4. **Hang and adjust the doors.**

   Tilt the top of the door away from you to hook the roller over the track.
   Do the rear door first. Then align the doors with the jambs by adjusting
   the height of the door hanger as directed. If the opening is not perfectly
   square the door may fit nicely on one side but not the other. If this is the
   case, you can scribe the one side of the door to the jamb. (See Step 2 in
   this chapter's section, "Replacing a door," or close one eye.)

   Secure the floor guide at the point where the two closed doors overlap.
   If necessary, raise the guide up by mounting it on a wood block. (Cut the
   block equal to the length and width of the guide, and as thick as needed.
   Don't forget to drill roomy clearance holes through the block so you
   won't split it with the screws.)

5. Install door pulls.

Because sliding doors pass by each other don't install doorknobs; finger pulls must be recessed. Drill these holes about 1½ inches in from the edge of the door and 36 to 40 inches above the floor to match other door hardware in the room or home. Remove the doors for finishing.

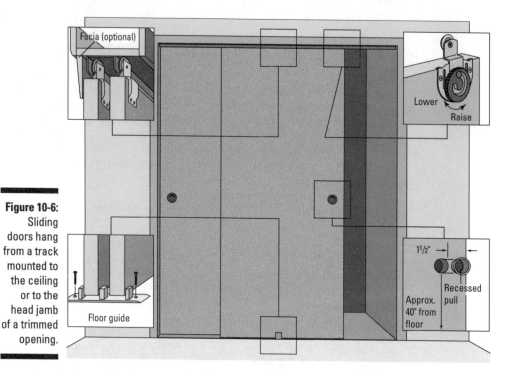

Figure 10-6:
Sliding doors hang from a track mounted to the ceiling or to the head jamb of a trimmed opening.

Replacing an Exterior Door

Although putting a new exterior door into an existing frame is possible, it's often as difficult as putting toothpaste back in the tube. With a prehung unit you are assured of a weatherproof seal. The installation (see Figure 10-7) is very similar to that of an interior prehung unit, but there are a couple of special considerations. Stock doors will often have exterior casing (a style called *brickmold*) already installed. This preinstalled casing usually presents a problem in a retrofit because you want your new casing to extend right up to the existing siding. So either plan on ordering a door with the proper size casing (an outside casing-to-casing dimension that equals the existing) or order it without casing and make your own from ¾ lumber. Any new door will come with detailed instructions, but you'll be following these basic steps:

1. **Remove the existing door and frame.**

   Remove the hinge pins and the door. Pry off interior casing (carefully, if you intend to reuse it). Pull the nails from the exterior casing with a claw-type nail puller. (You can usually locate the nails by looking for small dimples in the surface.) Cut through the wooden sill at the midpoint and rip it out. Pry the jambs away from the studs, working with a pry bar from inside. Be patient and try to avoid the urge to use brute strength. A more-controlled work style will result in little, if any, damage to the surrounding surfaces.

2. **Prepare the new door and opening.**

   Temporarily set the prehung door in the opening and determine if you need to shim it to the desired height relative to the finished floor. If necessary, install a solid, full-width spacer under the doorsill, sealing it with adhesive caulk on the underside. If necessary, shim the spacer to make it level, too.

   If the new door does not have exterior casing installed, do so. To determine the width of the casing, measure the siding-to-siding dimension at the top, bottom and middle. Choose the largest dimension and subtract the door width less twice the ³⁄₁₆-inch reveal. Divide the result by 2 for the casing width. With the door in place, also measure to determine the width of the top casing and drip cap. Install the exterior casing on the jamb. Slip the top flange of the metal drip cap up under the siding above the door.

3. **Screw the doorframe into the opening.**

   Test-fit the doorframe in the opening with the casing against the sheathing. Verify that the sill and the head jamb are level, shimming under the door, if necessary. Remove the door and apply two heavy beads of siliconized acrylic-latex caulk across the full width of the opening. Be careful not to step in any caulk or you'll track a sticky residue all over the house.

   Install the prehung door and screw it to the framing through the casing at the hinges. Nails are cheaper but screws are easy to remove if you later find that you need to adjust the jamb. Our experience tells us, "Use screws."

4. **Fasten the jamb to the rough opening through shims behind the hinges as described in "Installing a prehung interior hinged door," above.**

   To prevent a heavy door from sagging, remove the short screws that secure the top hinge and replace them with 3-inch or longer screws that can penetrate the framing.

5. **Weatherproof your door and install interior casing.**

   Caulk the joints between the siding and the exterior casing and the joints below the sill with siliconized acrylic-latex caulk. Fill the gaps between the jamb and the rough opening with fiberglass insulation before you install the interior casing.

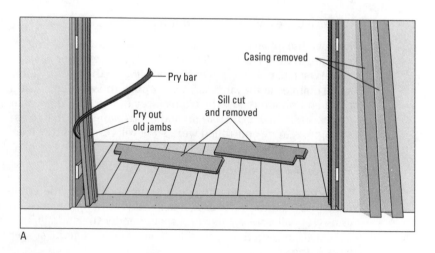

A

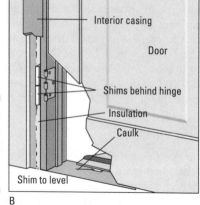

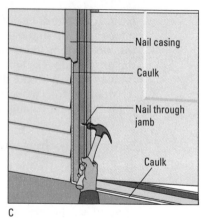

B

C

Figure 10-7:
Installing a
prehung
exterior
door.

Installing a Lockset

All door hardware will come with installation instructions that specify details
such as the exact size of pilot holes, but the steps are virtually the same for
all brands. If you have a prehung unit, the holes and mortises may all be done
and you just need to attach the various parts with a screwdriver. While the
internal mechanisms of tubular and cylindrical locksets differ, the installation
procedure, described in Figure 10-8 and the following steps, is nearly identical. The same approach is used to install recessed-style deadbolts, too.

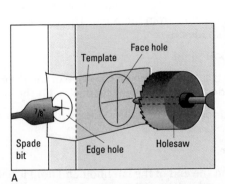

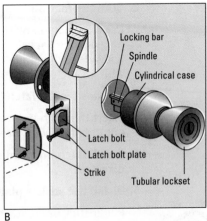

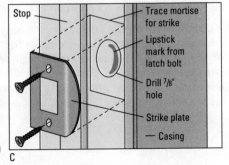

Figure 10-8:
Installing a
cylindrical
or tubular
lockset.

To install a lockset, follow these steps:

1. **Mark the centers for the cylinder and latch bolt holes on the door.**

   Fold the paper template as directed according to the thickness of your
   door, and place it over the latch edge of the door on the hinge face. If
   you do not have a template, make one or just measure. Use a combination square and pencil to lightly mark the face and edge of the door at
   36 inches above the floor (or at a height to match the other doorknobs
   in your home). Find the center of the door edge; the center of your latch
   bolt hole is where the points intersect. If you are installing the hardware
   in a new door in an existing opening, set the height of the latch to match
   exactly the center of the existing strike plate.

   Next, measure the distance from the faceplate on the latchbolt to the
   center of the lock. Measure from the edge of the door that same amount
   and you have your cylinder lock hole.

2. Bore the face and edge holes in the door.

Use a 2⅛-inch-diameter hole saw to bore the face hole. To prevent chipping out the backside, drill about three-quarters of the way through from one side and complete the hole from the other. Then bore the edge hole with a ⅞-inch-diameter spade bit.

3. Mortise for the latch bolt plate.

Insert the latch bolt to trace its outline on the edge of the door. Chisel out the mortise as needed so the plate will be flush with the surface.

4. Install latch bolt and door cylinder on the door with screws as directed.

5. Install the striker plate.

Put lipstick or crayon on the end of the latchbolt and hold it open (inside the door) while you close the door. Holding the door closed, release the latch with a snap several times to mark its location on the jamb.

Trace the outline of the striker plate on the jamb so it will align with the telltale "kiss" latch bolt location. Then drill the pilot holes for the screws, drill the hole for the latch bolt and mortise the jamb for the plate. Install the plate with screws provided. If the plate is slightly misaligned, refer to the section on warped door failing to latch in Chapter 15 — or wait for the movie version.

Chapter 11

Windows: A Whole New Way to Look at Things

. . . .

In This Chapter

▶ Understanding the benefits of replacing old windows

▶ Comparing installation options

▶ Looking at all approaches step-by-step

. . . .

*I*f money kept dropping out of a hole in your pocket, you'd fix the hole, right? (You should be nodding yes.) Well, it's the same for drafty, old windows: Fix them or money (in the form of high utility bills) will leak out through the cracks and gaps.

Replacing leaky, single-pane windows is often one of the first things people updating an older home do. Why? Because old windows create so many problems — and waste so much expensive energy — that you get a lot of bang for your buck when you put in new ones.

Installing efficient windows saves you money and increases your interior comfort. Today's insulated units keep the inside surface of the glass warm, and do a better job of sealing out drafts. Plus, interior condensation (and the peeling paint and water stains it causes) will be a thing of the past. In hot climates, modern high-tech glazing reflects solar heat without the need for dark tinting. Best of all, your windows will work for a change, and you'll reduce maintenance chores to just cleaning and occasional interior painting. If you elect for a tilt-in or lift-out option, you can easily clean the windows from inside — say goodbye to your extension ladder! In addition, installing new windows gives you the opportunity to update the style of your home. And thanks to the efficiency of modern windows, you can use larger windows, which bring the outdoors in, admit more light and give you (if you're lucky) better views. Try not to worry too much about cost — it balances out with the energy dollars you save and, ultimately, a higher selling price on your home.

Installation Options: You Make the Call

You can take one of three approaches to replacing windows — and simply nailing plywood over the window isn't an option (unless you're in the midst of a hurricane!):

- ✔ Remove the existing window entirely and replace it with a new one
- ✔ Install a replacement window within the existing frame
- ✔ Replace only the sash and counterbalance system

In the next three sections we describe the pros and cons of each approach. Then, starting with the easiest and least expensive approach, we run through the typical installation procedures so that you can determine the right approach for you. Obtain information from the manufacturer of your window, replacement window, or sash-replacement kit about measuring for your new windows. Better yet, have your dealer take the measurements (and assume the responsibility). While you're at it, obtain a copy of the installation instructions from your dealer or directly from the manufacturer so that you know exactly what you're getting into. And here's a radical thought: Read the instructions *before* attempting the installation!

While the representative is measuring your job, take the opportunity to talk over your ideas with him. Ask him how existing conditions, such as the type of exterior siding and the size and style of windows you're replacing, will affect the job. Share with him any plans that you may have for exterior or interior work on your home. Talk about any problems that you may have with your existing windows or wishes for the new ones. If he faints from exhaustion, stop asking questions.

When you have your final order for new windows in hand, don't place it right away. Let things sink in awhile. Give yourself time to go over the order several times. Walk around the inside and outside of your home, visualize your changes, and make sure that you are going to be happy with your choices.

New sash in a flash

Many homeowners don't know that instead of replacing the entire window unit they can replace just the window sash and the important operating parts. A sash-replacement kit usually includes two new sashes, two jamb liners, insulation, and installation hardware.

With sash-replacement kits you simply remove the old sash (the movable part of the window) and counterbalance system (the weights or springs that keep the window from slamming shut when you open it), then install new *balances* or *jamb liners* (the channels that the sash rides in), pop in the sash, and reapply the stops (the wood "rails" between which the sash slides).

You can do all the work from inside the house, and it only takes a couple of hours per window, so it's possible to complete an average-size room in a day.

Installation details differ slightly, but here are the basic steps for installing a replacement sash (as shown in Figure 11-1):

1. **Remove the existing sash and parting strips.**

   Keep in mind that if you're careful when you remove the stops, you can reuse them and get by with touch-up painting. Instead of replacing the weights, recycle them, knock out or unscrew the weight pulleys, and stuff the cavities with fiberglass insulation.

   If the *blind stop* (the outermost trim member that guided your old upper sash) has a buildup of paint, now is the time to deal with it. ("Oh, honey, could you come here a minute? And bring a scraper!") Scrape off the paint; sand the wood smooth, and prime and paint with a suitable exterior primer and topcoat.

2. **Install mounting clips or other hardware for the new sash balances.**

   Use the screws provided and install the clips in the locations specified for the particular size window.

3. **Install the balances.**

   With most balances, you simply press them onto the mounting clips and they sit against the blind stop. The new balances must be able to move in order to be able to insert and remove the sash, so don't caulk this joint. This is one problem with the system since it obviously cannot offer as tight a seal as a new window or replacement widow, which are caulked in place.

4. **Install the sash.**

   Install the upper (outer) sash first by inserting its pivot pins on the lower edge into the locations in the window channel specified by the maker. Then, tilt the sash up and press the top into the channel. Repeat the procedure for the lower (inner) sash.

5. **Cut and install a new horizontal parting strip in the head jamb (the top piece of the window frame) and reinstall the window stops.**

   Countersink the nails with a nail set, putty the holes, and touch up with interior paint as needed.

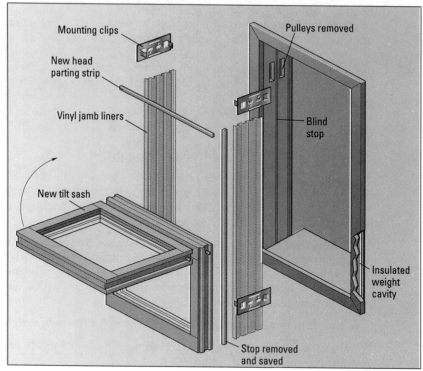

Mounting clips

New head parting strip

Vinyl jamb liners

New tilt sash

Pulleys removed

Blind stop

Insulated weight cavity

Stop removed and saved

Figure 11-1: A sash replacement kit makes quick work of upgrading old windows.

Out with the old and in with the new

The principal advantage of installing a new unit may be larger glass size — especially if you're removing double-hung windows that have 4-inch-wide weight cavities. Eliminating these spaces not only cuts down on tremendous heat loss, it lets you order windows that are several inches wider than your existing ones. A wider window means more glass and brighter interiors. When an entire window is built as a single unit under factory-controlled conditions, you get improved energy performance and easier operation, compared to sash-replacement kits.

The drawbacks to installing a new window unit are higher costs and additional labor. Replacing an entire window means you must retrim both the interior and exterior. Often, the work also requires cutting and/or patching exterior siding. Much of the work must be done from the outside, so don't save this project for the winter months (unless you live near the equator!). You also have to deal with more debris to haul away and, therefore, higher costs.

To minimize the disruption of your household and not get overwhelmed with the project, consider doing one room (or at least one side of the house) at a time. Complete all work before moving on to the next area. This approach may not always be practical but it is the best approach in most cases.

Before you begin, make sure that you have plastic sheets (not those flimsy painting dropcloths or trash bags) and duct tape to temporarily seal any openings that you might not be able to cover by the end of the day. And if security is an issue, have some plywood, screws, and a drill/driver on hand to batten down the hatches.

Windows come with detailed installation instructions, which you should obtain even before ordering the windows. Follow those instructions to the letter. The following steps and Figure 11-2 describe a typical installation:

1. **Remove the existing window.**

   Pry off the interior casing and remove the sash. Lift out the sash in sliding units and disconnect the hardware to remove the sash from casement and other windows with hardware-mounted sash. With double-hung units remove the sashes and counterweights as we describe in Chapter 13.

Figure 11-2:
Installing a new window versus a sash-only replacement usually results in a superior installation but requires a lot more work and additional cost.

New casing and drip cap

Nail through flange when window is leveled and square

Building felt

Caulk

A

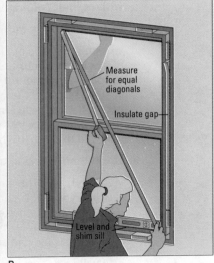

Measure for equal diagonals

Insulate gap

Level and shim sill

B

2. Remove the window frame.

Working from outside, use a claw-type nail puller to remove any nails that go through the casing into the framing. (You can usually spot the dimples over the putty-filled recesses of countersunk nails.) If the frame is sealed to the siding with caulk, cut through the caulk with a utility knife or stiff-blade putty knife. It will make the window easier to remove and lessens the chance of damaging the siding in the process. To get the window out, you may have to use a saw to cut through the sill, giving you a clear shot at the frame, making it easier to pry it (and the jambs) out.

Exercise extreme care when working around windows with the sash removed. Keep curious children at a safe distance. Don't hang from the inside of a window to work on the outside to save the time or expense of using a proper ladder setup. Observe proper ladder safety techniques. And make sure that you have a strong assistant to help you lift and carry both the old and replacement window — they're heavy and awkward to handle.

Standoffs for ladders are U-shaped braces that you attach to an extension ladder. The standoff allows you to center the ladder on a window opening. Rent or buy one if you're replacing many upper-story windows.

3. Clean up the opening (pull out old, bent nails and screws, and any odd chunks of wood), and then cover the exposed exterior sheathing with asphalt roofing felt (tar paper).

4. Install the new window.

Working from the outside, lift the window into the opening. Hold the unit in place while your helper (who has a level and is working from the inside) shims under it until the window is perfectly level. As shown in Figure 11-2a, nail the window in place through the flanges (or any factory-installed casing or brick mold) as directed by the manufacturer. Have your helper test each inside corner for square before and after you nail, and prior to driving the nails all the way home. (See Figure 11-2b.)

5. Extend the siding to the new window or install exterior casing.

What you do at this point depends on the type of siding you have and the look you want. The only material that is easy to patch is shingles, so in most cases it's better to plan your window sizes and casing widths to fill the existing hole. Maintain a ¼-inch gap between the window and siding or casing, and seal this space with caulk.

The nailing flange, while relatively thin, doesn't allow the exterior casing to sit flat against the sheathing, making it hard for you to get the joints tight and flat. Cut a rabbet ⅛ inch deep x 2 inches wide in the back of the casing so that the casing will fit over the flange; or place a ⅛-inch shim under the outside edge of the casing.

6. Fill all voids between the rough frame and the window frame with loose fiberglass insulation.

7. **Seal all exterior joints between the window and the casing or siding with a top quality siliconized acrylic-latex caulk.**

8. **Install interior trim.**

   Double-check the window operation before installing interior trim. Then install extension jambs to bring the window frame flush with the interior wall surface.

9. **Finish all exposed wood parts with stain or paint as soon as possible to protect the wood from moisture.**

   Be careful not to get paint, stain or other finishes on the hardware or weatherstripping.

Somewhere between the two

Vinyl replacement windows (see Figure 11-3) are made to order to fit your existing window frames after the sash and parting strips have been removed. You must prepare the opening as for a sash-replacement unit, described earlier in this chapter. But instead of installing separate jamb liners and sash, you install an entire window in one motion. This instant-window approach combines the performance and operating advantages of the new window with the convenience of a sash-replacement. On the downside, your new windows likely will have less glass area than the original windows, and your choices are also limited to vinyl windows — which is fine unless you want the look or stainability of wood.

1. **Remove the existing sash, parting strips.**

   See the section on replacing sash cords for information on removing the old sash. If you're careful when you remove the stops, you can reuse them and get by with touch-up painting. Remove and recycle the weights, knock out or unscrew the weight pulleys, and stuff the cavities with fiberglass insulation.

   Scrape off any paint buildup; sand the wood smooth; and prime and paint with a suitable exterior primer and topcoat.

2. **Caulk the inside edge of the blind stop — the outermost trim that the outer sash used to ride against — and press the window into place.**

   If necessary, install shims under the window frame to level it, and then carefully fasten the window by driving screws through the side jambs and into the old frame (as directed by the maker). And hey, Schwarzenegger, go easy with the drill/driver — if you overzealously overtighten the screws, you'll twist the window out of square. Be sure to check all corners with a framing square to make sure that you have not distorted the frame. Lower and raise the sash to check operation and, while you're at it, clean up any excess caulk ooze from around the outside.

3. Reinstall the interior stops with 4d finishing nails.

Countersink the nails with a nail set, putty the holes, and touch up interior paint as needed.

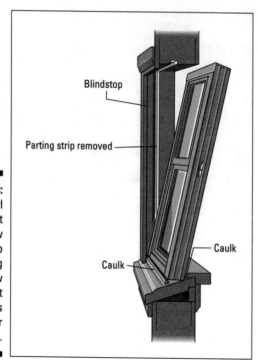

Blindstop

Parting strip removed

Caulk

Caulk

Figure 11-3:
A vinyl replacement window installs into the existing window frame, but it usually has a smaller glass area.

Chapter 12

Trimming Out a Room

. . . .

In This Chapter

▶ Understanding how casing and moldings add character to a room

▶ Removing trim with care

▶ Knowing why materials and finish choices matter

▶ Finding out how to miter-case a door

▶ Troubleshooting miter cuts

▶ Trimming windows and walls step-by-step

. . . .

Molding adds character to any room, plain and simple. It transforms ordinary walls because it adds a sense of detail and architectural interest, and it defines the space.

Minimum trim requirements usually include casing (the flat trim around window), doorjambs (frames), and baseboards. These moldings are required to cover the gaps between door and window jambs and the adjacent wall surface, and between the wall and the floor. Going beyond the basics, moldings may also be installed at the ceiling (crown and bed moldings), on the wall (chair rail, picture-hanging rail, plate shelf, corner guard), or on flat surfaces such as doors, walls, ceilings, or cabinets.

The principles and skills you pick up as you read this chapter and install moldings can be used again and again. For example, the only difference between installing a chair rail and base molding is a few feet on the wall! Applying molding to a door to create a panel effect is like applying mitered casing with two more miters.

Removing Trim for Reuse

Nice trim in a home is like gold these days. When a remodeling or repair project requires temporarily removing the trim, do it carefully, as shown in Figure 12-1. The other concern when removing trim is to minimize damage to the surface or base that it's attached to.

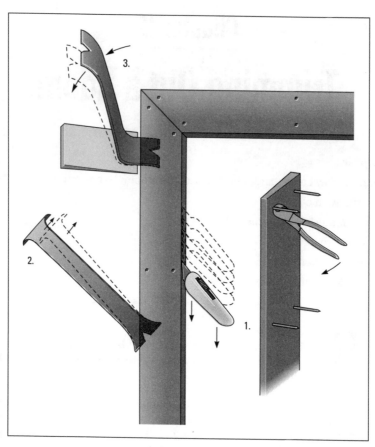

Figure 12-1:
Removing
trim for
reuse.

Following are a few tricks that can keep damage to a minimum:

- If the surface has been painted or varnished after the trim was installed, score the paint bond at the joint with a utility knife. Otherwise, you risk chipping the paint and even splitting the trim because the paint acts like glue.

- Use an appropriate pry bar not an old screwdriver, butter knife, or spatula to pry up the trim. The pry bar should have an end that is thin and pointed enough to get into the joint between the trim and the base. (See the section about trim bars in Chapter 9.) If your pry bar is too blunt, take a file to it.

- Locate the nails and insert the pry bar between two nailing points. (You have a better chance of getting the bar in at that location.) After you open up the joint, work your way over toward the nails by using the bent end of the pry bar.

✔ When prying, insert something between your tool and the base to protect the base. Keep a plastic laminate sample chip, a shingle tip, or a piece of sheet metal handy for this purpose.

✔ When the risk of damage to the base material is unacceptable, you may be able to drive the nails all the way hrough the trim with a nail set. (You can fill the holes later, when the trim is reinstalled.)

✔ As a last resort, use a nail puller — but not just any one. The nail puller needs to be sharp, pointed, and small enough to grab the nail and not so big that it carves a huge hole in the wood that resembles the aftermath of a crazed beaver attack. When the nail head is above the surface, pry the nail out with a hammer.

✔ If finish nails remain in removed trim, don't try to tap and pull them out from the face of the trim. To avoid damaging the face, pull out the nails from the back side by using end-cutting pliers (nippers) or locking pliers (Vise-Grip, for example).

Trimming a Room

Applying trim should be straightforward. (Yeah, right. Like raising teenagers.) When you cut two pieces of trim at a perfect 45-degree miter and then join and nail them to a door or window jamb, for example, the pieces should sit perfectly flat on the wall and form an equally perfect 90-degree corner. The miter will have no gaps at either the heel or toe. So why doesn't it work out like that? Well, it all starts with irregularities in lumber and other building materials and continues to be affected by the work of framers, drywallers, and carpenters who install and trim the windows and doors. If you did all that work, sorry, it's your fault entirely. If you're coming in on the tail end, you can blame the other guy. But in the end, you're the one who has to "make it nice," as a trim-carpenter friend always says.

Know what you're dealing with

The first step in every trim project is to evaluate the existing conditions and correct any problems that you reasonably can. While some tricks let you compensate for irregularities (in the house, not you), it's often easier and always better to start out with things as right as they can be. For a door, make sure that the jamb has square corners and that it's flush with and square to the wall. (See Chapter 10.) For a window, make sure that the jambs are square at the corners and that they extend flush to the face of the wall. Altering an out-of square wall generally isn't feasible, but you should still check corners for square, ceilings for level, and walls for general straightness. You can then make the appropriate compensation when cutting or installing trim such as base molding.

Use the best saw possible

In carpentry, lots of things can be beyond your control or skill level, so mastering certain techniques becomes even more important. Making perfect, square cuts and miters is one example. The way to perfect cuts and miters is to use a power miter saw. These incredible, accurate tools (which you can rent) can split a hair — and a finger if you're not careful. If you're not comfortable with this power tool, which like all power tools requires you to be familiar with the proper and safe way to use it, rent a *professional* quality miter box. Using miter boxes takes skill, but it, too, can deliver perfect miters. What a miter box can't do is make the fine adjustments to an existing cut, such as taking "a hair more" off the heel of a miter, that a power miter saw can do. The small wooden miter boxes you use with a back saw are marginal, at best, and in spite of the fact that they are sold for DIYers, the boxes take much more skill to use. Miter boxes offer no flexibility when you need any angle other than 45 degrees and 90 degrees.

Good news! Two standard casing profiles — colonial and clamshell — are often available for doors in pre-mitered trim packs. If everything is square and true (which isn't always the case) all you need to cut is a square cut at the bottom ends of the side pieces.

Material and finish choices matter

Applying molding is exacting work, and moldings are designed to attract attention, so it's important to "make it nice." The type of wood you use has a definite impact on how difficult it is to do a good job. Pine, cedar, and other relatively soft woods are much more forgiving than hardwoods such as oak, maple, and cherry. How you intend to finish the trim also makes a significant difference. Glue spots, sanding marks, and other imperfections tend to stand out when you use stain and clear finishes. And while paint, too, can sometimes emphasize imperfections, at least you can use fillers. For example, you can sand across the grain to level and smooth a slightly misaligned miter joint. And you can fill cracks between the trim and the wall with caulk. But you can't use these fixes with unpainted or stained trim.

 You'll find a variety of nonwood moldings at your friendly neighborhood home center: molding "systems" made of resin, vinyl, fiberglass, or reconstituted wood. These systems are designed to be used by unskilled DIYers. But you'll get better, more lasting results if you use actual wood instead of these imposters. And anyway, you're not "unskilled." You've read this book!

Trimming Doors and Windows

The casing around windows and doors can be cut and joined at the corners with either 45-degree miters or 90-degree butt joints. Contrary to popular thought, making a nice mitered joint on door or window casing is easier than making a square butt joint, so the decision is an aesthetic one.

If you choose to miter, the head and side casings must have the same profile and dimension. Furthermore, if you plan to use profiled casing (such as colonial style) for both head and side casing, you must miter the trim. When joined, the two 45-degree mitered members form a square corner that conceals undesirable end-grain, which doesn't smooth as well as other board surfaces and does not accept wood stains equally. Profiled moldings are always installed with the thinner (or lighter, more delicate) edge toward the opening.

With a butt joint, the head casing can be different from the side casing. For example, the head casing can be wider or thicker, or consist of two pieces instead one. The side casings can be fluted (have long half-rounded grooves) while the head casing can be flat. Usually, the head casing extends past the side casings. When it does, the ends can be cut square, at an angle or with a decorative profile.

In one traditional approach used in Victorian and other older homes, the lengths of molding all butt into rosette blocks (at the upper corners of windows and door), plinth blocks (where casings meet door openings) and at corner boxes (where base moldings meet at inside and outside corners). For the full scoop on installing this modular-type system check out *Home Improvement For Dummies,* by yours truly (IDG Books Worldwide, Inc.).

Also consider whether you want to trim windows with a *stool-and-apron* detail at the bottom edge of the window, or *picture-frame* them. The stool (what some people call the windowsill) is a horizontal piece of interior trim that overlaps the sloped sill, projects out beyond the wall surface, and extends beyond the edges of the casing. The apron fits under the stool to conceal the gap between the finished wall and the stool. This setup also adds visual weight to anchor the bottom of the window. A picture-framed window has a short, narrow stool that fits between the side jambs and extends only to the wall surface.

In this section we describe traditional mitered casing and square butt-jointed casing. Each approach can be applied to both windows and doors.

Almost all new windows require the *jamb* (the frame that the sash is set into) to extend to the interior wall surface. Doorjambs, however, are usually ordered to fit. Or larger jambs are ripped to width when they are installed.

However, if you resurface a wall with ¾-inch paneling, for example, you need to extend any existing doorjambs. Board stretchers exist only in our fantasies, so the way to extend a jamb is to add a knot-free piece of clear pine or other wood identical to that of the jamb.

Extending jambs

To install an *extension jamb* (see Figure 12-2), measure the distance from the jamb to the surface of the wall and various points along its length. If the measurement varies less than ⅛ inch, then you can *rip* a board (cut a board along its length) to the widest dimension. Unfortunately, you may find that required width of the extension is greater at one point than another. If it's more than ⅛ inch or so, scribe the extension jamb: Cut the jamb stock to length, place it in position, and mark it all along its length, using the wall to guide your pencil.

Interior wall surface

1½"

Figure 12-2: Extension jambs may be required to make a window or doorjamb flush with a wall surface.

Ripping a board is best done on a table saw. If you have a lot of extension jambs to install, consider renting a small portable table saw. If you're just doing one window or door and you own a circular saw, see Chapter 5.

Nail the extension jamb with its cut edge to the edge of the existing jamb and set back from the face about ⅛ inch. This *reveal* (the exposed part of the face) becomes an intentional detail that adds interest, rather than creating a visible joint, which looks like someone goofed and ordered a too-narrow jamb. Install the two sides first and then fit the top piece between them.

The edges of jambs are slightly beveled toward the wall. If they were cut square and then installed either slightly out of square with the wall or in a wall where the thickness varied slightly, the casing might not sit tightly against the jamb all along its length. To provide a "fudge factor," the edges of jambs are usually beveled about 5 degrees (see Figure 12-2).

Interior door frames for bypass or bifold doors can be extended on either edge of the jamb. Hinged doors should be extended only on the "outside" (door opens away from you). Extending the hinge side would either interfere with the proper placement of the hinge, not allow the necessary clearance for the door to open fully, or just plain look bad. So if you add paneling to walls on the hinge side of a door, you need to remove the jamb to reposition it flush with the new paneling and extend the jamb on the other side.

Miter-case a door

To case a door opening, you need to have inspected the opening and corrected any problems to whatever degree possible. You also have the best miter saw possible. (See this chapter's sections, "Know what you're dealing with" and "Use the best saw possible.")

To trim a door (or any similar framed opening) refer to Figure 12-3 and follow these steps:

1. **Mark the reveals.**

   Set a combination square at ³⁄₁₆ inch and mark the reveal (the distance that the casing will be set back from the inside face of the jamb) on the head and side jambs at the corners and midpoints, and at the bottom of the side jamb. A ³⁄₁₆-inch reveal is typical for a ¾-inch-thick jamb.

2. **Cut the head casing.**

   The short-point dimension should equal the width of the jamb opening plus two times the reveal. You can measure this amount, but it's easier (and safer) to just cut a miter on one end and position it on the jamb to mark the length.

3. **Install the head casing.**

   Align your trim so it just covers the pencil lines and is centered side-to-side. *Tack* the trim to the jamb with three 4d finish nails in the center and about an inch in from each end. (The term *tack* means to nail something just enough to hold it in place and so the nail can be easily pulled.)

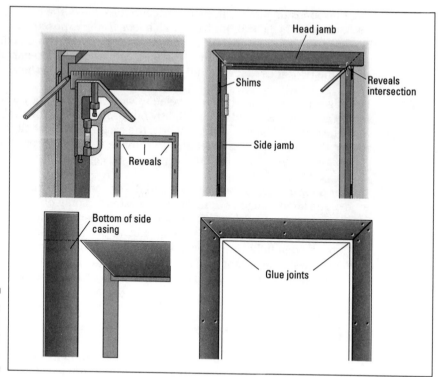

Figure 12-3:
Casing
a door
opening.

4. **Cut the side casings.**

Cut miters on the ends of the side casings. Then measure from the floor to the top of the head casing on each side and mark and cut the casing to that length. To eliminate the possibility of measuring errors, mark the casing in place: Stand each mitered side casing on its *point,* flat against the wall and parallel to the jamb; and mark the length where it touches the point of the head casing.

5. **Glue and nail the side casings.**

If all is well, you should be able to join the miters and nail the side casings in place. If the joint is acceptable, brush some wood glue on the end of the casing and tack it to the jamb with 4d finishing nails about 1 inch in from the corner. Then, drive a 6d or 8d finishing nail through the outside edge of the casing into the wall framing, again about 1 inch in from the end. Do the same for the head jamb. Next, *lock the miter* by nailing through the edge of the top casing down into the side casing. Use 3d finishing nails or brads for this to avoid splitting the wood. Complete nailing the side casings, first to the jamb and then to the wall.

Why use glue and nails? Because glued joints are less likely to open up over time. (See Chapter 8.)

6. **Complete nailing the head casing and countersink all nails just below the surface with a nail set. Then fill nail holes with putty, sand and finish.**

Troubleshooting poor miters

A poorly fitting miter is unattractive. Fortunately, you can remedy most with a little extra crafting:

- ✔ If the casing projects above the wall surface at a corner, the miter will open at the outside edge as the casings are pressed flat against the wall. Assuming that you cannot either move or plane the jamb to correct the problem, you can compensate for the problem by making each miter cut slightly less than 45 degrees and simultaneously *back cutting* the miter. This technique is feasible only with a power miter saw or by using a block plane.

- ✔ Another approach is to shim behind the outer edge of the casing the same amount as the jamb protrudes above the surface. To do this insert a shingle tip at the outside corner in as far as needed to close the joint; and when the nailing is complete, cut off the excess with a utility knife. The only problem with this approach is the gap that it leaves between the casing and the wall. If you are painting, you can easily fill the gap with caulk. If you aren't, *c'est la vie.*

- ✔ If the miter isn't tight because the jamb is out of square, then the best approach is to recut both miters to suit the out-of-square corner, both at 44 degrees, for example, to fit an 88 degree corner. This is feasible only if you have a power miter saw.

- ✔ If the drywall projects beyond the jamb and prevents the casing from sitting flat against the jamb, the first thing to do is take out your utility knife or surface forming tool and shave a little off the drywall (just the area that will be covered by the casing. As a last resort, you can plane some material off the backside of the trim at the outer edge.

Trim a window

Trim windows and doors with the same molding pattern (colonial, clamshell, and so on) and use the same type of joint (mitered or butted). This isn't the place to display your eclectic artistic bent. If you plan to picture frame a window, follow the same basic procedures that are described with miter-casing a door. Install the top casing and then the side casings; but leave the bottom half of the side casings untacked until you cut and install the bottom casing. Only when all joints are tight, complete the nailing and set the heads.

To trim a window by using a stool-and-apron approach with butted casings, see Figure 12-4 and the following steps:

1. **Cut stool to length.**

   The overall length should equal the inside width dimension of the jamb plus two times the width of the casing, plus two times the $\frac{3}{16}$-inch reveal, plus the same amount that will be exposed in front of the casing. Use a sander or router to give the ends the same profile that the front edge has.

2. **Scribe the stool.**

   Make a mark at the center of the stool and the center of the windowsill. Then hold the stool level and centered while you scribe it to the opening. Use a combination square to scribe it to the jambs and a compass to scribe it so the forward edge contacts the lower sash rail sash (or the edge of a finish sill) and the ears contact the wall. (See Figure 12-5.)

3. **Cut the stool.**

   Use a jigsaw or hand saw to cut the notches. Use a guided circular saw or jigsaw to make a nice straight cut where the stool will meet the lower sash rail. Trial-fit the stool and recut it as necessary for a perfect fit. Allow about $\frac{1}{16}$-inch clearance between the stool and the sash.

4. **Cut and prepare the apron.**

   Cut the apron to equal what will be the outside dimension of the casing. (Place each piece of side casing in place and mark the wall at the outer edge; and then measure between your marks.)

   Ideally, the profile on the ends of the apron should match the profile of the face. A professional approach calls for a return miter. The next best method is to cut the ends in a stepped fashion. The end grain will still be exposed but from the front it will look pretty good. The least you should do is cut the ends at a 5- to 10-degree angle to at least match the angle of the trim's profile. (See Figure 12-6.)

5. **Install the stool and apron.**

   Position the stool, making sure that it's square to the wall, and snug the apron up to it. Remove the stool while you nail the apron in place with four 8d finishing nails through the drywall and into the rough sill. Then nail the stool to the apron at the third points (one-third of the way in from each end) with 6d finishing nails.

6. **Install extension jambs.**

   If you need to extend the window jamb, install the head extension jamb first (see "Extension jambs," in this chapter). Then measure, cut, and install the side extensions to fit between the stool and head extension.

7. Mark reveals, and install side casings.

Mark ³⁄₁₆-inch reveals as described in Step 1 in this chapter's section, "Miter-case a door." Cut one end of a piece of casing square and stand it in place to mark its length at the reveal mark on the head jamb. Mark the other piece the same way, cut both pieces, and *tack* them in place.

8. Install the head casing.

Cut the head casing the same overall length as the stool so that it extends past the side casing the same amount as the stool does. If you are cutting the ends at an angle, the shortest dimension should equal the length of the stool.

Before you nail casings in place, spread wood glue on the top edges of the side casings. Nail the head casing to the head jamb first, and then to the wall at the center point. Then toenail through the top edge of the head casing into the wall so that you tighten the joint between it and the side casings.

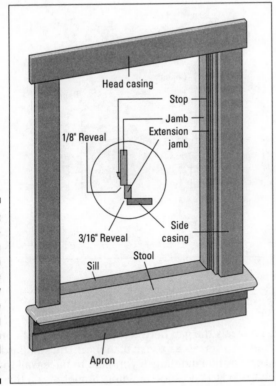

Figure 12-4:
A stool-and-apron approach allows more flexibility and is more interesting than a mitered casing.

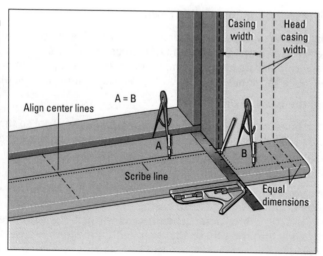

Figure 12-5:
Set your compass to the widest point between the sill and the lower rail of the sash, and scribe the stool to fit the window. (Step 2)

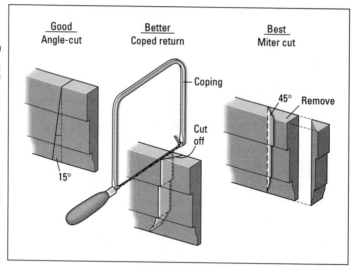

Figure 12-6:
The ends of the apron should have the same profile as the face. Good, better, and best approaches appear here. (Step 4)

Trimming Walls

Baseboard molding conceals the gap between the floor and wall, protects the wall from damage, and also serves as a visual anchor. The standard base trim consists of the base and a shoe molding. If you plan to have wall-to-wall carpeting, then you don't need to add shoe molding. Sometimes a third member, called a *base cap* or *base molding*, sits atop the base. (See Figure 12-7.)

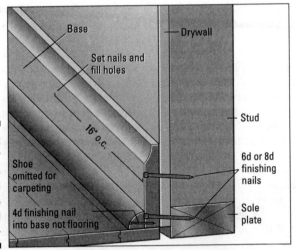

Base — Set nails and fill holes — Drywall — 16" o.c. — Stud — Shoe omitted for carpeting — 4d finishing nail into base not flooring — 6d or 8d finishing nails — Sole plate

Figure 12-7:
The proper sequences, jointing methods, and nailing of base trim.

To trim the walls, evaluate the existing situation. Test inside and outside corners with a framing square. The application of metal corner bead on outside corners and tape and joint compound on inside corners usually make the corners somewhat out of square. Often, the trim bends a little to conform to the wall, and you'll be able to caulk small gaps that remain. In the worst cases, however, the corners are so out of whack that it's best to apply additional compound as needed to create a flat surface for the trim to lay against.

Before you install base trim, take some time to locate the wall studs. (See the section on locating studs in Chapter 4.) Mark two or three locations on the floor and later, when you're nailing, open up your tape measure and align the layout marks (every 16-inches) to your marks and the remaining studs will also be at layout marks.

Trim the most visible wall first. This wall is usually the wall opposite the entry door — the wall you first see when entering the room. Fit a full length of trim between the two walls with square cuts on both ends. Nail the trim at every bearing point (stud location) with two nails — one about ½ inch down from the top of the trim and one about ½ inch up from the bottom. (Shoe molding or carpeting will conceal the lower nail.)

If the wall is so long that you can't trim it with a single length, then square-cut one end, butt it into one corner and mark the other end for cutting over a stud location. Cut that end with an open 45-degree miter. Then work your way around the room, starting at the square-cut end.

Generally, plan to cut and test-fit inside corners first and, when you're sure they look nice, mark the length (short point) at the outside corner. The same applies when a door breaks up a wall. Cut the trim a little long and make the necessary cuts at the inside corner. Then mark the piece for length at the door casing.

At inside corners, cut the end of the first piece square, and butt it into the corner (or between two corners if you are able to cover one wall with a single piece). If the molding is profiled, cope the end of the next piece. For information on how to use a coping saw and make this cut, see Chapter 5. If you are using flat, square-edge stock (called S4S), make a square cut and use a butt joint. If the other end will extend to the next wall, cut it square and butt it into the corner.

Thanks to metal corner bead that you apply to protect drywall corners, the outside corners are often slightly less than 90 degrees. You need to cut the trim at slightly less than 45 degrees. So after you make a nice fit at an inside corner, mark the length at the outside corner in place. Cut the piece and nail it.

Keep handy a couple of 3- to 4-foot-long pieces of trim with miters cut on both ends. Use these pieces to test the fit at outside corners. After you establish the exact required angle of cut, you can position the good piece, mark it for length and know you will be cutting the correct angle. If you had cut a 45 degree and later found out you needed to cut a 44-degree angle, your board would be short either at the corner or back at that cope joint that you worked so hard to make perfect.

Chapter 13

Laying a Prefinished Wood Floor

. . . .

In This Chapter

▶ Buying and acclimating the flooring

▶ Nailing down a prefinished floor

▶ Installing parquet tiles

▶ Floating floor — the easiest system for do-it-yourselfers

. . . .

*P*refinished wood flooring is an ideal material for the do-it-yourselfer. The flooring is seasoned, sanded, and finished at the factory under ideal conditions, so none of these critical steps are left to the amateur. The product is ready for installation right out of the box. It practically climbs out of its packaging and lays itself down. The finish is either a combination of wood stain plus durable polyurethane, or a clear polyurethane that protects and enhances the natural wood tone. Prefinished flooring is commonly available in oak, birch, hard maple, and pine.

For any flooring work, invest in a pair of kneepads — wear them and save your knees!

The method of installation depends on the type of flooring and the manufacturer's specifications:

✔ You can lay some hardwood flooring over an adhesive-coated subfloor.

✔ You can nail some flooring in place or join it with tongues and grooves.

✔ You can lay one type of flooring over a resilient base, gluing the individual flooring strips together at the edges, instead of gluing the flooring directly to the subfloor.

Buy enough flooring at one time to do the entire job. Be aware that you must make some allowance for end-matching and waste. In fact, you may need to buy an extra 10 percent of flooring for these allowances. You can always return unopened (or skillfully repackaged) bundles. The easiest way to estimate your flooring needs is to carefully measure the floor size in square feet (room width multiplied by room length). Take the measurements to your flooring dealer for an accurate estimate of the amount of flooring you need.

When you choose flooring, read and heed the manufacturer's directions for installation. For adhesive application, use only the adhesive or mastic the manufacturer suggests. Substitution of a cheaper adhesive may lead to job failure and void the product warranty.

Because of the danger of moisture damage to a wood floor, most manufacturers prohibit the use of wood flooring over any concrete floor that is below grade; that is, lower than the ground level at the exterior foundation. Check with the manufacturer for further advice on below-grade wood floor applications.

The factory properly dries the wood flooring which makes it relatively stable. That's great, but you're not installing it at the factory. Any wood product is subject to some expansion and contraction as the temperature and humidity change. Many experts suggest putting the wood flooring in the room where you are going to lay it. You should leave the flooring in the room for two or three days to acclimate to the temperature and humidity conditions there.

Plan to lay the flooring perpendicular to the floor framing. You must also provide a small space between the flooring and the walls or other immovable objects to allow the wood flooring to expand without buckling. Typically the expansion space should be equal to the flooring thickness. You can use base trim and/or shoe molding to cover the gap.

Nailing Down a Prefinished Floor

Ladies and gentlemen, start your hammers! The manufacturer supplies instructions for nailing down prefinished wood flooring. The following general directions apply to any installation of nailed-in-place, prefinished wood flooring:

1. **Pry off any existing shoe molding and save it for reuse. (For tips on removing molding, refer to Chapter 12.) In new construction, install the base molding after the floor.**

2. **Clean the subfloor with a shop vacuum using a crevice tool for removing dust and debris. Cover the floor with builder's paper.**

   This paper, sometimes called red rosin paper, helps prevent future squeaks and retards the passage of moisture vapor from underneath, a source of warping.

3. **Place spacers equal to the width the flooring maker suggests against the starting wall.**

4. **Position the first row of flooring against the spacers with the grooved edge toward the wall.**

   Stretch a string along the outer edge to verify the row is straight; and check that it is perpendicular to the adjacent wall using a 3-inch by 4-inch by 5-inch right triangle, as described in Figure 13-1.

Figure 13-1:
Face-nail the first and last few rows but blind-nail the remaining flooring with a power nailer.

A

B

5. **Scribe first row, if necessary.**

If the wall is not square to the adjacent walls or is crooked, scribe the first row to the wall. Snap a square, straight guideline with a chalk line; align the row parallel to the guideline. Use a compass/scriber to mark the floor for cutting. (For details on scribing refer to Chapter 4.)

6. **Start nailing the first row, by hand — it must be *face-nailed*. Then *blind-nail* the first couple of rows — you need to make enough room to position a power nailer (see sidebar, below, for more on power nailers). Nail at every bearing point (over each joist location).**

Face nailing means to drive the nail into the top surface of the floorboard, and not into the tongue. The face nailing is nearly invisible if you orient the heads so they are parallel to the grain. Use a hammer and nail set to drive the nails below the surface, then fill the holes with a suitable colored wax crayon or putty stick. Blind nailing doesn't mean closing your eyes; it means that you drive the nails at an angle through the tongue so you can't see them when the next board is in place. You can use flooring nails or just break off strip nails that you use for the power nailer.

7. **After you establish the starter rows, lay out six or eight rows of flooring. The name of this process is *racking* the floor.**

Racking enables you to arrange the floor pattern and do most of the cutting in one operation, saving you time and energy. Manufacturers bundle the flooring in random lengths. As you rack the floor, stagger the end joints so that they're no closer than the manufacturer-specified minimum distance apart. Alternate the strips by length. Set aside the shortest strips for use in closets or for filling in small spaces. Scatter the rest of the short lengths so that they fall randomly amongst the long boards over the floor.

8. **Blind nail the rest of the flooring in place using a power nailer.**

   To prevent damage to the floor, to get the joints tight, and to vastly speed the process, always use a power nailer. Power nailers are fun to use — and they emit a great "pow" with each nail driven.

   As you install the racked flooring, move out and rack more flooring. When you get to the end of a row, use the cut-off piece (if it's at least 12 inches long) to start the next row at the opposite end of the room.

9. **When you can no longer use the power nailer because you are getting close to the far wall, face-nail by hand and set the nails as you do in Step 5.**

10. **Cut the last row of flooring to width, allowing the proper expansion space.**

    To install the last row, insert a pry bar between the wall and the strip to push it tightly against the previous row, then tap it down into place. Protect the wall with a block of wood. Face-nail and set the last row.

If you're laying wood flooring in more than one room and have to change the direction of the flooring strips, the tongues and grooves may not match up. In this case, you can cut a thin wood strip, called a *spline,* the thickness of a tongue and double its width. Insert the spline into the groove edge of one board to act as the missing tongue and fitting into the grooved ends of the adjacent flooring. Pretty groovy, huh?

Laying Parquet Tiles

Parquet tiles are usually 12-inch by 12-inch tiles made from an alternating pattern of small bonded wood strips. Some versions of parquet are composed of a veneer laminated to a plywood backing. The solid-wood type is usually made up of individual pieces of wood held together with a wire backing.

Laying parquet is similar to laying resilient floor tiles, but you want to pay special attention to placement because the tiles are made of four smaller squares of alternately oriented strips. Lay them so that the parquet squares form a pattern. They look best in parallel, woven, or herringbone patterns depending on the look you want. Use a trowel to apply plank parquet acrylic urethane adhesive, available where the tiles are sold, usually at home centers or tile stores.

Putting power into your nailing

If you're nailing down the flooring, rent a power nailer. A power nailer holds a magazine full of barbed cleats and is so darn easy to use that it makes the job fun (Pow! Pow! Pow!). There are two types of power nailers: pneumatic and manual. The pneumatic kind is only necessary for production work, so save a few bucks and rent a manual one.

Despite its name, the manual nailer offers you a lot of power. All you have to do is strike the plunger with a special hammer and the nailer drives the nail home.

The special hammer has two faces: You strike the plunger with steel face and you lightly tap the flooring strips together at the ends and edges (before nailing) with the rubber face.

You'll need to practice with the power nailer to gauge how hard you need to strike the plunger. The blow must be sufficiently heavy to drive the nail all the way in, because you don't get a second chance — the next nail drops into position right away (sort of like a stapler). If you miscalculate a little, set the nail with a hammer and nail set. If you're even close, pull the nail and drive another rather than risk the damage associated with hammering it in.

Because parquet is real wood, it is more sensitive to moisture than resilient flooring materials. We don't recommend that you install parquet on a below-grade basement floor. You can do it, but it's a project best left to a professional.

The preparation for laying parquet tiles is the same as for laying resilient tiles. Use a sharp hand saw to undercut the bottom edge of door casings, as shown in Figure 13-2 so that you can slip the edge of the tile under the casing. Prepare the room by thoroughly cleaning the grit and dirt from the floor.

Figure 13-2:
Use a piece of flooring to guide your saw when you undercut the casings.

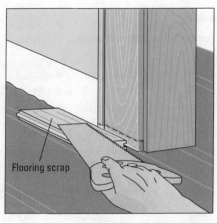

Flooring scrap

The right time to renail squeaking floors is when you're laying a new floor or floor covering. Before beginning any flooring project, walk over the floor(s) to test for squeaks. If you locate a squeak, drive spiral-shank flooring nails through the floor/subfloor and into the joists. Spiral-shank nails have a twist in their shaft that enables them to act more like screws than nails, but be careful: These nails are nearly impossible to yank out once they're more than halfway in. If one bends, break it off using pliers. Trying to pull a spiral-shank nail out could ruin the floor board, break your hammer handle and cause you to use words that would embarrass a sailor. Drive these nails in at an angle — or, as a carpenter would say, *toenail* them. Nails that you drive in at an angle hold two boards together better than nails that you drive straight into the wood. Walk over the floor to be sure there are no more squeaks before proceeding with your new flooring project.

Follow the steps below to lay parquet flooring tiles:

1. **Measure out from the starter wall a distance of 4 or 5 tile widths. Mark this distance on each side of the room.**

2. **Find the centerline for the length and width of the room and use a chalk line to mark these two lines.**

   Begin installation in one quadrant, at the corner, formed where the two chalklines intersect, which is the center of the room.

3. **Use a notched trowel to spread adhesive on the existing floor.**

   The type and size of the proper notched trowel is noted in the instructions on the can of adhesive, often the best choice is a trowel with a $\frac{3}{32}$-inch notch. To ensure that you're applying the adhesive at the right spread rate, push the trowel against the floor and hold it at a 45-degree angle as you smooth out the adhesive. You generally want to apply the adhesive to a 3-foot-square area at a time so that the adhesive doesn't dry out. Check the instructions on the can. As you apply the adhesive, be careful not to cover the layout lines.

4. **Lay all the full-size tiles first.**

5. **Cut border tiles to the proper size, then install.**

   At the borders, lay a full tile face up and centered over the last full tile that you laid. Then take a second tile and position it on top of the first tile with the back edge of the second tile about ½ inch away from the wall or base trim. The ½-inch gap allows for expansion of the wood tiles. Make a pencil mark on the first tile using the front edge of the top tile as a guide. Use a handsaw to cut the lower tile along the pencil mark, and then install it at the border. Proceed in this manner until you finish cutting and laying all the border tiles — or you pass out from exhaustion.

Parquet tiles are factory-finished with a tough polyurethane coating. Do not use floor wax over any flooring that has a polyurethane finish; the wax interferes with refinishing when the floor must be renewed.

Concrete floors that are at or below grade level (the level of the soil on the outside of the building) are prone to moisture from absorption or condensation. The moisture can destroy the bond between the adhesive and the tiles and may warp or stain wood flooring. For this reason, don't install parquet or strip-wood flooring directly on any concrete floor that's below grade level. If you want to install a wood floor over a concrete basement floor, consult the manufacturer about using their product on concrete floors that are below grade. Some manufacturers prohibit any such installation; others require that you first waterproof the concrete slab, lay down a plastic vapor barrier film, and then glue or nail wood strips or sleepers at intervals 16-inches OC (on center) — that is, measuring 16 inches from center to center. Then install a subfloor of ½-inch-thick exterior plywood, and install the wood flooring on top of the plywood.

Use a sharp hand saw to undercut the door casing or trim moldings so that the new flooring can slip beneath the casing. If you are installing a floor over a resilient backing or are using adhesive, add a strip of cardboard of the same thickness.

Floating a Floor

Perhaps the easiest of all prefinished floors to install is *floating floors*. (No water is involved, and no flood insurance is required.) You install veneered strips or tiles with precision-engineered tongue-and-groove edges over a foam cushion without any attachment to the floor. Instead, you glue the pieces together and the floor becomes a single unit. The walls around the floor and the furniture on top of it are all that contains it. You can install this type of flooring over hardwood, tile, or any existing flooring. You can also lay a floating floor directly over concrete or underlayment. Most manufacturers do not recommend that you install their products over below-grade concrete floors, in bathrooms or laundry areas because of moisture problems (or potential ones).

The floors are available with a variety of real wood veneers and recently include a wide array of plastic laminate designs and colors. These laminates have a special wear-layer (which makes them more abrasion-resistant than countertop laminates) that is bonded to particleboard, flakeboard, or fiberboard. You must install some brands side by side, while you may install others so that the panels or tiles are at right angles. The design flexibility of the latter type of panels and tiles allows you to introduce borders, inset "stone tiles," and install other design elements.

Installation requires only a hammer, utility knife, tape measure, glue, knee pads, and a saw or two. (Most cuts can be made with a handsaw but you may find use for a jigsaw to notch around doorways.) A circular saw speeds cutting, especially cutting rips for the final row. All manufacturers supply detailed instructions (and, yes, you must read them) but the basics steps are as follows:

1. **Prepare the existing floor by removing existing shoe or base moldings. While you can install over some irregularities, make sure the existing floor is secure and squeak-free. Cover concrete with a vapor retarder, usually heavy (8-mil) polyethylene sheeting, overlapped at any seams.**

   The installation requires that you leave about a ¼-inch gap at all walls and immovable objects. Pry off any existing shoe molding and save it for reuse (for tips on this process, refer to Chapter 12). In new construction, install the base molding after the floor.

2. **Roll out the foam cushion. You can cut the foam cushion easily with a utility knife but if you have a polyethylene sheet on the floor, backup your cut with the backside of a strip of flooring so you don't accidentally cut the polyethylene. Butt the edges of the foam cushions and tape over the seams.**

3. **Install spacers. Cut some wood blocks or plywood spacers and set them against a long, straight wall and the walls adjacent to it.**

4. **Lay the first row.**

   Position the first plank in the corner with its grooved side and grooved end against the spacers. Apply glue in the groove at the end of the next panel according to the manufacturer's instructions. (With some floating floors you must glue along the entire length, some you don't.) Tap the panel into the end of the first panel using the tapping block the manufacturer supplies (or one that you make yourself using a short cutoff of the grooved side of the flooring). Measure and cut the last piece in the row so it fits tightly against the spacer at the far end.

5. **Lay the second and third rows.**

   Start the second row with the cutoff from the first row (assuming that it's at least 12 inches long). Apply glue in the grooves of this and subsequent pieces as you lay them. Tap the pieces together so that they fit tightly at both the ends and along the sides. Wipe off excess glue with a damp cloth after the pieces are together. Repeat the above for the third row.

   The panels that you lay in the first few rows, may tend to pop apart when you install a new row. Some manufacturers offer professional installation kits that include special web clamps that are used to hold the first few rows together. Your dealer may rent this kit to do-it-yourself installers. Alternately you can use vinyl electrician's tape to hold these first few panels together.

6. **When your floor passes through a doorway, cut the bottom of the door casing to allow the floor to slip under it. Refer to Figure 13-2 to see how to guide your cut. Cut or notch the flooring so that it extends under the casing but not all the way to the framing behind it.**

7. **Cut the panels for the last row.**

The easiest way to determine the width for the final plank is to place each full-width piece face up directly on top of the second-to-last row. Then lay another strip on it and against the spacers, which, in turn are against the wall. Mark a cut line along the edge as shown in Figure 13-3.

8. **Install the last row.**

   Glue and position the strips as usual but instead of tapping the sides together, use a pry bar inserted between the wall and the side of the panel to force the pieces together; and insert a tapered shim between the spacer and the edges to hold the pieces together until the glue dries.

9. **Install base or shoe molding.**

   When the glue is dry, remove all spacers at the walls. Nail base molding to the wall and shoe molding to the base molding. Remember that the floor must be free to expand and contract so do not toenail the shoe molding into the floor.

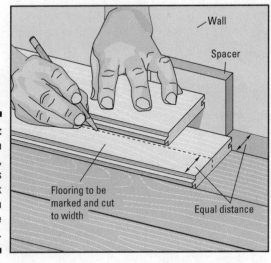

Figure 13-3: Rather than measure, use this trick to mark the width for the last strip.

Wall

Spacer

Flooring to be marked and cut to width

Equal distance

Chapter 14

Hanging Things on Walls

. . . .

In This Chapter

▶ Decking the walls

▶ Discovering what to do with hollow walls

▶ Figuring out fasteners (anchors, bolts, hooks, and nails)

▶ Working with brick, masonry, and tile surfaces

▶ Attaching wall shelving

▶ Installing a wire closet-shelving system

. . . .

*L*ife would be pretty dull and floors would be laden with junk if you couldn't take advantage of wall space for decorative items, such as framed art, or for storage systems, such as bookshelves and closet shelving systems. (In fact, we're working on inventing a wall-mounted sofa!) This chapter should give you the confidence to select the right anchor to mount nearly anything to the walls, ceilings, and floors in your home. You may never use some of the more exotic anchors we mention, such as wedge and sleeve anchors, but you can drop the names into coffee shop conversation and sound like an expert.

Decking the Walls

When you need to hang something on a wall (or a ceiling), consider the type of surface you're working with and the size and weight of the object to be hung; and the additional forces that the object may be subject to, such as shock, vibration, or a fat sleepy cat. A lightweight, framed poster doesn't require the holding power of a heavy architectural plaque or that nifty moose head. And fastening a hanger into hollow drywall is a whole different process from mounting an entertainment center on a brick wall.

Other important factors to consider include whether the mounted object needs to be easily removable and, in the case of apartment dwellers, how much damage is acceptable when you remove an item to take with you.

When you're shopping for anchor hardware, know the following:

- ✔ **Approximate size and weight of the object.** Get out your tape measure and the bathroom scale. No, you're not getting fitted for a tux or prom gown — are you? For shelving and cabinets, don't forget to weigh the items that you may load on or in it.

- ✔ **The type of wall surface.** Is the wall drywall, plaster, brick, or concrete? Hollow or solid? If hollow, how thick is the face piece, and how big of a void is behind it?

- ✔ **The types of forces likely to be applied.** Will anything tend to pull out on the fastener (tensile force) or primarily pull down on it (shearing force)? Will it be subjected to shock or vibration?

As you look at various types of hanger hardware, notice the package instructions. You often can find out the weight and dimension requirements. The more demanding the application is, the more you need to know. Read the labels, consult knowledgeable sales staff, or call the manufacturer for advice.

Hollow walls

In most walls in your home, the wall studs create a handy cavity that builders use to run electrical and plumbing lines. Building codes generally require protection for these lines so that you can nail and drill into most walls and be fairly sure that you don't damage one of these lines.

Before you hang, cut, drill, nail, or screw into walls, however, try to find out if anything is behind them. You can damage heating and water pipes and electrical cables, turning a $10 shelf installation into a major plumbing, electrical, drywall, and painting repair job. You can't even begin to imagine the amount of damage you can cause if you drill into a copper water pipe. "Thar she blows!"

Remember these tips to stay out of trouble:

- ✔ **Watch for clues.** Notice, for example, the position of wall receptacles. Cables may travel up or down the stud that they are attached to, or run horizontally on a line a little above them. Radiators stacked one floor above the other may connect to each other, and A/C and heating registers will have ductwork that extends either above or below them within the same wall cavity. If bathrooms stack above one another or over a kitchen sink, figure that water and drain lines run vertically between their fixtures.

- ✔ **Be careful.** Use special caution when proper fastening requires screws or nails that will penetrate more than 1 inch into studs, especially if you have 2x4 stud walls. Electrical lines and pipes that pass through studs generally run through holes drilled in the center of the studs, including the ones at corners.

✔ **Slow down.** High-speed drills and electric drill/drivers work so fast that you won't know that you hit a copper water line until you hear mice singing in the shower. When in doubt, drill and screw by hand or use power tools at low-speed settings so you can feel the resistance or hear a change in sound, as you pass from drywall or wood into metal. If you encounter unexpected resistance or hear a metallic sound while drilling, *stop!* Drywall, plaster, and wooden studs are rather soft compared to steel or copper pipes. Don't push harder on the drill; instead, back off and investigate the source of the resistance.

Similarly, you tool freaks out there should avoid using your power nailers with long fasteners in uncertain situations.

Use the following items to hang lightweight objects on hollow walls:

✔ **Small finishing nails and brads** driven at a 45-degree angle into drywall or plaster

✔ **Hook-type hangers** that nails hold in place

✔ **Duct tape or adhesive tape.** When driving a picture nail into plaster, put a piece of the tape over the nailing location to prevent chipping the plaster; and lubricate the shaft of the nail. (If you don't have any 3-in-1 oil handy, carefully rub the nail against the side — not the *inside* — of your nose . . . yes, really!).

✔ **Adhesive hangers.** These little squares feature a sticky side and a little hook.

✔ **Plastic screw anchors** fit snugly into predrilled holes in the drywall. As you drive a screw into the plastic plug, the slotted base of the plug spreads and locks against the perimeter of the hole.

To hang medium-weight objects on hollow walls, use one of these items:

✔ **Molly anchors or hollow-wall anchors.** Casing surrounds these combination screws. As you tighten the screw, the casing around the screw collapses against the wall interior. You can hammer in some types; for most of these anchors, predrill a hole, insert the anchor, then turn the screw to collapse and tighten.

✔ **Toggle bolts** have spring-loaded wings that expand inside the wall. Predrill a hole, remove the winged toggle from the screw, and place the screw through whatever you want to hang. Then replace the toggle and insert the assembly into the wall. Tighten the screw to pull the toggle tight against the inside of the wall.

Traditional toggle bolts can be awkward to use because you must position the object and fastener at the same time. They also drop into the wall cavity if you ever need to remove the fixture. A greatly improved version, called the *Toggler* toggle bolt, uses a toothed strap and retainer ring to clamp the anchor tight against the inside of the wall. Then you mount the fixture and drive the fastener, which you can remove and replace as needed.

Heavy items and objects that receive a lot of shock need special handling — you can't mount them to just the drywall or plaster. Heavy items can include shelving, cabinets, and wall-mounted lavatories; items subject to shock include stair handrails and tub grab bars. You need to secure these elements into framing (or to solid backing installed between the framing); and you may need two or more anchors for support.

Where's the stud?

Whenever possible, use screws driven into wall studs rather than hollow wall anchors. Whatever method you use to find framing, it helps to understand how most homes are built. Wall studs, ceiling joists (flat ceilings), and roof rafters (cathedral and vaulted ceilings) are all regularly spaced, so when you find one or two framing members you can usually locate all the others on a wall or ceiling by measurement.

To locate a stud, joist, or rafter, you may be able to go the high-tech route and use an electronic *stud finder* — a gadget that locates studs in the wall by measuring the density of various points in the wall. When you pass the stud finder over a wall stud, a light signals the stud location. (Sorry folks — this device often fails to detect framing behind a thick plaster-and-lath wall finish.)

For a low-tech way to find the framing behind drywall remove the shade from a lamp and set the lamp with bare bulb about a foot away from the wall or ceiling surface. This side-lighting highlights the slight depressions or raised bumps at fastener locations. Or, get down on your hands and knees and look at where the baseboard molding has nail dimples showing. Putty and fillers that conceal nailheads shrink a little, so if you look carefully, you can usually find the dimples. Wherever you see a dimple, especially if it appears to be 16 inches apart from another one, you likely will find a stud.

Receptacle outlets also provide a strong clue to where you can find studs. The receptacle inevitably is attached to one side of the stud or the other. With drywall, you can usually determine the site by tapping the wall on each side of the receptacle to see which sounds hollow and which sounds solid. If you can't tell, or if you have plaster walls, remove the cover plate to see. If necessary, probe just *outside* the box with a nail or small screwdriver to feel for the stud. Measure 16 inches from one edge of that stud to the same edge of the next stud. A light-switch outlet near a door is a less reliable indicator of the location of framing, at least beyond the one stud it is attached to. Typically, these boxes are attached to the *king stud* of a doorframe, which is positioned without regard for the 16-inches-on-center layout.

Brick, masonry, and tile surfaces

Extra-hard surfaces like brick, masonry, and tile require fasteners designed to stay in their holes. Masonry nails are probably the most common fasteners, but they aren't very reliable. So use construction adhesive with masonry nails. Plastic plugs are next in popularity, but with a few exceptions they're not very strong (especially in applications where "pull-out" tensile strength is important). Masonry screws, available with hex-nut or Phillips heads, hold better than nails and most plastic anchors. Use screws for any light-to-medium-duty applications. Be sure to buy the masonry bit suggested by the screw manufacturer.

To hang lightweight items on brick or masonry surfaces by using a plastic plug or similar friction-type anchor, follow these steps:

1. **If necessary, bore a clearance hole through the fixture that you wish to attach; position it to mark the installation hole.**

2. **Drill a hole in the masonry that is the same depth and diameter as the anchor and blow the dust out the hole. Wear goggles.**

3. **Tap the friction plastic plug or anchor into the hole.**

4. **Position the fixture and drive a screw through the fixture and into the plug to expand it and lock the plug into place.**

If you need to use more than one mounting screw, complete the procedures in each step for all the screws before going on to the next step.

To hang medium-weight items (or items that while not necessarily heavy, are subject to greater stress) on brick or masonry surfaces, you can use special plastic anchors rated for these loads, such as the _Alligator_. Or use an expansion-type anchor, such as an expansion screw anchor or a machine screw anchor, following the same procedure as described above.

Plastic anchors aren't new, but the Alligator anchor works differently from most. The friction of driving the screw extrudes the anchor and drives the molten plastic into all the pits and ridges in the pilot hole. The resulting bond is far stronger than standard plastic anchors and may even be stronger than steel anchors of the same size. These vibration-resistant anchors are perfect for attaching shelf standards or hanging light fixtures to block, brick, or solid concrete walls.

Alternatively, you use masonry screws by following these two steps:

1. **Position the fixture and drill through the fixture or any predrilled mounting holes.**

Use a carbide-tipped masonry bit of the size specified for the screw size that you plan to use. Don't use a bit that is even 1/64-inch larger or smaller in diameter, and don't use a badly worn bit. Masonry screws require a nearly perfect pilot hole.

2. **Drive the screw with a drill/driver or by hand with the appropriate driver.**

Unlike using anchors, which require you to drill clearance holes and position all anchors before the fixture is set in place, you drill for and install masonry screws as you go. If you wish, or if required, predrill clearance holes in the fixture before positioning it.

To install a light- or medium-duty fixture with a *hammer anchor,* drill through the fixture and into the base material 1/2 in. deeper than the desired embedment depth; and then hammer the fastener in. Hammer anchors have a spring-loaded crook or a split in the shank that compresses against the walls of the pilot hole. These anchors are faster than screws for rough work such as attaching wall plates to concrete floors or furring strips to concrete or block walls. Use S-shaped anchors for block and brick, and split-shank anchors for hard materials such as poured concrete and stone.

For medium to heavy-duty applications, the holes and anchors get bigger and more expensive, but the stakes are higher. Pay special attention to the ratings and if you aren't sure how to evaluate factors other than weight and size, be sure to discuss your situation with a well-informed salesperson, a reliable contractor or the anchor manufacturer.

Following are a few types of anchors for heavy-duty applications:

✔ The bolt in a *sleeve anchor* causes a steel sleeve to expand in the pilot hole, distributing tension evenly, so this anchor works better in relatively "soft" masonry such as brick or old concrete. To install, drill a hole through the fixture and into the base material. Insert the sleeve and finger-tighten the bolt; and then turn the bolt with a wrench three to four turns or to the manufacturer's recommended torque. Over-tightening the anchor can crack the base material.

✔ The mother of all anchors is the *wedge* anchor. It will keep a 2-year-old in place — not quiet, mind you, just in place. A wedge anchor compresses with such force that it will commonly crush or crack soft materials such as block and brick, so use it only in concrete or stone. You rarely need such an anchor, but it's nice to know it's available. Wedges have removable nuts so that you can remove and replace fixtures, but it's nearly impossible to withdraw the anchor body from its hole. Installation is easy — simply drill a pilot hole through the fixture and base material. The hole should match the diameter of the anchor and be one anchor diameter deeper than the desired embodiment.

Drilling in hard materials

Drilling holes in hard surfaces like brick and concrete is difficult, and some tile is practically impervious. For this job, you need an electric drill with a carbide masonry bit to predrill a hole. For some particularly hard materials, or when you need to drill many holes, you may need to use a hammer drill. This drill delivers very rapid, sharp blows to the surface as the bit turns. Check out your local tool-rental store if you need one for your project. Be sure to purchase the special bits required for these tools.

When drilling into ceramic tile, use a steel punch to chip the surface of the tile. Apply just a light tap on the punch with a hammer or you may crack the tile. The tiny hole helps keep the masonry bit on target and gives the bit a little head start when penetrating the hard surface.

When you need to drill a large hole, start with a ⅛-inch bit and work in increments up to the final bit size.

> ✔ *Chemical* anchors (also called *epoxy* or *bonded* anchors) work by bonding the fastener to the walls of the pilot hole. Epoxy is an ideal way to attach a metal handrail to a concrete stoop: The epoxy requires a smaller hole than embedding the post in anchoring cement would. Epoxy is also a permanent way to install an eyebolt in your garage floor to lock items such as bicycles. Some hardware stores and home centers now carry kits that mix and dispense the two-part resins that form the epoxy.

Shelving

A novice carpenter, with just a few basic tools, can install all types of shelving, from the simplest utility shelf mounted on a basement wall to expensive wall systems for stereo equipment or clothes closets.

Putting up a closet shelf and rod

A simple closet shelf and rod like the one shown in Figure 14-1 consists of the shelf itself; cleats attached to the back and sidewalls, and a bracket to support the center of the shelf and the rod at the midpoint. (Well, you're not building an aircraft carrier.) Your layout, bracket position, and shelf length may vary, depending on the project, but the principles are the same.

The shelf itself secures either to the brackets and cleats or, sometimes, just rests on top of them. A wide, single shelf typically has at least one intermediate bracket fastened to the wall framing; more brackets may be necessary for longer shelves or to support the end of a shelf that doesn't terminate at a wall. Simple shelf or shelf-and-rod brackets are available in hardware stores and home centers. You can choose from a wide variety of decorative brackets in all kinds of stores, catalogs, and just about anywhere that household furnishings are available.

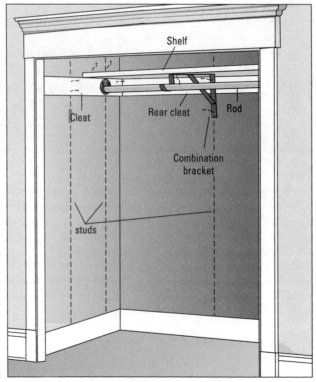

Figure 14-1: Install a shelf-and-rod on cleats nailed to wall studs. If the unit spans more than 3 feet, install a support bracket at the midpoint.

Follow these steps to install a closet shelf and rod, supported with one bracket and wall cleats and one shelf:

1. **Draw a level line across the back wall of the closet by using a carpenter's level.**

   The line should be ¾ of an inch below the desired shelf height. Draw two shorter, level lines at the same height on the sidewalls.

2. **Locate the wall studs and mark their location just above your three lines.**

   Use a small tick mark at the side of the stud and an X to indicate which side of your mark the stud is located.

   Follow the instructions in the sidebar titled, "Where's the stud?," in this chapter, to locate the studs.

3. **Cut the 1x4 side cleats so that they extend at least as far as the first stud from the corner. Position them with their tops aligned with your level line and nail them to the studs. Nail at an angle into the corner(s).**

To avoid splitting the boards when nailing close to the ends of the boards, drill a pilot hole for the nail.

4. **Cut the back-wall cleat to fit between the sidewall cleats, and fasten it to the studs in the same fashion.**

5. **Mount the bracket.**

Hold a shelf support bracket in place, centered over a stud at about the midpoint (or ⅓ points if you're using two brackets on a very long wall) of the wall. Use the bracket as a template to mark the location of the mounting screws. Secure the bracket to the cleat at a stud location with screws that are long enough to penetrate the wall stud by at least an inch or so.

6. **Install the shelf.**

Secure the shelf to the cleats with finishing nails, and secure the bracket to the underside of the shelf with short screws.

7. **Attach the closet rod brackets to your side cleats with the screws provided.**

Cut your closet rod ⅛-inch shorter than the inside dimension between the brackets, and set it in place. Secure the shelf support bracket to the pole with a screw through the mounting hole.

Installing a wall shelving system

A wall shelving system, shown in Figure 14-2, consists of three basic components: the shelves, the vertical standards (the long, metal, slotted strips fastened to the wall), and brackets that fit into grooves at any desired height along the length of the standards. Before you invest your hard-earned dollars in a shelving system, consider these shopping tips:

✔ Make a preliminary shopping/learning expedition to select a shelving system and pick up a planning brochure that details with the system's standard and bracket specifications. Pack a lunch — this trip may take a while.

✔ Decide how many shelves you want and how you want to arrange them. Make a sketch of the wall, noting the location of wall studs so that you can plan the design.

✔ Choose the standard size and shelf depth and style to fit the items you plan to store and display, such as deep shelves for large items, narrower ones for smaller things. Plan to space the standards about 32 inches apart and allow a maximum overhang of ⅙th of the shelf length.

✔ If you must fasten the shelf to a hollow wall, choose mounting anchors based on their weight-bearing capacity. Don't be embarrassed to ask for help!

✔ Read the directions on the package, noting how many uprights and brackets and what width and length of shelves are included. Most systems have brackets for at least two shelving widths, so make sure that you buy the correct sizes. Some systems include the mounting hardware; some don't. Don't leave the store without everything you need.

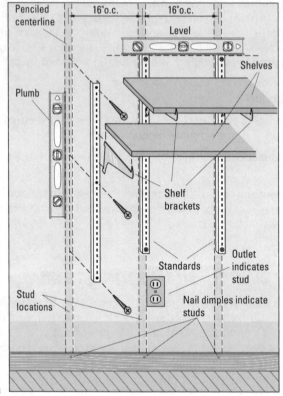

Figure 14-2:
Choose a shelving system that is designed for the weight and size of the things you plan to store on it.

Follow these steps for installing a component shelf system with standards and brackets:

1. **Find the studs, following the instructions in the sidebar called, "Find framing behind walls and ceilings," in this chapter.**

   Plan to install each standard on the center of the stud. Make light pencil marks on all the wall studs in the vicinity of the spot where you plan to install the shelving unit. (You may have to adjust the exact location slightly so that the standards will be attached to the studs.)

2. **Mark the location for the top screw hole on the first standard and drill a small pilot hole through its top hole.**

   Using a Phillips-head screwdriver, fasten the bracket with a screw at that location, but don't tighten it yet.

3. **Mark the placement of the other mounting screws.**

   Use a carpenter's level to position the standard so that it's plumb, and then mark the location of the other mounting screws by inserting a pencil point into the mounting holes in the bracket.

4. **Swing the bracket to one side and then drill pilot holes for the mounting screws.**

5. **Reposition the upright and install the remaining mounting screws.**

6. **Locate the proper position of the second standard.**

   To position the second standard, place a shelf support bracket in the standard hanging on the wall. Then, install another shelf support bracket in the same slot of a second standard. Hold the second standard over the next wall stud and then place a level (alone or on a piece of shelving) across the two brackets and move the second standard up or down until the shelf is level.

7. **Mark the location on the wall of one of the mounting screws for the second standard and install it as you did the first one.**

8. **Repeat with the remaining standards, if any.**

9. **Install the shelf support brackets into the standards.**

   These brackets usually slide down into slots that lock them in place, you'll probably have to tap them down into place. Don't pound too hard or you may move the standard.

10. **Install the shelves.**

Adding a wire shelf system to a closet

You can tame closet clutter with a bulldozer or by installing a closet organizer with ventilated wire shelves, as illustrated in Figure 14-3. You still have to hang up your clothes, but opening the closet door is far less intimidating when you don't face a potential avalanche. By reorganizing the inside of your closet, you can almost double your closet space — making the chore of sorting through your stuff to install shelving well worth the effort. The installation is the easy part; the real work is cleaning out the closet and realizing that you used to actually fit into some of those clothes.

These systems are sold as individual components to fit any size closet and as closet kits designed for various sizes. For example, a kit for an 8-foot closet includes four shelves, one support pole, a shoe rack, and mounting clips and screws.

Here's what you need to install a wire shelf system:

- ✔ Carpenter's level
- ✔ Screwdrivers
- ✔ Measuring tape and pencil
- ✔ Hacksaw for cutting the metal shelving to length
- ✔ A free afternoon

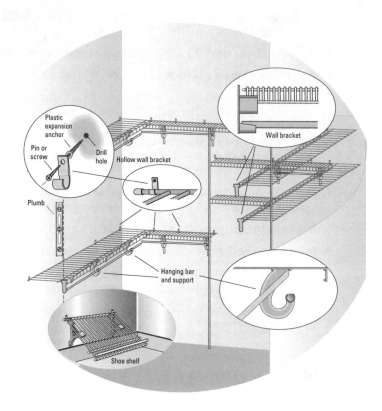

Figure 14-3:
Easy- to-
install wire
shelving
offers a
great deal of
design
flexibility.

Plastic expansion anchor

Pin or screw

Drill hole

Plumb

Hollow wall bracket

Wall bracket

Hanging bar and support

Shoe shelf

Getting ready — the worst part of the job

Before you can install a closet wire-shelving system in your closet, you have to do the following prep work. (Trust us. The extra effort at this point will pay off every time you open the closet door.)

1. **Remove all the stuff inside the closet. If you don't come out by morning, we'll send in the dogs.**

   Just do it! Think of this as an opportunity to get rid of items you don't wear or use. Donate the booty to charity or to anybody who can use it.

2. **Remove the existing shelving and the clothes rod.**

   Remove the screws or pull the nails that hold the shelf and rod in place. If you need to use a pry bar, place a thin board against the wall under the heel of the pry bar to minimize damage to the wall.

3. **Patch any nail holes with a fast-drying spackling compound.**

4. **If the walls are dirty and dingy, give them a quick coat of paint.**

Wire shelving step-by-step

To install the shelving system, follow these steps (refer to Figure 14-3):

1. **Read through the instructions that came with the shelving a few times.**

2. **Determine the height for the main shelf.**

   Hold a carpenter's level on the wall about ½ inch above that height, and pencil a very light level line on the wall.

3. **Mark the locations for the wall clips.**

   Make a mark 2 ½ inches in from either end of the shelf line and ½ inch above the shelf line. Then mark 1-foot intervals along a level line connecting the two marks.

4. **At each mark, drill a hole ¼-inch deep and insert the wall clip.**

5. **Insert a screw into each wall clip and tighten them into the wall. Erase your level line.**

6. **Put the end caps on one end of the shelf and measure and cut the shelf to length on the other side.**

7. **Put the other end caps on the cut end.**

8. **Hang the shelf on the wall clips.**

9. **Hold the shelf level, with the lip of the shelf toward you and facing down.**

10. **Position the wall brackets on the sidewalls so that the shelf lip fits into the "U" and mark the holes.**

11. **Lift up the shelf until it's level (perpendicular to the wall) and drill holes for the anchors.**

12. **Insert the anchors.**

13. **Position the wall bracket, insert the screws, and tighten.**

14. **When both ends are installed, tighten the screws of the wall mounting brackets.**

15. **Go shopping for clothes that fit!**

Part IV
The Part of Tens

The 5th Wave   By Rich Tennant

"I swear, Frank, it's not a pyramid scam. You help a few guys with their home improvements and then, after you bring in ten friends, you'll be enjoying each and every Saturday as much as I do."

In this part . . .

Personal growth: Now all of us have different takes on what that means, but here it refers to practicing the carpentry skills you've developed. What good is knowing how to cut a miter joint in a piece of wood if you can't do it where it counts? In this part of the book, you'll find suggestions on ways to put your carpentry skills to work, not just for yourself, but to help others as well. And if you want to further enlighten yourself we've chosen some Web sites about carpentry that we've found to be especially helpful in our home improvement, carpentry, and woodworking activities. Enjoy!

Chapter 15

Ten Ways to Put Your Skills to Work

In This Chapter

▶ Practicing your skills to teach and help others

▶ Making things around your house more safe and more useful

▶ Putting unused space in the attic and basement to better use

Teaching Your Kids

There isn't a parent who isn't a little nervous when a child first learns to swing a hammer let alone crank up a power tool, but if you work with your children from the beginning, they will grow up comfortable with tools. No doubt this early experience may make them independent homeowners some-day, but the skills, the comfort around tools, the sense of how things go together generally will serve them well as scientists, engineers, and — who knows — maybe surgeons.

Working with kids requires that you always practice good safety procedures yourself (and that won't hurt you a bit either!). Make sure that the tasks you choose are ones your child can accomplish well and watch his or her confidence and enthusiasm grow. Projects may all take a bit longer, at least in the beginning, but it's what they call "quality time."

Helping Your Neighbor

In our many years as do-it-yourselfers, we have come to value working with others, helping and being helped, and putting our skills to work for the community. Our contact with hundreds, even thousands, of people through HouseNet, the Web site that we founded for do-it-yourselfers, made us realize that there are lot of others that feel the same way. It's sometimes incredible how much people are willing to help each other, just for the joy of it.

Sometimes working together is just easier and more fun. A painting party comes immediately to mind, but there are lots of hard chores that people working together can turn into pleasant, rewarding experiences. Sometimes you can make a contribution to your community by helping an elderly neighbor with some repairs or by working with volunteer organizations to help improve your larger community.

Making Your Home Safer

Little problems can become serious hazards. We all procrastinate to some degree, but if you don't have the tools or skills yourself to make a simple repair and must go through the hassle and expense of hiring a carpenter, it's not surprising for these things to go unattended for many years. As an official *...For Dummies* carpenter, tend to repairs such as loose railings or broken steps as soon as you notice them. Not only is the task usually easier when done quickly, you may prevent an avoidable accident.

Aside from correcting problems, there are also many little things you can do that to make your home a safer place. Put up a child-height handrail for a few years if you have very young children. You know how to buy, measure and cut the lumber and how to hang things on walls (and even patch the screw holes in the drywall when it's time to take the handrail down). Install safety locks on that toxic waste dump under your kitchen sink or install a new medicine cabinet with a lockable section for prescription drugs. Just keep your mind open to safety and you may find lots of little easy-to-do projects that can make you and your family safer.

Accessorizing Your Kitchen Cabinets

With basic carpentry skills and a free weekend you can make and install a host of kitchen cabinet accessories that increase usable storage space that are so convenient you'll wonder why you waited so long!

One of the best accessories you can make and install yourself are roll-out shelves in the base cabinets (one on the floor of the cabinet and one to replace that nearly useless 12-in.-deep shelf). Made from plywood edged with 1x4 pine (glue and nail on the sides first and then the fronts and back), the shelves use standard drawer-slide hardware, which attaches to the sides or lower side corners of the shelf and to the sides of the cabinet. If you have face frames on your cabinets you will need to install the slides on 1x furring strips attached to the sides of the cabinet.

Making a Bath Vanity More Useful

Inspired by an elderly couple's need for more accessible bath vanity cabinet storage space, we built two simple two-tier plywood boxes, open on one long side and the top (like a little one-shelf bookcase without a top). We installed them on drawer slides behind the two vanity doors of their bath vanity. I swear, so many people have said what a great idea that we could make a business of it!

When you make a rollout such as this, you can often make things even more convenient if you remove the hinges on the door (or doors) of the cabinet and secure the door to the rollout like a drawer front. The taller the front of the roll-out, the better you can place screws for a secure connection without drilling through the face of the door. Install screws — usually quite a few of them — through the face of the rollout into the back of the door. Just be careful choosing an appropriate screw length and drill a proper clearance and pilot hole.

Organizing Attic and Garage Clutter

The bare bones of an unfinished attic or garage can be finished with simple shelving to provide a lot of storage possibilities. Hang a closet pole between roof rafters and voilà, there's room for hanging garment bags. On unfinished garage walls you can get fancy installing shelves between the wall studs or take the instant hook approach by banging in large nails to hang rakes and other lawn equipment. These unfinished spaces offer a lot of usable storage space — it's there for the taking.

Installing a Whole-House Fan

Basically, the task involves cutting a hole in the drywall ceiling in an upstairs hall and installing a louver on the hall side of the opening and the fan on the other side. Don't worry. You don't have to cut any ceiling joists if you choose the right model fan. Then you may need to enlarge existing vents in the attic or install new ones. Typically, you will be able to install simple rectangular or triangular louvered vents in the gable end (the triangular endwalls) of your house. How you do that, of course depends on the type of siding you have and the style vent. Installation instructions come with the fan or the vent. Have a licensed electrician set you up with the necessary new wiring and a conveniently located timer-switch.

Finishing a Basement

Although it might not seem so at first, an unfinished basement for a do-it-yourselfer is like a blank canvas for an artist. For a quick fix, simply paint the walls, but to create more finished rooms, there are a lot of options. You can install wallboard, paneling, or a combination of both using the paneling as wainscoting. Finishing off the space with doorways and openings will give you plenty of practice cutting miters installing trim. That untapped space down under is well worth the effort to finish and won't hurt the resale value of your house either.

Making Simple Furniture

A box is a box and once you know how to put one together that looks nice and will stay together, you can build sturdy, practical furniture. Children's furniture is a great place to start. You can build things a lot stronger than the typical melamine/particleboard stuff for less money. Talk about a great project to work on with your kids! Try a bookcase or toy box, a platform bed or a simple desk. Use "paint grade" birch plywood for the parts that show and check out the decorative painting section in our *Painting and Wallpapering For Dummies* book for some fun and easy finishing ideas.

If this is an area of carpentry that appeals to you and you have more ideas than you know what to do with, it may be time to step up your tool collection to include either or both of the following power tools: a small 10-inch table saw and a bisquit joiner.

Making Wooden Toys and Gifts

After you've mastered some of the basic carpentry skills, transfer them to woodworking, which is probably one of the most popular hobbies around. Working with wood can be enjoyable and relaxing, and if you can turn that time into creating gifts for others, so much the better. There's a plethora of plans available in magazine and books, at home centers, and of course, on the Internet. Start with a simple project to hone your skills, and before you know it you'll be creating your very own masterpiece crafts.

Chapter 16

Web Sites for Carpenters

. . . .

. . . .

*H*aving been involved in the growth of the Internet and particularly the World Wide Web, we know what a great resource this collection of electronic files, networks, and services can be. The Internet is accessed through your home computer or television via phone lines. For your guide to the Internet we recommend *The Internet For Dummies,* 4th Edition, by John Levine and Margaret Levine Young (published by IDG Books Worldwide).

Oh, there's a lot of fluff and misinformation, too. So consider the source before you act on advice or information. We've put together a list of some of our favorite web sites with reliable information on carpentry, woodworking and related subjects. When a site has something particular that we like we've noted it, but you'll find lots of good stuff surfing on your own.

Thinking of Buying a Power Tool?

Before you buy a tool read the Tool Reviews at www.augusthome.com to get the latest news and reviews. Armed with the information that enables you to compare features, you'll be able to make a better decision about which tool is appropriate for your needs and is a good value. By reading good tool reviews, such as those found on this site, you'll get to better know the criteria for choosing tools or the right questions to ask when buying any tool, even if no review is available.

Associating with the Right People

Who knows better about working with redwood than the California Redwood Association (CRA) at www.calredwood.org, about plywood and engineered wood products than APA, The Engineered Wood Association at www.apawood.org, or about cedar siding, paneling and roofing than the Western Red Cedar Lumber Association (WRCLA) at www.wrcla.org and the Cedar Shingle and Shake Bureau at www.cedarbureau.org?

The CRA offers a great deck planning kit, outdoor project plans and technical information relating to redwood construction and finishing. Turn to the APA for literature about basic wood-frame construction and recommendations for floor, wall and roof construction. In addition to the information on the installation, repair and care of wood siding, the WRCLA site features how-to information and D-I-Y plans on outdoor projects such as fences and gates. The Cedar Shingle and Shake Bureau is *the* online source for information about installing, repairing, maintaining cedar shingle and handsplit cedar shakes on sidewalls or roofs.

Don't Get Stuck in the Mud

For anyone interested in hanging, repairing, or finishing drywall take a look at www.usg.com. USG is the leading manufacturer of drywall in the country. Its brand name, Sheetrock, like Bandaid, Kleenex, and Skilsaw, is often synonymous with the product.

USG's Web site has a "DIY Workshop," where you can find everything you always wanted to know about drywall and drywall finishing products, and clear step-by-step instructions on the whole process from choosing the right product to applying the paint. And if you're looking for a specialty wallboard, such as flexible ¼-inch thick panels that allow you to create very cool rounded wall corners, you'll find it in their product information.

Getting in the Pink

Looking for a way to save big bucks and make yourself more comfortable at the same time? Well, if your home is uninsulated (or under-insulated) or if you are refinishing a basement or attic, then be sure to check out the Pink Panther at www.owenscorning.com. This Owens Corning site has the most in-depth coverage we've seen, called "Around Your House," that helps you visualize how and where and why to insulate. While you're there take a look at the information about windows, roofing siding, and a host of other building materials that the company manufactures.

Conquering Closet Clutter

If closet clutter has gotten the best of you and you're hell-bent on getting organized, get help at `www.homebase.com`. In addition to added information on installing prefabricated wire closet organizers, which is discussed in Chapter 14, this Web site has particularly useful step-by-step advice that you can print about installing both prefabricated and custom-built closet organizers.

This Site Will Floor You

Check out `www.pergo.com`, the site of the Scandinavian company that is invading home centers with its extensive line of floating floors. Floating floor installations are perhaps the easiest floor system to install and Pergo offers a premium plastic laminate flooring that they claim is 30 times more abrasions resistant than laminate countertops (and backs its claims with a solid warranty).

Working the Wood Web

For the ultimate woodworking resource, look to `www.woodweb.com`, the information resource for the woodworking industry. The ever-growing site includes a database of woodworking machinery, supplies and services, an online bookstore with hundreds of titles, and interactive forums where you can get your specific questions answered.

It's great fun to find all the resources in one place on the Net. Although Wood Web is designed for professionals, even wannabe-woodworkers will learn from this extensive site.

Motivating Couch Potatoes

Inspired by projects they may have enjoyed watching on Dean Johnson's _HomeTime_ on Public Television, fans of this will appreciate having an online source for all the step-by-step information that makes it more likely that they make the move from the couch to the workshop. Take a look at `www.hometime.com` even if you don't catch the show. It's good stuff.

Working with Hardwoods

If you're a more skilled craftsman you'll appreciate the installation instructions the Hardwood Council offers on its site, www.hardwoodcouncil.com. This trade group has taken its extensive line of color brochures and placed them online, just waiting for you to download or print. There's a booklet on hardwood lumber grades and one on various hardwood flooring installations. The council's built-in cabinet is a showstopper we'd love to build.

Mail Ordering Made Easier for Woodworkers

Browsing these woodworking mail-order catalogs is always a revealing experience. You'll discover neat tools, hardware, and other woodworking supplies that will make your tasks easier to accomplish with more professional results. Many of the nation's leading woodworking mail-order companies are online. Here are some that are ready to serve surfers:

- Rockler: 800-279-4441 or www.rockler.com
- Constantines: 800-223-8087 or www.constantines.com
- Garrett Wade: 800-221-2942 or www.garrettwade.com
- Woodcraft Supply: 800-225-1153 or www.woodcraft.com

Getting Caught in the Net (HouseNet, that is)

We couldn't talk about Web sites without mentioning www.housenet.com, the site we founded. Some of the best carpentry advice comes from the visitors who share their best tips in the Handy-at-home tip database, with hundreds of clever ideas. Project of the Week provides simple, step-by-step instructions for a variety of carpentry-related home improvement and maintenance projects. The ever-popular Project Calculators will help you figure out how much material you should buy for a job. Browse the message boards to get help and help others. There's tons of info here to use right away for a project you're about to undertake or to file away for future reference.

Index

Discover Dummies Online!

The Dummies Web Site is your fun and friendly online resource for the latest information about ...*For Dummies®* books and your favorite topics. The Web site is the place to communicate with us, exchange ideas with other ...*For Dummies* readers, chat with authors, and have fun!

Ten Fun and Useful Things You Can Do at www.dummies.com

1. Win free ...*For Dummies* books and more!

2. Register your book and be entered in a prize drawing.

3. Meet your favorite authors through the IDG Books Author Chat Series.

4. Exchange helpful information with other ...*For Dummies* readers.

5. Discover other great ...*For Dummies* books you must have!

6. Purchase Dummieswear™ exclusively from our Web site.

7. Buy ...*For Dummies* books online.

8. Talk to us. Make comments, ask questions, get answers!

9. Download free software.

10. Find additional useful resources from authors.

Link directly to these ten fun and useful things at **http://www.dummies.com/10useful**

For other technology titles from IDG Books Worldwide, go to **www.idgbooks.com**

Not on the Web yet? It's easy to get started with *Dummies 101®: The Internet For Windows® 98* or *The Internet For Dummies®, 6th Edition,* at local retailers everywhere.

Find other ...*For Dummies* books on these topics:

Business • Career • Databases • Food & Beverage • Games • Gardening • Graphics • Hardware
Health & Fitness • Internet and the World Wide Web • Networking • Office Suites
Operating Systems • Personal Finance • Pets • Programming • Recreation • Sports
Spreadsheets • Teacher Resources • Test Prep • Word Processing

IDG BOOKS WORLDWIDE BOOK REGISTRATION

Register This Book and Win!

We want to hear from you!

Visit **http://my2cents.dummies.com** to register this book and tell us how you liked it!

✔ Get entered in our monthly prize giveaway.

✔ Give us feedback about this book — tell us what you like best, what you like least, or maybe what you'd like to ask the author and us to change!

✔ Let us know any other ...*For Dummies*® topics that interest you.

Your feedback helps us determine what books to publish, tells us what coverage to add as we revise our books, and lets us know whether we're meeting your needs as a ...*For Dummies* reader. You're our most valuable resource, and what you have to say is important to us!

Not on the Web yet? It's easy to get started with *Dummies 101*®: *The Internet For Windows*® *98* or *The Internet For Dummies*®, 6th Edition, at local retailers everywhere.

Or let us know what you think by sending us a letter at the following address:

...*For Dummies* Book Registration
Dummies Press
7260 Shadeland Station, Suite 100
Indianapolis, IN 46256-3945
Fax 317-596-5498

™

**BESTSELLING
BOOK SERIES
FROM IDG**